KU-305-053

Film Production Management

Third Edition

Bastian Clevé

AMSTERDAM • BOSTON • HEIDELBERG • LONDON • NEW YORK • OXFORD
PARIS • SAN DIEGO • SAN FRANCISCO • SINGAPORE • SYDNEY • TOKYO

ELSEVIER

Focal Press is an imprint of Elsevier

Acquisitions Editor: Elinor Actipis
Associate Editor: Becky Golden-Harrell
Assistant Editor: Robin Weston
Marketing Manager: Christine Degon
Cover Design: Eric DeCicco

Focal Press is an imprint of Elsevier
30 Corporate Drive, Suite 400, Burlington MA 01803, USA
Linacre House, Jordan Hill, Oxford OX2 8DP, UK

First published 1994
Second edition 1999
Third edition 2006

Copyright © 2006, Elsevier Inc. All rights reserved.

No part of this publication may be reproduced, stored in a retrieval system, or transmitted in any form or by any means, electronic, mechanical, photocopying, recording, or otherwise, without the prior written permission of the publisher.

Permissions may be sought directly from Elsevier's Science and Technology Rights Department in Oxford, UK: phone: (+44) (0) 1865 843830; fax: (+44) (0) 1865 853333; e-mail: permissions@elsevier.co.uk. You may also complete your request on-line via the Elsevier homepage (http://elsevier.com), by selecting "Customer Support" and then "Obtaining Permissions".

 Recognizing the importance of preserving what has been written, Elsevier prints its books on acid-free paper whenever possible.

Library of Congress Cataloguing in Publication Data
A catalogue record for this book is available from the Library of Congress

British Library Cataloguing in Publication Data
A catalogue record for this book is available from the British Library

ISBN-13: 978-0-240-80695-2
ISBN-10: 0-240-80695-6

05 06 07 08 09 10   10 9 8 7 6 5 4 3 2 1

For information on all Focal Press publications visit our website at:
www.focalpress.com

Typeset by Charon Tec Pvt. Ltd, Chennai, India
www.charontec.com

Printed in the United States of America

Working together to grow libraries in developing countries

www.elsevier.com | www.bookaid.org | www.sabre.org

ELSEVIER   **BOOK AID** International   **Sabre Foundation**

UNIVERSITY OF WESTMINSTER

791.430232
~~068~~ CLE
3 weeks

Failure to return or renew overdue books on time will result in the
suspension of borrowing rights at all University of Westminster
libraries. To renew by telephone, see number below.

Due for return on:

1 7 NOV 2005

Information Systems and Library Services **Harrow LRC**
Watford Road Northwick Park Harrow Middlesex HA1 3TP
Telephone 020 7911 5885 (direct line)

26 0146903 7

This book is dedicated again to Marietta Celine and Marlies

Contents

Appendix 1: Selected Addresses 199

Appendix 2: Example Agreement Forms 205

Index 215

Introduction

Five years have passed since the second edition of this book was published. Technological changes have been dramatic since then, most notably the arrival of digital filmmaking. There is hardly a motion picture nowadays that does not use computer generated or altered images. Whole features have been shot not on film but on High Definition HD Video—whole features have been shot without real live actors or sets—yet they look convincingly realistic.

Well-established directors and producers such as George Lucas have been at the forefront for many years in advancing the medium, and rely completely on digital artistry—and movies such as the *Lord of the Rings* trilogy are virtually impossible but for the wizardry of computer generated special effects. The entertainment industry is in the midst of a technological revolution that changes the way theatrical motion pictures are produced and—more seriously and with yet unknown consequences—the way motion pictures will be distributed throughout the world.

Nevertheless, the basic standards and procedures of how filmmaking is being organized, how locations are chosen, how actors are made ready for shooting, those and most other related procedures for getting the film in the can—or getting the video digitalized—remain the same.

Wherever possible I have tried to provide fresh and updated information. The consequences of digital filmmaking have been incorporated into the text whenever it affects procedures in preparing, shooting and finishing a movie. Other areas—such as the use of the Internet—have been deleted from this edition; I don't think there is anyone any more who is not highly sophisticated in using this medium; it has become standard, just as knowing how to read and write. Also the section on film festivals has not been expanded. There are film festivals on almost any day of the year throughout the world, catering to specific filmic interests, and filmmakers should find out for themselves which festivals suit their individual purposes the best. There is a vast amount of information on this topic on the Internet and the information will and does fill a variety of books.

Bastian Clevé

1

The Production Manager

Movies are make-believe. They are designed to portray reality to such an authentic degree that even stories taking place millennia ago in far-away galaxies look true and convincing. In historical movies or science fiction films this becomes obvious, as there is no such "reality" which might be used to film in—but of course this is true for stories set in everyday life as well, and even for documentaries to a certain degree. Considering that it takes a small "army" of technicians, actors, and other personnel to create this illusion it becomes clear that there is no "let's just go ahead and shoot" without meticulous preparation, planning, and legal work far in advance to any first day of cameras rolling. This book will try to offer an insight into the mechanics of organizing for and accomplishing shooting of motion pictures, especially from the viewpoint of a production manager.

Few people grow up with the goal of becoming a motion picture production manager. Everyone knows what a director does and what producers do. Everyone can identify with an actor or a star. Even director of photography is a generally known profession. But who knows what a production manager does?

Admittedly, it sounds boring. Yet this field of work is one of the most complex, responsible, and diverse in the whole process of motion picture production. It poses challenges in vastly different areas and requires legal, technical, organizational, and psychological expertise. This profession demands the very best from those who pursue it; it is a job that starts first thing in the morning and closes late at night—the production manager is usually available at all times during the day and night, acting as emergency help, and should be relied on at any time during preproduction, shooting, and postproduction. It is normal to expect competent and up-to-date answers from the production manager to any and every question, however strange—he or she is the person who embodies the complete production and has a clear overview of what has happened, what is happening, and what is going to happen. The production manager sets the mood of the overall production and often serves as a go-between to restore balance and common sense if necessary. This business being what it is, this personal quality might be called upon more often than can be imagined. The production manager's work gives a production the necessary structure within which artists can create their visions.

If your ultimate goal is to become a producer—for theatrical motion pictures, commercials, music videos, corporate image films, documentaries, or TV—you will probably proceed through the levels of production management, from assistant director to production manager to independent producer. To do a thorough and creative job as a producer, it is wise to get as much experience as possible guiding a production from conception through to final screening. The best way to do this is through hands-on, detail-oriented, nitty-gritty production work on the set and in the production office. The production manager is one of the few people working on a production who is involved from beginning to end. Few others know and are responsible for as many details about the production. The knowledge you gain as a production manager will be invaluable when you achieve the title of producer. It will give you the power and authority to seize control of the production; through personal experience, you will know the limits of what can be done. As a producer, your creative ambitions will be set free. You will decide on story ideas, developments, and creative aspects of the screenplay; you will make choices in casting and all other artistic aspects of production; and you will be fully responsible for making your vision a reality.

The Production Manager's Job

The Directors Guild of America (DGA) has a very precise job description for the position of production manager. In reality, though, the areas of authority often become hazy, particularly in the field of independent nonunion production. The job titles, also, may become indistinct. Virtually the same position might carry the title production manager (PM), unit production manager (UPM), line producer, or producer. The title depends on the size of the production, the staffing of the production department, and the relationship of the position to the producer and executive producer.

Here is how the DGA describes the production manager's role (from Directors Guild of America, Inc., Basic Agreement of 1993):

> A Unit Production Manager is one who is assigned by the Employer as a Unit Production Manager of one or more motion pictures as the term "Unit

Production Manager" is customarily used and understood in the motion picture industry. A Unit Production Manager (UPM) may be assigned to work concurrently on one or more productions, whether theatrical and/or television. . . . After a picture is approved for production there shall be no delegating to other employees (except First Assistant Directors where no UPM is assigned to the production involved) the duties of UPMs.

It is an element of good faith of, and part of the consideration for, this Directors Guild of America Basic Agreement of 1984 (BA) that no Employer will make a general rearrangement of duties among such categories, change classifications of employment for such categories, employ persons not covered by this BA or delegate the duties ordinarily performed by UPMs to persons other than First Assistant Directors acting in the dual capacity of UPMs or to bona fide Producers for the purpose of eliminating UPMs who otherwise would have been employed hereunder. There shall be no restriction on delegation of duties ordinarily performed by UPMs where a UPM and a First Assistant Director both are assigned to the production.

The UPM under the supervision of the Employer is required to coordinate, facilitate, and oversee the preparation of the production unit or units (to the extent herein provided) assigned to him or her, all off-set logistics, day-to-day production decisions, budget schedules and personnel. Without limitation, among the duties which the Employer must assign the UPM or First Assistant Director are the supervision of or participation in the following:

1. Prepare breakdown and preliminary shooting schedule;

2. Prepare or coordinate the budget;

3. Oversee preliminary search and survey of all locations and the completion of business arrangements for the same;

4. Assist in the preparation of the production to insure continuing efficiency;

5. Supervise completion of the Production Report for each day's work, showing work covered and the status of the production, and arrange for the distribution of that report in line with the company's requirements;

6. Coordinate arrangements for the transportation and housing of cast, crew, and staff;

7. Oversee the securing of releases and negotiate for locations and personnel;

8. Maintain a liaison with local authorities regarding locations and the operation of the company.

In principle, the production manager's job is not one of artistic creativity. The PM is not involved in the process of screenwriting, has no influence on the choice of actors, and does not make directing decisions. The PM's responsibility is to facilitate the work of the executive producer, producer, and director and to provide them with the best possible working conditions. Without the production manager, the director would not have the creative room to work with actors and other personnel to turn the screenplay into a work of art.

The PM is directly responsible to the producer or the executive producer (for an organizational chart, see Figure 2.1 in the next chapter). The PM protects the interests of the production company. During preproduction, all other units, such as the art department, the camera department, the special effects department during digital postproduction, and so on, must follow the directives of the production office, as represented by the production manager. The same is true throughout the other stages of production. During the shoot, however, some authority is delegated to the director. On the set, the director's word is law. Still, the PM must protect the company's interests—if necessary, also against the director. The PM is charged with the control of all organizational, managerial, financial, and logistical aspects of the production, in collaboration with and subject to the executive producer's or producer's directives.

The PM epitomizes the eternal conflict between art and commerce, and with this position, conflicts between the two fields come into focus. Whereas the director strives to get the best possible results on film, regardless of cost, the production manager is responsible for avoiding budget overruns. The PM's job is to finish the production "on time, on budget". Clearly, someone in this position should be able to live with stress and conflict, and still be enough of a psychologist and diplomat to avoid hurt egos and bad feelings on the set. Inevitably, the holder of this position will never win popularity contests with the crew; generally, the PM's work is underrated and unappreciated by most of the crew and cast. If ever there was a "bad guy" doing "hatchet jobs" for the executive producer, it is the production manager.

The PM's position is one of great trust. He or she is responsible for spending, and not spending, large amounts of money and is also highly instrumental in hiring staff and crew personnel. This position involves quite a lot of office-based work; only rarely is the PM needed on location or on the set. There, the assistant director (AD) is in charge. The AD organizes the daily procedures on location in cooperation with the PM and reports to the PM at least daily, usually several times a day, on the progress of the shoot. (More on the relationship between PM and AD can be found in subsequent chapters.)

The Process of Production Management

The following chapters clarify the process of production management, from the first steps of a screenplay breakdown through the ever-more complex postproduction period. The focus is on nonunion productions—that is, those in which only one union, generally the Screen Actors Guild (SAG), is involved. It generally is correct to assume that the novice production manager will be involved in nonunion shoots for quite some time because the entry requirements for the Directors Guild of America (DGA) are absurdly high and can only be passed after extensive practical work on nonunion productions.

At what point in time does the production manager join the production? The PM usually becomes involved after the production company has approved a screenplay, has some of its financing in place, and is ready to go into preproduction. The PM accompanies the project through the shoot until all shooting-related tasks have been accomplished. Sometimes this takes weeks after the shooting period, and sometimes the PM is asked to remain for the postproduction phase, as due to the growing digital effects work more and more aspects of postproduction work have to be integrated and discussed with the Director and the Director of Photography from the very first planning and layout as soon as the screenplay is available. As this is usually less work-intensive than the preproduction and production phases, the PM may at the same time become involved in preproduction on another project.

Seasoned production managers can handle more than one production at a time. In television, a PM frequently supervises the production phases of single episodes of a series or sitcom that are in progress at varying stages of development. Of course, this is only possible when a well-oiled crew of assistant directors and production secretaries is available to assist the PM.

Once the project gets a "green light", it enters the preproduction phase, and the production manager must juggle many, often interdependent, processes simultaneously. Only very few people in the "business" have the authority to "green-light" a production, which means that the final "go ahead" and start of production has been given. A "green light" usually is the result of years of development and contractual negotiations—also called "development hell". Up to such a "green light" any production is a rather fragile endeavor that might equally result in total abortion and loss of commitments, hard work, and financial investments. However, the PM usually will not enter a production before "green-lighting" has taken place.

Before arranging shooting permits, the PM must find and secure locations; before renting equipment, the PM must arrange for insurance and must obtain the best deal from a multitude of various offers; and before asking for official location permits, the PM must make sure that the schedule is in place and that other insurance requirements are fulfilled. At the same time, the casting and hiring of the crew take place, and some of these decisions are dependent on the budget or the distribution agreements. In addition, the distribution agreements may determine the caliber of the actors who will be cast, and vice versa.

Preproduction is a time of both order and chaos, of plans that must be revised, of tentative schedules and possible budget changes, of revisions to the screenplay and changing structures. Eventually, all the elements come together: a truly mystifying process of things falling into place and procedures being secured. Preproduction is the least expensive part of the filmmaking process. The staff is fairly small, and the activities mostly center around a production office (requiring only chairs, phones, calculators, computers, and online-communication—the usual office equipment and furniture). During this stage, the groundwork for all later activities is laid.

Practical Tips

As a production manager, you will be expected to know every detail about every unit during all phases of production. Therefore, it is advisable to keep telephone logs that contain notes on your conversations: when the call took place, with whom you spoke, what you discussed, and any decisions or agreements you reached. It is also a good idea to create a paper trail of memoranda that details recommendations, suggestions, directives, and opinions expressed by and to anyone involved in the production (above-the-line as well as below-the-line personnel—above-the-line meaning creative individuals such as authors, directors, composers, producers, and most of all: actors; below-the-line meaning crew). If possible, have these memos countersigned by the people to whom they are addressed.

Put in writing all deals involving commitments, finances, permits, and other agreements. Not only is this important for internal use, it is also mandatory when dealing with third parties, such as government agencies, agents, location owners, and rental companies.

For your own protection, you always should be able to retrace how a decision was made, by whom, and after what consideration. Not uncommonly, PMs are made scapegoats when things go wrong and are forced to defend their decisions in court. In fact, this occurs in Hollywood at all levels.

In nonunion situations, you might be asked to join a production before financing is available. The production company will want you to establish a budget so that it can raise the necessary funds. As you will see, it is quite a difficult, time-consuming, and tedious process to come up with a detailed budget. It can be achieved only when a complete screenplay is available, and even then it might take several days or weeks, depending on the complexity of the production.

This is a "catch-22": the producer cannot try to raise financing without a budget that shows how much money is needed, but to get a budget the production company must put up the money for development and must compensate the PM for time and labor required to compute the budget. If you are asked to work "on spec" (common in independent filmmaking), insist that any deferred-pay agreements are put in writing. Make sure you will be hired as PM for the production when the time comes and you will be paid the salary due. If the producer is not willing to make such commitments in writing, do not get involved.

2

The Business of Film

Next to the producer or executive producer, the production manager is one of the few people on a production who stays with the project from beginning to end. The four distinctive phases in any production are development, preproduction, production (principal photography), and postproduction. This chapter looks at the role of the PM at each phase.

Development

The production manager is usually spared the most nerve-racking and frustrating phase of all: development. In this phase, the producer conceives an idea for a movie, develops it into a presentable package and tries to raise production funds to get the project into preproduction. To put it bluntly, filmmaking is all about business and earning potentially vast amounts of money. This statement might sound harsh and cynical to a novice filmmaker, but it accurately reflects the dealings and philosophy of the entertainment business.

The development process sounds simple, but let's take a closer look. First, the producer searches for material that can be turned into a successful (that is, *financially* successful) motion picture. Inspiration might come from an original screenplay, novel, stage play, short story, book, periodical, real-life story, pop song, or another motion picture. Regardless of its source, the producer must acquire or option the rights to it before making the movie. If an intellectual property is being optioned it means that there is usually a certain time limit (mostly one year with the possibility of a prolongation for another 12 months) during which time the producer must be ready to pay the full amount of the previously agreed-upon full price. This does not necessarily mean the producer must get shooting, but it means he has to purchase the property completely.

Buying the exploitation rights to an existing screenplay can involve a considerable amount of money. It all depends on the market value of the script, whether it is brand new or has been shopped around for a while, and the "name value" of the screenwriter. In any case, the producer must consult (and pay) a lawyer to ensure that exploitation rights are cleared and obtained. The lawyer must also make sure the story of the screenplay does not violate other rights, such as the right to privacy. Even if the producer believes the screenplay must be rewritten, either by the original author or by another writer, buying an existing screenplay is still the easiest and quickest way to obtain a property ready for "pitching"—that is, for presenting, packaging, and trying to sell it. To obtain the rights, the producer must have up-front money. If the producer does not have a development deal with a studio or a production company, he or she personally must advance the money. Of course, an author may grant the producer the right, without financial compensation, to try to sell the project and agree to get paid once the production is secured and green-lighted. There are no hard-and-fast rules in this regard, so whatever deals can be made, will be.

If the screenplay will be based on an existing novel, play, short story, or book, the producer first must obtain the rights to have the screenplay written (assuming the property is not in the public domain). The time needed to negotiate adaptation rights and then to obtain a finished, presentable screenplay, including rewrites and the like, can be considerable—several months to a year or two. The process is similar if the producer wants to base the film on an article from a periodical. The rights must be cleared, and the screenwriter found, motivated, and paid. Once again, rewrites by other authors might be required—contractual provisions for such a case must have been previously implemented.

The process is slightly different with a real-life story. If the story is "hot", fierce competition will be had for the right to create a film about it. This means that cash is necessary to secure the rights. In any case, the producer must obtain the rights from those involved. In addition, of course, a screenwriter must be found, and the screenplay must be written. Lawyers must be involved in negotiating any agreements. The rights of those who might be affected by the story must be cleared. All this can be quite an exhausting enterprise.

If an existing motion picture is involved, the original producers or holders of the copyright will probably want to retain their rights for a sequel if they can. Otherwise, the author must be contacted, and the rights purchased as described earlier. If you plan to make a sequel to your own movie and you retained the right to do so, the process is somewhat easier. If you want to use the original cast, negotiations might prove to be expensive unless a provision was made in the original contract for a sequel.

Finally, if the movie is to be based on the plot or lyrics of a song, the producer must obtain the adaptation rights. Besides the songwriter and singer, a record company might be involved. Whoever owns the copyright must participate in the negotiations. It is easy to see why a seasoned entertainment lawyer should be at the producer's side at this early but essential phase of any production: exploitation rights that have not been obtained from the very beginning—and this list must be complete, exclusive, worldwide, and for all media—are very difficult to clear at a later stage.

Next, to raise money for production, the producer must find a production company or studio willing to provide financing. This is where the process of packaging begins. The producer must create an attractive overall package. "Name" actors who will guarantee the film's success must be found. The producer might also seek a well-known director to guarantee the financiers that a professional and superior product will be created. However, "name" actors and directors will only agree to be in a movie if distribution is guaranteed, and to get a distribution contract, commitments are required from the actors and director. It is a vicious circle.

When dealing with "name" talent (in reality, this means dealing with their agents, managers, personal advisers, astrologers, friends, and trustees), the producer must accept their "right" to creative participation. In the end, it is the talent's face and name that are remembered with the screenplay. As a result, the screenplay must often go through new rounds of rewrites to accommodate the wishes of the talent. All this takes time—and money. The process is successfully concluded when the producer has all the names he or she wants—or is satisfied with—and has obtained their written consent to be part of the production. At this point, the package is presentable, and the producer will pitch it again to studios, networks, financiers, and distributors.

Clearly, film is a product, and entertainment is a business. Everything and everyone involved in the business is judged by a simple criterion: Will the involvement of this thing or this person improve the product's chances of being sold, being seen, and turning a profit—a huge profit, if possible? In the entertainment industry, everything and everyone has a value. Disturbingly, these values can go up or down dramatically within a day (contributing further to the exhaustion occurring during the development phase). For example, an unknown actor becomes a sought-after star if the movie turns out to be a surprise hit; the same is true of the unknown director, the unknown studio executive, and the unknown writer. By the same token, if a star has one or more box office flops, he or she will become undesirable, and his or her participation in a project will virtually destroy all chances the screenplay may have had with another performer. This, of course, is true regarding known directors, established studio executives, and expensive writers. Everyone must be very successful all the time—and success always means financial success.

Let's return to the development process. After the producer has found inspiration for a film, has cleared the rights to the screenplay or other material on which the film will be based, and has obtained commitments from actors and a director, he or she is ready to pitch again. This is the point at which a production manager might sign on. The producer must have a budget to know the amount of money to request. Producers who cannot or do not want to break down the screenplay or work out the budget themselves hire a PM to do this.

Independent nonunion production being what it is, producers usually try to find a PM who will do this free, in exchange for a guarantee that he or she will be hired as PM on the production once it has been green-lighted. Production managers who accept this deal should be sure to get it in writing. The agreement should spell out the amount of money owed to the PM for work on speculation. Without an agreement, no producer can actually guarantee that the PM will be hired. The financier might want to install a friend or relative in an important career position. The financier's nephew, for example, would love to have the PM credit, despite having neither the qualifications nor the desire to do the nitty-gritty work. Under such circumstances, the nephew might easily be made an associate producer, a credit typically given out for favors.

Assume a happy ending: the producer has all the talent desired, a final screenplay, and financial backing. A substantial amount of money has been advanced and is on account and ready to be drawn. The producer might even have distribution. In other words, it's a go! The production is now ready to move into preproduction.

Preproduction

Much of this book deals with work the PM must accomplish during prepro-duction. This includes screenplay breakdown, shooting schedule, location scouting, budget, casting and unions, permits, hiring staff and crew, unit supervision, permit clearance, equipment rental and stock, lab supervision, payroll service, insurance, postproduction preparation, and so on. Because these subjects are treated in greater detail later in the book, this section is quite brief. Figure 2.1 illustrates how the production team is organized and where the PM fits. The lines of authority and chain of command are indicated.

Production (Principal Photography)

Once all the preproduction tasks are complete, the film enters the production phase, during which the film is actually shot. The PM is responsible for a glitch-free shoot and must handle both logistics and overall organization.

If editing has already begun, the PM's responsibilities might include some postproduction work, such as dealing with digital special effects houses, the film lab, watching dailies, and possibly starting work on the soundtrack. The budget must be monitored according to the cash-flow chart; preliminary press work and public relations must be started. Together, the PM, in the production office, and the assistant director, on the set, are responsible for the flow of information. They must ensure that everyone involved with the production—staff, crew, and cast—knows what is going on, when, and where. The PM again coordinates and supervises the cooperation of the various units, as depicted in Figure 2.1.

The main action has shifted from the production office to the set or location. The assistant director is responsible for the flow and continuity of activities on the set. He or she keeps the PM informed on the status of the production and is responsible for the observance of union regulations, including timely

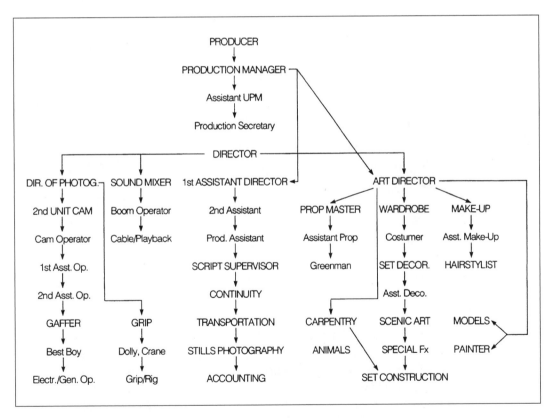

Fig. 2–1. Organizational chart of the motion picture production team for preproduction and principal photography.

lunch breaks and correctly completed paperwork. The AD alerts the PM to any difficulties that arise.

What happens on the set? The four distinctive phases of set operations are blocking, lighting, final rehearsals, and shooting. Let's take a closer look at what happens during each phase.

Blocking

During blocking, the director sets up the shot, determining the look of the scene and the film. This is the time for creative decisions and work with actors. Cast members must repeat their actions several times until perfect compositions and movements are found. Actors do not actually perform during this phase. Instead, they walk through the scenes to determine positions.

During blocking, conversation between crew members and working actors is prohibited. If the director and talent are permitted to work without interruption, the production will progress smoothly and quickly. Nothing is deadlier on a shoot than the slow pacing caused by disturbances and lack of concentration.

Only the following personnel are required on the set for blocking:

- Actors in the scene and being blocked;
- Director;
- Director of photography;
- Special effects supervisors—if required;
- Assistant director;
- Script supervisor;
- Gaffer.

Everyone else must stay off the set and be quiet. The AD must make sure that these rules are not violated and that the work advances at a good pace.

Lighting

During this phase, the director of photography (DP), gaffers and grips, and electrical and camera crews begin to establish the technical structure within which the scene will be shot. This is possible only after blocking has been completed, positions have been marked, and the DP understands what the director wants. Stand-ins, usually extras, may take the actors' places during lighting. They should have the same height as the actors they are replacing, otherwise precise lighting cannot be accomplished. No one else is required on the set, with the possible exception of set dresser and prop master. Everyone else should not disturb the work of the technical crews. With ever more complicated postproduction special effects work to be done, SFX personnel frequently work on the set to make sure that principal photography incorporates all necessary aspects for a later problem-free workflow. During this time, the actors are in wardrobe, hair, and makeup, getting ready for final rehearsals and the shoot. They may go over their lines or just relax. The DP estimates when the set will be ready, and the AD communicates this information to wardrobe and makeup so that the actors will be available when needed. The AD must know the whereabouts of the actors at all times. He or she cannot permit the talent to leave the location, even if they are done with wardrobe and makeup. When the DP declares the set ready, no further changes should be made. It is highly disturbing when the DP starts to make changes in lighting once the director and the actors are back. The AD must make certain this does not occur.

Final Rehearsals

The extent of the final rehearsals varies from scene to scene, from director to director, from actor to actor. These rehearsals involve all units working on the scene. Actor–camera–sound relations are fine-tuned to perfection. The actors must be completely ready to perform before final rehearsals begin. No further wardrobe or makeup alterations—except slight touch-ups—are permitted. Members of props, wardrobe, and makeup crews must stand by to be instantly available if needed. The AD must make sure that no one who might be requested on the set is permitted to leave. The DP and gaffers should not be allowed to change lighting. The AD is responsible for ensuring that no delays occur.

Shooting

Shooting commences immediately after final rehearsals, when everyone is ready and knows exactly what to do. Absolute silence is mandatory once these commands are given: "Sound rolling. Camera rolling. Slate number x. Action". Crew members not directly involved should remain absolutely still to avoid making disturbing background noises. The shooting stops when the director calls "Cut". If additional takes are necessary, wardrobe, hair, and makeup people check on the actors, and the props crew replaces items if necessary. Once the scene is completed and in the can, the director says "Print", and the still photographer may take pictures as long as the set is lit.

After the first scene is completed, the next one goes through the same cycle of blocking, lighting, rehearsal, and shooting. The AD already should have the next scene prepared. The location should be readied as much as possible, the

CALL SHEET

PRODUCTION COMPANY _____   DATE _____

SHOW _____   DIRECTOR _____

SERIES EPISODE _____   PRODUCER _____

PROD # _____ DAY # _____ OUT OF _____   LOCATION _____

IS TODAY A DESIGNATED DAY OFF? ☐ YES ☐ NO   SUNRISE _____   SUNSET _____

CREW CALL _____   ANTICIPATED WEATHER _____

LEAVING CALL _____   ☐ Weather Permitting   ☐ See Attached Map

SHOOTING CALL _____   ☐ Report to Location   ☐ Bus to Location

SET DESCRIPTION	SCENE #	CAST	D/N	PAGES	LOCATION

CAST	PART OF	LEAVE	MAKEUP	SET CALL	REMARKS

ATMOSPHERE & STAND-INS					

NOTE: No forced calls without previous approval of unit production manager or assistant director. All calls subject to change.

ADVANCE SCHEDULE OR CHANGES

Assistant Director _____   Production Manager _____
© ELH

Fig. 2–2. Call sheet forms.

PRODUCTION REQUIREMENT

SHOW:			PROD #:			DATE:	
Production Mgr.			Gaffer			Cameras	
1st Asst. Dir			Best Boy				
2nd Asst. Dir			Lamp Oper.			Dolly	
2nd 2nd Asst. Dir			Lamp Oper.			Crane	
DGA Trainee			Lamp Oper.			Condor	
Script Supervisor			Local 40 Man				
Dialogue Coach						Sound Channel	
Prod. Coordinator			Prod. Designer				
Prod. Sect'y			Art Director			Video	
Prod. Accountant			Asst. Art Dir.				
Asst. Accountant			Set Designer			Radio Mikes	
Location Mgr.			Sketch Artist			Walkie/talkies	
Asst. Location Mgr.							
Teacher/Welfare Worker			Const. Coord.			Dressing Rooms	
Production Assts.			Const. Foreman			Schoolrooms	
			Paint Foreman			Rm. For Parents	
Dir of Photography			Labor Foreman				
Camera Operator			Const. First Aid			Projector	
Camera Operator						Moviola	
SteadyCam Operator			Set Director				
Asst. Cameraman			Lead Person			Air Conditioners	
Asst. Cameraman			Swing Crew			Heaters	
Asst. Cameraman			Swing Crew			Wind Machines	
Still Photographer			Swing Crew				
Cameraman-Process			Drapery				
Projectionist							
			Technical Advisor			**SUPPORT**	
Mixer			Publicist			**PERSONNEL**	**TIME**
Boomman			**MEALS**			Policemen	
Cableman			Caterer			Motorcycles	
Playback			Breakfasts			Fireman	
Video Oper.			Wlkg. Breakfasts rdy @			Guard	
			Gallons Coffee			Night Watchman	
Key Grip			Lunches rdy @ Crew @				
2nd Grip			Box Lunches				
Dolly Grip			Second Meal				
Grip							
Grip							
Grip			**DRIVERS**			**VEHICLES**	
			Trans. Coord.			Prod. Van	
Greensman			Trans. Capt.			Camera	
			Driver			Grip	
S/By Painter			Driver			Electric	
Craftservice			Driver			Effects	
First Aid			Driver			Props	
			Driver			Wardrobe	
Spec. Efx			Driver			Makeup	
Spec. Efx			Driver			Set Dressing	
			Driver			Crew Bus	
Propmaster			Driver			Honeywagon	
Asst. Props			Driver			Motorhomes	
Asst. Props			Driver			Station Wagons	
			Driver			Mini-buses	
Costume Designer			Driver			Standby Cars	
Costume Supervisor			Driver			Crew Cabs	
Costumer			Driver			Insert Cars	
Costumer			Driver			Generators	
			Driver			Water Wagon	
Makeup Artist			Driver			Picture Cars	
Makeup Artist			Driver				
Body Makeup							
Hairstylist			Stunt Coord.				
Hairstylist			Wranglers				
			Animal Handlers			Livestock	
Editor						Animals	
Asst. Editor							
Apprentice Editor							

DEPARTMENT	**SPECIAL INSTRUCTIONS**

© ELH

Fig. 2–2. (continued)

SHOW _____   PROD# _____   DATE _____

NO	STAFF & CREW	TIME	NO	STAFF & CREW	TIME	NO	EQUIPMENT
	Production Manager			Gaffer			Cameras
	1st Assistant Director			Best Boy			
	2nd Assistant Director			Lamp Operator			Dolly
	2nd 2nd Assistant Director			Lamp Operator			Crane
	DGA Trainee			Lamp Operator			Condor
	Script Supervisor			Local 40 Man			
	Dialogue Coach						Sound Channel
	Production Coordinator			Production Designer			
	Production Sect'y			Art Director			Video
	Production Accountant			Assistant Art Director			
	Assistant Accountant			Set Designer			Radio Mikes
	Location Manager			Sketch Artist			Walkie-Talkies
	Assistant Location Manager						
	Teacher/Welfare Worker			Construction Coordinator			Dressing Rooms
	Production Assistants			Construction Foreman			Schoolrooms
				Paint Foreman			Room for Parents
	Director of Photography			Labor Foremen			
	Camera Operator			Construction First Aid			Projector
	Camera Operator						Moviola
	SteadyCam Operator			Set Decorator			
	Assistant Cameraman			Lead Person			Air Conditioners
	Assistant Cameraman			Swing Crew			Heaters
	Assistant Cameraman			Swing Crew			Wind Machines
	Still Photographer			Swing Crew			
	Cameraman-Process			Drapery			
	Projectionist						
				Technical Advisor			
	Mixer			Publicist			
	Boomman			**MEALS**			**SUPPORT PERSONNEL**
	Cableman			Caterer			Policemen
	Playback			Breakfasts			Motorcycles
	Video Operator			Walking Breakfasts ready @			Fireman
				Gals. Coffee			Guard
	Key Grip			Lunches ready @ Crew @			Night Watchman
	2nd Grip			Box Lunches			
	Dolly Grip			Second Meal			
	Grip						
	Grip						
	Grip			**DRIVERS**			**VEHICLES**
				Transportation Coordinator			Production Van
	Greensman			Transportation Captain			Camera
				Driver			Grip
	S/By Painter			Driver			Electric
	Craftservice			Driver			Effects
	First Aid			Driver			Props
				Driver			Wardrobe
	Special Effects			Driver			Makeup
	Special Effects			Driver			Set Dressing
				Driver			Crew Bus
	Propmaster			Driver			Honeywagon
	Assistant Props			Driver			Motorhomes
	Assistant Props			Driver			Station Wagons
				Driver			Mini-buses
	Costume Designer			Driver			Standby Cars
	Costume Supervisor			Driver			Crew Cabs
	Costumer			Driver			Insert Cars
	Costumer			Driver			Generators
				Driver			Water Wagon
	Makeup Artist			Driver			Picture Cars
	Makeup Artist			Driver			
	Body Makeup						
	Hairstylist			Stunt Coordinator			
	Hairstylist			Wranglers			
				Animal Handlers			Livestock
	Editor						Animals
	Assistant Editor						
	Apprentice Editor						

COMMENTS—DELAYS (EXPLANATIONS)—CAST, STAFF, AND CREW ABSENCE

© ELH

Fig. 2–2. (continued)

needed actors should be standing by, and everyone should know where the next set is and which scene to prepare. When this structure is followed and a quick pace is maintained, the production will run efficiently and smoothly. Otherwise, the production will sink into chaos and frustration, and is likely to go over budget and fall behind schedule. Any questions of overtime should be passed on to the production office, where the PM or the producer decides whether the extra expense is warranted. Neither the director nor anyone else on the set can authorize overtime; this is the producer's prerogative. At the end of each shooting day, the AD, together with the PM and possibly the director, details the next day's schedule and draws up the appropriate call sheets. The call sheets describe the next day's work and indicate who will be required and when. The shooting schedule is drawn up during the preproduction phase, but frequently minor changes must be made daily. The call sheets reflect these changes. They are distributed or exhibited where everyone can read them. A sample call sheet is shown in Figure 2.2. The AD makes sure that the actors sign off on the actors' production time report, which is forwarded to the Screen Actors Guild every week. These time reports keep track of each actor's arrival time, time in makeup, breaks, and end of workday. They serve as the basis for computing salaries, overtime, night-work premiums, and fines. Figure 2.3 shows a sample actors' production time report. The AD also fills in the daily production report. Additional information provided by the script supervisor helps the PM complete this form, which must be kept not only to record the progress of the shoot, but also to document it for the insurance company. The PM can use the production report to determine quickly if the production is on track, if film stock use is as initially intended, if the scenes are being shot as planned, if delays are occurring, and if cost overruns are likely. A sample daily production report is illustrated in Figure 2.4.

Postproduction

When principal photography is completed, the production moves into the final stage: postproduction. Depending on the amount of work to be organized, the production manager might be asked to stay on. Often, the PM simply concludes the tasks related to the production office—communication with the SAG, rental houses, lab, insurance, payroll, accounting, and book-keeping—and then leaves the production.

Generally, the PM organizes the editing phase in advance, including sound effects, music production, opticals, and mixing. The supervision of postproduction in the past has not been usually a full-time task, and with traditional

SCREEN ACTORS GUILD
ACTORS PRODUCTION TIME REPORT

EXHIBIT G

PICTURE TITLE________________ PROD. NO.________ PRODUCTION CO.________________ DATE

CONTACT________________ PHONE NO. (   )________ ADVERTISING AGENCY________________

☐ THEATRICAL ☐ TV ☐ COMMERCIAL ☐ INDUSTRIAL ☐

WORKED — W STARTED — S TRAVEL — TR REHEARSAL — R HOLD — H FINISHED — F TEST — T		W H S F R T	Makeup Wdbe.	WORK TIME			MEALS				TRAVEL TIME				Stunt Adjust.	ACTORS' SIGNATURES
CAST	CHARACTER	TR		Report On Set	Dismiss On Set	BKFST	1st MEAL		2nd MEAL		Leave For Location	Arrive On Location	Leave Location	Arrive At Studio		

Fig. 2–3. Actors' production time report form.

DAILY PRODUCTION REPORT

	1st Unit	2nd Unit	Reh.	Test	Travel	Holidays	Change Over	Retakes & Add. Scs.	Total	Schedule	
No. Days Sched										Ahead	
No. Days Actual										Behind	

Title _____ Prod. # _____ Date _____
Producer _____ Director _____
Date Started _____ Scheduled Finish Date _____ Est. Finish Date _____

Sets _____
Location _____
Crew Call _____ Shooting Call _____ First Shot _____ Lunch _____ Til _____
1st Shot After Lunch _____ 2nd Meal _____ Til _____ Camera Wrap _____ Last Man Out _____
Company dismissed at ☐ Studio ☐ Location ☐ Headquarters   Round Trip Mileage _____ Is Today A Designated Day Off? ☐ YES ☐ NO

SCRIPT SCENES AND PAGES			MINUTES		SETUPS		ADDED SCENES			RETAKES	
	SCENES	PAGES								PAGES	SCENES
			Prev.		Prev.		Prev.		Prev.		
			Today		Today		Today		Today		
Script			Total		Total		Total		Total		
Taken Prev.			Scene No.								
Taken Today											
Taken to Date			Added Scenes								
To Be Taken			Retakes					Sound Tracks			

FILM STOCK	FILM USE	GROSS	PRINT	NO GOOD	WASTE	1/4" ROLLS	FILM INVENTORY	
	Prev.						Starting Inv.	
	Today						Additional Rec'd Today	
	To Date						Total	

FILM STOCK	FILM USE	GROSS	PRINT	NO GOOD	WASTE		FILM INVENTORY	
	Prev.						Starting Inv.	
	Today						Additional Rec'd Today	
	To Date						Total	

FILM STOCK	FILM USE	GROSS	PRINT	NO GOOD	WASTE		FILM INVENTORY	
	Prev.						Starting Inv.	
	Today						Additional Rec'd Today	
	To Date						Total	

CAST - WEEKLY & DAY PLAYERS		W H S F R T TR	MAKEUP WDBE.	WORKTIME		MEALS		TRAVEL TIME				STUNT ADJ.
Worked – W Rehearsal - R Finished - F Started – S Hold - H Test - T Travel - TR				REPORT ON SET	DISMISS ON SET	OUT	IN	LEAVE FOR LOC.	ARRIVE ON LOC.	LEAVE LOCA- TION	ARRIVE AT HDQ.	
CAST	CHARACTER											

XX = N.D. BREAKFAST   * = DISMISS TIME INCLUDES 15 MIN. MAKEUP / WARD. REMOVAL
X = NOT PHOTOGRAPHED   S = SCHOOL ONLY

EXTRA TALENT												
No.	Rate	1st Call	Set Dismiss	Final Dismiss	Adj.	MPV	No.	Rate	1st Call	Set Dismiss	Final Dismiss	Adj.	MPV

Assistant Director _____ Production Manager _____
© ELH

Fig. 2-4. Daily production report form.

filmmaking still is not. However, with the advent of digital filmmaking and digital special effects work it frequently nowadays turns into a production by itself. Careful preproduction-planning, on-the-set execution and often time-consuming computer-guided work have created a new profession called the SFX supervisor. The UPM works closely together with this person to make sure all necessary budgetary and deadline-requirements are met. Overall super-vision may be handled by the production secretary, or specific aspects may be guided by a postproduction producer or supervisor.

3

Preparing for Production

Script Breakdown

The very first step the production manager must take to evaluate a project's overall size and scope is completing a thorough breakdown of the finished screenplay. With an initial "first-glance" reading of a screenplay, an experienced producer or PM can get a good estimate of the size of a production—that is, how long the shooting period, how many necessary cast members, how much required travel, how expensive the props and sets, and much more. However, a reliable budget estimate only can be calculated after the screenplay has been broken down professionally.

In the screenplay breakdown process, all elements of the screenplay are defined and listed for later reference. Because of this, all screenplays must follow the industry standard. Each new scene is assigned a scene number, given a "day" or "night" designation, and described in terms of location—INTerior or EXTerior. If these procedures are not followed, the missing information makes a reliable prediction of shooting schedules and budgets impossible.

Similarly, it is next to impossible to accurately estimate a project's budget with no screenplay. No production manager can reliably forecast final costs from just a story outline or a twenty-page treatment. Many elements that later give the film color and "production value", such as props, sets, and locations, may not be included in the story outline. Cast and extras are sometimes added during screenwriting, and completely new subplots and scenes also might emerge during that process, and what amount of computer-created imagery or visual effects are implemented will be discussed between Director, Director of Photography, and the SFX Supervisor. With experience, however, a producer or PM can tell from a treatment whether a project will fit a given budget. If the budget limitation is $500,000, for example, travel around the world with the whole crew and cast obviously is not affordable, nor are costly special effects or sophisticated computer-generated postproduction trickery.

The situation may seem somehow different with projects that look less restricted or are not completely scripted, such as documentary films. However, preplanning is as much a factor in this genre as it is with films scripted in every detail. Duration of shoot, size of crew, travel expenses, and so on are factors all filmmakers must evaluate before they consider a realistic budget.

Script Breakdown Sheet

The script breakdown sheet is the single most important production form during this phase because all future reference and production work will be based on it. Anything missing in the breakdown sheet is likely to be missed during the shoot on the set, and thus will be missed on the screen. It is essential that the utmost care be taken during this step of production. The PM creates a separate breakdown sheet for each scene in the screenplay. Eventually, the number of breakdown sheets must equal the number of scenes in the screenplay.

The sample script breakdown sheet illustrated in Figure 3.1 shows the required information. The numbers in the descriptions that follow correspond to the numbers on the sheet.

1. *Date of current screenplay version.* To minimize confusion, it is important to distinguish the breakdown sheets for various versions of the screenplay. A screenplay often can go through many drafts and revisions. All these revisions must be evaluated, new breakdown pages drawn up, and old ones replaced. Previous breakdown sheets should be put aside when the new pages are available for replacement.

2. *Date when breakdown sheet is written.* If a development period extends over a period of time (certainly the case on most projects— sometimes years are required to put together financing), it is helpful to know when the script breakdown was prepared. This date serves as a safeguard but may be omitted (it will appear on budget forms).

3. *Name of production company.* Also included here should be the names and telephone numbers of those who will handle any problems that arise.

4. *Title and number of production.* On a television series, such as a weekly sitcom, single episodes are frequently given numbers in addition to titles. In theatrical motion pictures, though, production numbers are uncommon. When the production manager is working on different projects at the same time, this information becomes crucial.

5. *Breakdown sheet page number.* This information helps confirm that the breakdown is complete.

CODE – BREAKDOWN SHEETS/STRIPS

Day Ext. – Yellow
Night Ext. – Green
Day Int. – White
Night Int. – Blue
Numbers refer to budget
categories

SCRIPT
BREAKDOWN SHEET

① ② _____ DATE

③ _____
PRODUCTION COMPANY

④ _____
PRODUCTION TITLE/NO.

⑤ _____
BREAKDOWN PAGE NO.

⑥
SCENE NO.

⑦
SCENE NAME

⑧
INT. OR EXT.

⑨
DESCRIPTION

⑩
DAY OR NIGHT

⑪
PAGE COUNT

CAST Red (1301-2-3) ⑫	**STUNTS** Orange (1304-5) ⑬	**EXTRAS/ATMOSPHERE** Green (2120) ⑭
	EXTRAS/SILENT BITS Yellow (2120) ⑮	**SECURITY/TEACHERS** ⑯
SPECIAL EFFECTS Blue (2700) ⑰	**PROPS** Violet (2500) ⑱	**VEHICLES/ANIMALS** Pink (2600/4500) ⑲
WARDROBE Circle (3400) ⑳	**EST. NO. OF SETUPS** ㉑	**EST. PROD. TIME** ㉒
SPECIAL EQUIPMENT Box ㉓	**PRODUCTION NOTES** ㉔	

© 1984 Lone Eagle Productions, Inc.

Fig. 3–1. Script breakdown sheet.

6. *Scene number*. The importance of numbering scenes extends into the whole organization of a production, from start to final mix. Some screenwriters do not care to number their screenplays. In this case, the PM or production secretary must do it. Without scene numbers, no further work on the production makes sense because all planning and cross-referencing are determined by scene numbers. Never change these numbers! Even when new scenes are added or old ones are deleted, use the numbering system already established. Label new scenes by adding A, B, C, and so on. For example, scene 23A would be the correct number for a new scene that follows scene 23. When scenes are deleted, just make a note, such as "Scene 23 deleted".

7. *Name of location or set where scene takes place.* This does not mean the name of the site where filming will be done. It describes the setting of the scene in the context of the screenplay's story line, not in the context of production logistics. The name of the setting must be identical to the name used in the screenplay. If the screenplay states "mansion", for example, this is the term that should be used on the breakdown sheet. This consistency cuts down on confusion in later planning. The description should be as precise as possible. For example, "fireplace/living room" is clearer than just "living room" or "fireplace".

8. *Interior or exterior.* This information defines where the scene is to be shot, whether at an inside or outside location. The location will have consequences for planning and scheduling, and thus this information is important. Even if the dialogue or content of the scene makes clear where it takes place, this data must be part of the breakdown sheet heading to avoid confusion. The PM sometimes must clarify the precise location with the screenwriter or director. For example, "front door" could mean that the scene is being shot from the inside looking out or from the outside looking in. From the standpoint of logistics and organization, this could mean a big difference and could result in different time schedules.

9. *Scene description.* In this portion of the breakdown sheet, the PM describes in a few sentences the action or activity that takes place in the scene. This serves as a reminder of the content and scope of the scene and makes unnecessary the constant rereading of the screenplay.

10. *Day or night.* This indicates the time of day during which the scene *takes place*. It does not necessarily mean that the scene must be *shot* at that particular time of day. For example, a scene designated "INT DAY" or "INT NIGHT" can be shot at any time of day, provided no windows on the set or location reveal the actual time of day. In an artificially lit, windowless room, a night scene can be shot during daytime, of course,

because the difference cannot be ascertained visually. If the screenplay does not clearly indicate when a scene is to take place, the PM must clarify this with the author or the director as soon as possible.

11. *Page count.* This section of the breakdown sheet indicates the length of the scene in the screenplay. Each screenplay page is divided into eighths. The page count is not an absolutely reliable method of determining the length of the actual shooting of the scene. A scene only one-eighth of a page long might take days to shoot if it involves a complicated military action, for example, and a scene of seven-and-a-half pages, consisting of a simple stream-of-consciousness monologue, might be shot in two hours. However, experience shows that the page count usually serves as a workable indication of the production effort needed to get the scene "in the camera".

12. *Cast.* Here, the PM lists all speaking parts that appear in the scene, whether big or small. The parts may also be numbered, starting with "1" for the leads and continuing with lesser parts. It is helpful to mark the parts played by minors (those under 18 years of age) by either adding "M" or noting the actors' ages in brackets. Minors require special treatment during shooting, and this has a direct effect on scheduling and logistics.

13. *Stunts.* Because stunt work is usually rather time-consuming, a reminder about stunts that must be performed is important here for planning. Also listed should be those who will perform and direct the stunts.

14. *Extras/atmosphere.* In this section, the PM lists all general extras required (such as for a crowd scene) and divides them into categories: male, female, juvenile male, juvenile female. The PM also indicates how many minors, if any, are needed. Generally, this information is determined in cooperation with the director.

15. *Extras/silent bits.* Included in this category are all extras who must perform in such a way that they stand out from the general extras—for example, a waiter serving a drink without speaking. Should the waiter have a line, the character would be listed under "Cast". Here again, the number, sex, and perhaps age of these extras should be noted.

16. *Security and teachers.* This portion of the breakdown sheet serves as a reminder of when a scene requires additional personnel. Although security people and teachers do not appear in front of the camera, extra attention (and expense) is required when they are necessary. Teachers are always mandatory when shooting with minors, and security personnel may be needed under certain circumstances, such as crowd

control, work with explosives, and so on. The conditions that, by law, require the presence of private security are well defined. In this section, the PM also lists fire marshals, children's guardians, nurses, first-aid personnel, and military security, if applicable. For out-of-state productions, local laws must be checked and observed.

17.   *Special effects.* Here, the PM indicates all the special effects the scene requires, including optical, mechanical, pyrotechnic, and makeup effects. All special effects, especially when executed on the set during the actual shooting, require extra time and preparation, and thus careful scheduling. Digital effects to be finished during postproduction frequently require special care and attention during the original shoot. These may be time-consuming in preparation and execution and a SFX supervisor most likely will be on the location to make sure everything will fit together later on.

18.   *Props, set dressing, greenery.* This section lists all items that are part of the scene and will be seen. Props are items used by an actor or extra, such as a book a character reads, puts down on a table, and picks up later. Special care must be taken of props that are part of the plot and are used by actors. Frequently, more than one of the same prop must be available in case it becomes damaged. Set dressing refers to items that decorate a set and will not be moved, such as books on a library shelf. Once a set has been dressed, unless the story line makes changes necessary, the set dressing usually remains untouched. Greenery describes all plants not part of the original location.

19.   *Vehicles and animals.* All vehicles seen on screen, the so-called picture cars, are listed here. Cars used as production vehicles or for transportation of equipment are not included. Working with animals can be unpredictable, so the PM may have to arrange for special time allowances. Also, some animals are more difficult to handle than others. Dogs tend to be easy; cats and birds can be difficult. For most animals, an extra animal handler may be needed to guide the animal through the action. This person also might be mentioned under "Security/teachers". In all matters that require special knowledge, the PM should not hesitate to talk to experts—special effects people, animal handlers, heads of departments, and so on.

20.   *Wardrobe.* Only those pieces of clothing that stand out from the general wardrobe and that require special attention belong here. This includes items that may get damaged, stained, or wet, and that must be replaced to maintain continuity.

21.   *Estimated number of setups.* This section has special importance because it describes the number of different camera setups the director

needs to cover the scene. The coverage may vary greatly from director to director. Each new camera setup usually means moving the equipment around, relighting the set or location, and restaging the action of actors. All this is very time-consuming and affects the speed and economy of the production. Thus, the number of setups determines the amount of finished, usable film at the end of a shooting day. Getting a grip on the working style of the director and the DP, who lights the set, is one of the production manager's most important activities.

22. *Estimated production time.* Using the information on the breakdown sheet, the PM estimates how long the production of the scene will take, from the crew's arrival at the location to its departure. It includes time spent unloading, positioning, and hooking up the equipment; shooting the various setups; and wrapping. The length of time required for these tasks is very difficult to estimate because particular circumstances of location, access to the shooting site, amount of equipment needed, and number of actors to be prepared in wardrobe and costume make each scene different. As a rule of thumb, however (and use this guideline with caution), it takes one hour to set up equipment and lights and to get the location in shape for filming; it takes slightly less to wrap. The PM should walk the location with the director and the DP and talk over each and every detail. This is the only reliable way of predicting how long it will take to shoot a given scene.

23. *Special equipment.* This section serves as a reminder of any special equipment needed for the scene—that is, any equipment that will be rented for just one scene, rather than the entire shooting period. Examples include Steadicams, special cranes, and camera helicopters.

24. *Production notes.* The final space on the breakdown sheet is where the PM lists anything of special importance to the production. For example, this might be a comment that the scene is a flashback and requires period props and wardrobe or that special contacts are required. In other words, the PM notes here anything out of the ordinary. If a still photographer will be used only for certain scenes and days of the production, this fact can be mentioned. One more person on the set requires one more meal, for example, and in this case additional time must be scheduled so the photographer can take publicity stills.

The information recorded in sections 6, 7, 8, 10, and 11 will later be transferred to the heading of the scheduling strips used on the production board for scheduling the shoot. The production board is discussed later in this chapter.

Sample Script Breakdown

Two pages from a screenplay are shown in Figure 3.2, and the corresponding script breakdown sheets appear in Figures 3.3 through 3.6.

1. Scene 70, script breakdown sheet 70 (Figure 3.3).

    a. The lead, as learned earlier, is MELISSA.

    b. The number and types of extras were determined after discussion with the director.

    c. Minors are involved, requiring a teacher on the set. In this case, the shoot occurs in Thailand, so the PM must check local laws and requirements.

    d. Because some physical action occurs in the scene, a first-aid person is needed.

    e. Animals play a part in this scene. It is assumed they do not require a special animal handler, but will be handled by extras (their owners), who will receive additional pay.

    f. The director will capture this scene in six setups.

    g. Because of the animal involvement, the PM schedules an entire working day.

2. Scene 71, script breakdown sheet 71 (Figure 3.4).

    a. Because the director has determined MELISSA will be seen, she must be present for the shooting of this scene. However, a stand-in will most likely be needed as well. The PM must take this into consideration for catering and budget.

    b. More extras will be needed than in the previous scene because the entire bus will be visible. In scene 70, it was possible to create the illusion of a packed bus by reusing extras in different positions, according to the camera angle. This is not possible here.

    c. The bus driver is noted as an extra, although he will not stand out as he does in scene 70. A professional stunt driver may be needed to drive the bus. The PM should check with authorities, the producer, and insurance representatives.

    d. Minors will take part in this scene, so a teacher again is needed.

    e. Note some inconsistency in terms on sheets 70 and 71: The vehicle is described as an "old Viet Nam bus" in the former, but simply as "bus" in the latter. Although confusion seems unlikely in this instance, it is wise to use the same terms throughout the breakdown sheets and possibly make alterations in the

70 INT.   OLD VIETNAM BUS--MELISSA--THE OTHER PASSENGERS--THE DRIVER--DAY

The bus is absolutely packed with Vietnamese. Near MELISSA, in another
seat, a small pig sticks his head around a passenger, squalls, and lunges
for freedom. He lands on MELISSA, squeals again, and bounces to the floor.
MELISSA swallows. Several Vietnamese try to catch the pig as it runs for
the front of the bus. It is bedlam. A little boy sticks his head up again
an a chicken pokes his head out to watch MELISSA.

71 EXT.   VIETNAM ROAD--THE BUS--PANNING SHOT--DAY

The bus is loaded with people and baggage piled on the roof almost as high
    as the bus.

                                                               DISSOLVE TO:

72 INT.   BUS--MELISSA--AS SHE SLEEPS--DAY

MELISSA has fallen asleep with a makeshift pillow of her small traveling
bag piled against the window. ARTILLERY IMPACTS EXPLODE OUTSIDE OF HER
WINDOW and WALK AWAY FROM THE BUS FOR FIVE OR SIX MORE EXPLOSIONS. The bus
driver pulls to the ditch. An F-100 JET SCREAMS IN LOW AND DROPS NAPALM
about two hundred yards from the bus. MELISSA lurches into the aisle.

73 EXT.   ROAD--BUS--THE PASSENGER--MELISSA--BLACK PAJAMA VC--ARVIN VIETNAMESE
           SOLDIERS--GREEN BERET ADVISOR--CAPTAIN CHAU--DAY

A firefight has started and the bus is directly in the middle of it. SIX
VC GUERRILLAS rise up out of the grass and fire offscreen at the ARVN
SOLDIERS. FIFTEEN ARVN SOLDIERS rise up, fire back. The VC retreat. The
PASSENGERS head for a ditch. The ARVN SOLDIERS run between them as they
attack the VC. The VC halt, turn, and fire again. The ARVN and the
PASSENGERS are hit. Melissa stands in bewilderment. CAPTAIN CHAU, the
ARVN commander, runs into the shot and knocks her down to the ground. The
F-100 returns and drops bombs. They hit among the VC. The ARVN attack
again. An AMERICAN GREEN BERET runs into the scene.

74 EXT.   ROAD--THE BUS--THE PASSENGER--MELISSA AND CHAU--DAY

MELISSA pushes CHAU off of her.

                            MELISSA
                           (screams)
                       Get off of me!!!!

                             CHAU
                           (shocked)
                          American!!!

                            MELISSA
                       (scared to death)
                         Of course!!!
                             CHAU
                       (shoving her down)
                         Stay down!!!!

THREE PASSENGERS get up and start to run. TWO go down from VC fire.
Suddenly, it is absolutely quiet.

Fig. 3–2. Screenplay pages from *Endless Voyage*, scenes 70 to 74.

SCREENPLAY VERSION DATED: 17 May 1990

SCRIPT
BREAKDOWN SHEET

1.15.91
DATE

CODE — BREAKDOWN SHEETS/STRIPS
Day Ext — Yellow
Night Ext — Green
Day Int — White
Night Int — Blue

name, contact	Endless Voyage	70
PRODUCTION COMPANY	PRODUCTION TITLE/NO.	BREAKDOWN PAGE NO.
70	old Viet Nam bus	INT
SCENE NO.	Location or Set	INT. OR EXT.
Chasing of a pig in a crowded bus		D
DESCRIPTION		DAY OR NIGHT
		1/8
		PAGE COUNT

CAST	STUNTS	EXTRAS/ATMOSPHERE
Melissa (1)		Vietnamese (18 F)
		Vietnamese (8 M)
		Viet children (m/f 4)
	EXTRAS/SILENT BITS	SECURITY / TEACHERS
	little Viet boy (7)	Teacher
		First Aid
SPECIAL EFFECTS OPTICAL / MECHANICAL MAKE UP	**PROPS** / SET DRESSING GREENERY	**VEHICLES/ANIMALS**
	boxes /chicken	small pig old bus chicken
WARDROBE	EST. NO. of SET UPS	EST. PROD. TIME
	6	12 hrs
SPECIAL EQUIPMENT	**PRODUCTION NOTES**	

Fig. 3–3. Script breakdown for Scene 70.

SCREENPLAY VERSION DATED: 17 May 1990
1·15·91
DATE

CODE — BREAKDOWN SHEETS/STRIPS
Day Ext. — Yellow
Night Ext. — Green
Day int. — White
Night int. — Blue

SCRIPT
BREAKDOWN SHEET

name , contact	Endless Voyage	71
PRODUCTION COMPANY	PRODUCTION TITLE/NO.	BREAKDOWN PAGE NO.

71   Viet Nam Road   ExT
SCENE NO.   Location or Set   INT. OR EXT.

the bus drives by   D
DESCRIPTION   DAY OR NIGHT

                                                1/8
                                           PAGE COUNT

CAST	STUNTS	EXTRAS/ATMOSPHERE
Melissa (1)		Vietnamese (40 F) Vietnamese (40 M) Viet children (m/F 10)
	EXTRAS/SILENT BITS bus driver	SECURITY / TEACHERS Teacher
SPECIAL EFFECTS OPTICAL / MECHANICAL MAKE UP	**PROPS** / SET DRESSING GREENERY baggage on bus roof	**VEHICLES/ANIMALS** old bus
WARDROBE	EST. NO. of SET UPS 1	EST. PROD. TIME 3 hrs
SPECIAL EQUIPMENT	**PRODUCTION NOTES**	

Fig. 3–4. Script breakdown for Scene 71.

screenplay itself. Scene 71 might be shot on a different day than scene 70, and uncertainty might arise regarding the bus required, especially if other buses are used in the film.

3.   Scene 72, script breakdown sheet 72 (Figure 3.5).

    a.   Although this scene is only one-eighth of a page, it includes complicated military action, special pyrotechnical effects (b), and coordination. The entire shooting takes place inside the bus (c), but the staging of the scene will be time-consuming. For these reasons, the PM has scheduled two full days (d).

    e.   Special personnel will be needed on the set, and the PM must make provisions for them, with catering, for example.

    f.   Melissa's props will be visible. If these props are in danger of being damaged, replacements must be on hand. The production manager checks with the prop master for this information. The PM also checks with the AD or the script person to determine whether the props will be needed in the other scenes of this sequence.

    g.   A scene like this must be cleared with local authorities and will involve detailed preproduction and coordination. The PM must check with the insurance company for special requirements.

4.   Scene 74, script breakdown sheet 74 (Figure 3.6).

    a.   Another leading part, CHAU, is introduced.

    b.   The PM should check whether this action must be executed by stunt people.

    c.   An added time allowance must be made for preparation of special makeup effects.

    d.   Here, the PM has written a reminder to check with the director to determine the extent to which the action of scenes 72 and 73 is continued in scene 74. Perhaps only battle sounds (to be added in postproduction) are required.

These breakdown sheets demonstrate the process of finding the right information for the production. This can only be done in cooperation with the director. For example, in scene 74, the scope of background activity will be determined by where and how the director wants to set up the camera to cover the scene.

Ideally, complicated scenes like scene 74 should be storyboarded (as most of the film should be). In addition to a regular storyboard, which has comic-book-like drawings, a technical storyboard should be made. A technical storyboard generally shows a bird's-eye view of the set or location and marks the

SCREENPLAY VERSION DATED: 17 May 1990

**SCRIPT
BREAKDOWN SHEET**

DATE 1·15·91

name, Contact
PRODUCTION COMPANY

Endless Voyage
PRODUCTION TITLE/NO.

BREAKDOWN PAGE NO. 72

CODE — BREAKDOWN SHEETS/STRIPS
Day Ext. — Yellow
Night Ext. — Green
Day Int. — White
Night Int. — Blue

72
SCENE NO.

old Viet Nam bus
Location or Set

INT. OR EXT. INT

bus gets attacked
DESCRIPTION

DAY OR NIGHT D

PAGE COUNT 1/8

CAST	STUNTS	EXTRAS/ATMOSPHERE
Melissa (1)	F100 jet low flying	Vietnamese (12 F) Vietnamese (12 M) Viet children (m/F 6)
	EXTRAS/SILENT BITS bus driver	SECURITY / TEACHERS Military advisors Teacher First Aid Security
SPECIAL EFFECTS OPTICAL / MECHANICAL MAKE UP 6 artillery impacts napalm drops	**PROPS** / SET DRESSING GREENERY pillow traveling bag	**VEHICLES/ANIMALS** old bus F-100 jet
WARDROBE	EST. NO. of SET UPS 10	EST. PROD. TIME 2 days
SPECIAL EQUIPMENT	**PRODUCTION NOTES** Contact Military base for plane + pilot Insurance	

Fig. 3–5. Script breakdown for Scene 72.

CODE — BREAKDOWN SHEETS/STRIPS
Day Ext. — Yellow
Night Ext. — Green
Day Int. — White
Night Int. — Blue

SCREENPLAY VERSION DATED: 17 May 1990
1.15.91
DATE

SCRIPT
BREAKDOWN SHEET

name, contact	Endless Voyage	74
PRODUCTION COMPANY 74	PRODUCTION TITLE/NO. Viet Nam Road / bus	BREAKDOWN PAGE NO. EXT
SCENE NO. Melissa and	Location or Set Chau meet during	INT. OR EXT. D
DESCRIPTION the battle		DAY OR NIGHT 3/8
		PAGE COUNT

CAST	STUNTS	EXTRAS/ATMOSPHERE
Melissa (1) Chau (4)	2 Vietnamese get killed	Vietnamese (10 F) Vietnamese (10 M) Viet. children (m/F 4)

	EXTRAS/SILENT BITS Vietnamese (3 M)	SECURITY / TEACHERS Teacher First Aid

SPECIAL EFFECTS OPTICAL / MECHANICAL MAKE UP gunfire-wands	PROPS / SET DRESSING GREENERY	VEHICLES/ANIMALS

WARDROBE	EST. NO. of SET UPS 4	EST. PROD. TIME 8 hrs

SPECIAL EQUIPMENT	PRODUCTION NOTES does background action from Scene #72 and #73 continue, to what extent ?

Fig. 3–6. Script breakdown for Scene 74.

positions of the actors at the beginning and end of each shot. In relation to these movements, it also marks the camera's positions, the camera's movements (if any), and its final position for each setup, that is, for each coverage of the scene. The two storyboards illustrated in Figures 3.7 and 3.8 permit all members of the crew, especially heads of departments and the production staff, to anticipate the needs and scope of the shooting.

As should now be clear, the process of putting together a production requires continual back-and-forth communication. Understanding a screenplay and how the director visualizes what is written is another important part of the producer's and PM's work. The director's vision largely determines the size of the production. However, the producer-as-financier clearly can and should give budgetary guidelines and artistic opinions that confine the size of the production.

Other Breakdown Sheets

In addition to the script breakdown sheets, the production manager normally puts together two additional forms: cast/scene number breakdown and location/scene number breakdown. The cast breakdown lists every actor and extra and the scene numbers in which they appear. With this breakdown, the PM can quickly determine how busy a particular actor will be during the shoot and in how many scenes he or she will appear. A standard cast breakdown form appears in Figure 3.9.

The location breakdown lists all the locations (as labeled in the screenplay) and provides an overview of how many scenes take place in a specific location. Figure 3.10 illustrates a location breakdown form. The PM sometimes goes beyond this form and lists information about sites where the actual filming will take place, including addresses, contact people, phone numbers, and so on. Frequently, one shooting location may offer appropriate sites for more than one screenplay location. For example, a factory may house such diverse locations as "office", "workplace", "hallway", "staircase" and so on.

Usually, the PM does all this breakdown work, especially on low-budget independent films. In addition, most heads of departments are required to make their own breakdown lists. The wardrobe designer lists the wardrobe required in each scene for each actor; the prop master lists all props required for the film and when and where each item will be used. All heads of department are required to read the screenplay according to their specific needs and tasks. The assistant director and script supervisor will have different breakdowns than those of the art director or stunt coordinator. (The individual roles the crew members play in a production are discussed in detail in Chapter 4.)

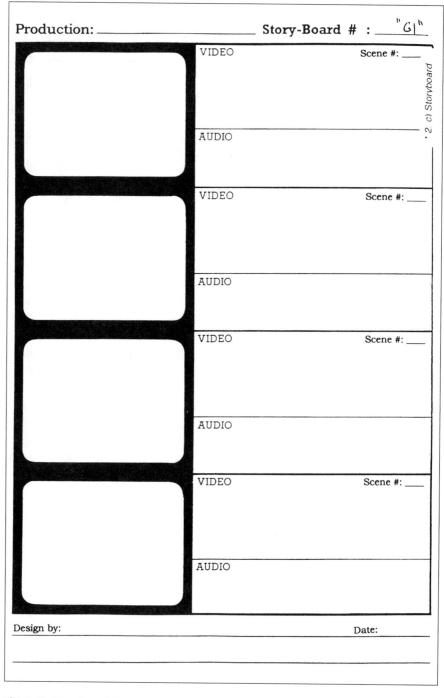

Fig. 3–7. Storyboard form.

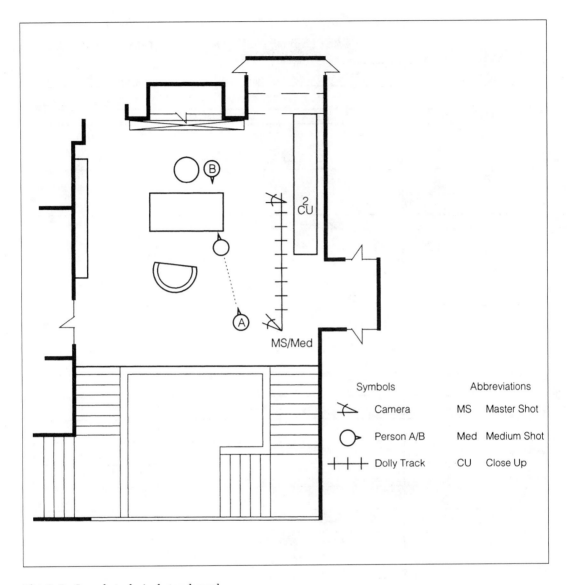

Fig. 3–8. Sample technical storyboard.

All these various breakdowns are channeled back to the PM. These too become the basis for time estimates, scheduling, and cost budgeting. After all the information has been obtained and all the questions answered—which, in many instances, is possible only after further location scouting, surveying, and on-site research—the script breakdown sheets will be complete. The production manager's next step is the creation of the shooting schedule.

CAST MEMBER	SCENE NUMBER(S)
EXTRAS/SILENT BITS	
EXTRAS/ATMOSPHERE	

CAST / SCENE NUMBER BREAKDOWN

PAGE _____ OF _____

PRODUCTION COMPANY_____

PRODUCTION TITLE: _____

NO. _____   DATE:_____

SCREENPLAY VERSION DATED_____

Fig. 3–9. Cast/scene number breakdown form.

LOCATION / SCENE NUMBER
BREAKDOWN

PRODUCTION COMPANY_____ PAGE_____OF_____

PRODUCTION TITLE_____ DATE_____

SCREENPLAY VERSION DATED_____

LOCATION (EXT/INT)	SCENE NUMBER(S)

Fig. 3–10. Location/scene number breakdown form.

Shooting Schedule

Various ways can be utilized in putting together a shooting schedule, but the industry standard is the production board with its movable production strips. The same principle is still in effect with the computer-software version that has become common. Software programs can ease the workload considerably, because information once provided—such as into the breakdown sheet—will be transferred automatically into the next steps—such as the production board. The danger of losing information is eliminated; however I still find it quite valuable to do some of this work by hand, using a pencil—the slowness of this "hand-made" process helps me to get thoroughly acquainted with the screenplay and its specifics. The PM puts the production board together with the help of the AD, who controls and directs all organizational aspects on the actual location. The production board is discussed, checked, and rechecked with the director of the film. The director must be comfortable with the workload and shooting pace because he or she ultimately will be held responsible for cost overruns and delays. The director must sign off on the shooting schedule. One copy of the production board remains in the production office with the production manager; another copy is with the AD on the set.

A shorter overview of the production schedule, called the actors' day-out-of-days, is illustrated in Figure 3.11. This sheet is put together after the production board has been finalized. It gives a smaller, more compact impression of the production flow, but its form clearly does not allow for easy changes. The SAG requires this form for computing salary estimates.

Production Board

A production board is illustrated in Figure 3.12. The PM completes the board by first filling in the information required for the heading: title of production and names of producer or production company, director, assistant director, and production manager. The PM adds the name of each part and the actor who plays the part. The speaking parts are numbered consecutively, starting with "1" at the top. (These numbers are carried over to other phases of the production. For example, they appear on the daily call sheets.) If appropriate, the PM adds subheadings for extras/silent bits—persons who show a certain "personality" or character as opposed to, extras/atmosphere, which are for nondescript crowd-scenes, animals, and stunts. Roles in the first category are numbered, but the others are marked only with an "X".

The PM devotes one strip of cardboard to each individual scene. These strips list much of the information contained in the script breakdown sheet, including "D" or "N" (day or night), "I" or "E" (interior or exterior), scene number, page count, estimated production time (in hours), and location or set

SCREEN ACTORS GUILD

CASTING DATA REPORT

48

See Reverse
For Instructions

THIS FORM MUST BE COMPLETED FOR EACH MOTION PICTURE AND EACH EPISODE OF EACH SERIES PRODUCED FOR THE QUARTER IN WHICH PRINCIPAL PHOTOGRAPHY WAS COMPLETED.

1) PRODUCTION COMPANY _____

2) QUARTER and YEAR _____

3) PROJECT (Title, Prod. No., etc.) _____

4) DESCRIPTION (Feature, M.O.W., TV Series, etc.) _____

5) TOTAL NO. OF DAYS OF PRODUCTION (Principal Photography Only) _____

6) DATA SUBMITTED BY _____ NAME

TELEPHONE NUMBER (___) ___ - _____

7) CHECK IF APPROPRIATE ☐ NO STUNTS

PART I

8)

CATEGORY		FORM OF HIRING			9) CAST TOTALS	10) NO. OF DAYS WORKED	11) AGE:		
		DAILY	WEEKLY	SERIES			UNDER 40	40 and OVER	UNKNOWN
MALE	LEAD								
	SUPPORT								
FEMALE	LEAD								
	SUPPORT								

PART II

12)

CATEGORY		FORM OF HIRING						13) NO. OF DAYS WORKED		14) AGE					
		DAILY		WEEKLY		SERIES				UNDER 40		40 and OVER		UNKNOWN	
		M	F	M	F	M	F	M	F	M	F	M	F	M	F
ASIAN/PACIFIC	LEAD														
	SUPPORT														
BLACK	LEAD														
	SUPPORT														
CAUCASIAN	LEAD														
	SUPPORT														
LATINO / HISPANIC	LEAD														
	SUPPORT														
N. AMERICAN INDIAN	LEAD														
	SUPPORT														
UNKNOWN / OTHER	LEAD														
	SUPPORT														

Fig. 3-11. Actors' day-out-of-days form.

INSTRUCTIONS

(After reading the following, if you have any further questions, please call 213/549-6644.) (For your convenience, our fax number is 213/549-6647.)

1. Indicate the name of the signatory Production Company (e.g., "THE ABC COMPANY").

2. Indicate the quarter/year when ***principal photography*** was completed (e.g., "1st quarter 1981"). Make one report only for full project even though it might span more than one quarter.

   The quarters consist of:

January	-	March	(1st)
April	-	June	(2nd)
July	-	September	(3rd)
October	-	December	(4th)

3. Indicate the <u>name</u> of the film for which you are reporting.

4. Indicate the <u>type</u> of project (feature, television movie, television pilot, television series, animation).

5. Use a number to respond to this question.

6. Indicate the name of person completing this form and the telephone number for same.

7. Two separate reports are required, one for <u>Performers</u> only and one for <u>Stunt Performers</u> only. If there were no Stunt Performers employed on the film, check the "No Stunt" box. If Stunt Performers were employed, complete the casting data report form for Stunt Performers.

8. **Part I.** Indicate the total number of lead and supporting Performers in each of the applicable categories. Series performers column is provided for episodic TV shows only. Daily column is for daily contract & 3-day contract performers only. Weekly column is for weekly contract and run-of-the-picture performers. A day contract performer upgraded to a weekly contract performer in a drop/pick-up situation should be listed in the weekly column (**do <u>not</u> count** the performer twice).

9. Use numbers only to indicate the total number of Performers in the category.

10. Use numbers only to indicate the total number of days worked by <u>ALL</u> Performers in the category. (Include all days paid for including hold, rehearsal days, etc.)

11. Use numbers only to indicate how many Performers were in each age group.

12. **Part II.** Indicate the total number of males and females in each category.

13. Use number only to indicate the total number of days worked by <u>ALL</u> the Performers in male and female category.

14. Use numbers only to indicate how many Performers were in each age group.

<u>NOTE</u>: PLEASE MAKE EVERY EFFORT TO INSURE THAT YOUR NUMBERS CORRESPOND ACROSS AND AMONG <u>PART I AND PART II.</u>

Fig. 3–11. (continued)

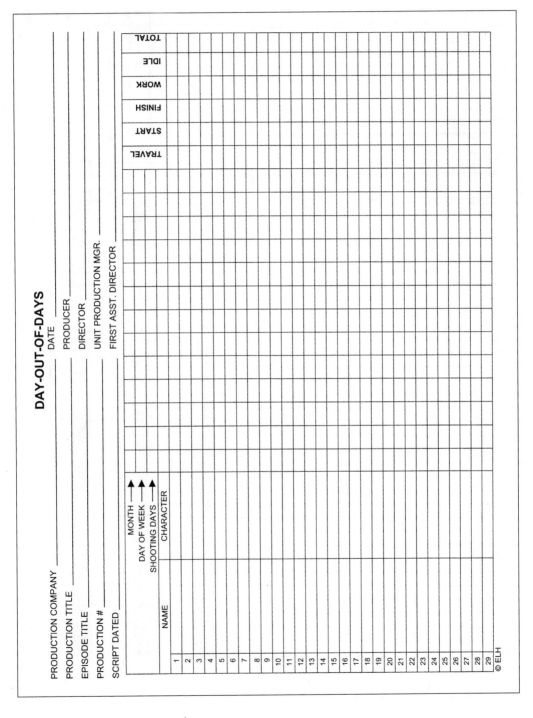

Fig. 3–11. (continued)

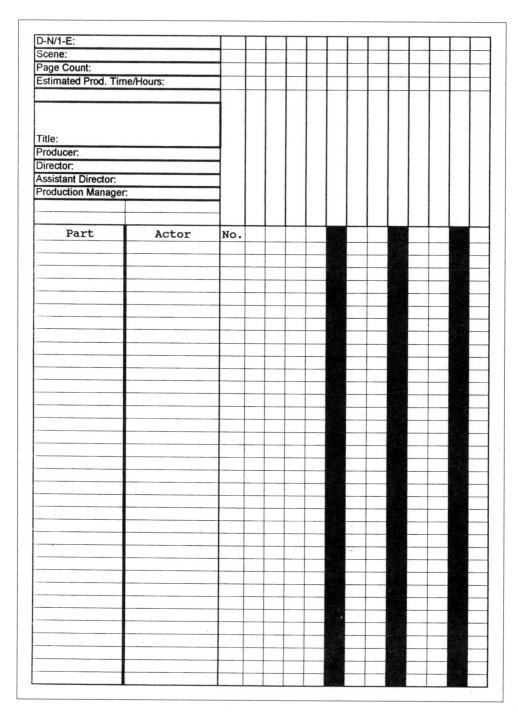

Fig. 3–12. Incomplete production board.

name. These strips come in many colors. Production managers and assistant directors are free to design their own systems, but the following classification scheme has become the standard:

Yellow   Day/exterior
White   Day/interior
Green   Night/exterior
Blue   Night/interior

Black strips are used to separate individual shooting days, and gray strips show free days, such as weekends.

When these classifications are observed, those involved in the production can understand and evaluate a complete shooting schedule and its flow almost at a glance. Turnaround times—required hours of rest between two shooting periods—are clearly indicated, as are switches from day to night shoots.

Sample Production Board

Let's now consider how the scenes and breakdown sheets illustrated earlier translate into strips for the production board. Note that because the scenes are taken out of context, the sample production board shown in Figure 3.13 does not reflect the actual position of these scenes in the overall shooting schedule. It illustrates only the information that is to be transferred and how. The figure shows how the strips would be assembled if the scenes were shot in the same sequence as they appear in the screenplay. In reality, though, this almost never occurs. For convenience, similar shots are filmed together, regardless of their screenplay order.

Figure 3.14 shows the production board, with scheduling information, for these scenes. Scene 70 is shot on one day, scene 72 on the next two days, and scenes 71 and 74 on the fourth day. Notice how the production board is marked when one scene requires more than one day to shoot. An identical strip is added for the scene, they are marked "first day" and "second day", and a black strip is used to separate them. During a low-budget independent production, this situation probably will never arise.

The interior scenes have been grouped together because once the equipment, lighting, and rigging are arranged inside the bus, it is best to shoot all interior scenes in one stretch. It would be inefficient to set up the equipment inside the bus, then move it all outside the bus, only to go back into the bus some hours later.

After completing all the script breakdown sheets and transferring the appropriate information onto strips for each scene, the PM groups the strips together according to shooting location. If the actual locations have not yet been determined, this procedure must wait.

D-N/1-E:			D/1	P/E	D/1	P/E						
Scene:			70	71	72	74						
Page Count:			1/8	1/8	1/8	3/8						
Estimated Prod. Time/Hours:			12	3	24	8						
Title: *Endless Voyage* Producer: name/company Director: name Assistant Director: name Production Manager: name			Old Vietnam Bus	Vietnam Road	Old Vietnam Bus	Old Vietnam Road/Bus						
Part	**Actor**	**No.**										
Melissa	name	1	1		1	1	1					
name	name	2										
name	name	3										
Chau	name	4					4					
name	name	5										
Extras/Silent Bits												
Viet. boy (7)	name	21	21									
Bus driver	name	22			22	22						
Viet. man	name	23					23					
Extras/Atmosphere												
Viet. female	name	41	X		X	X	X					
Viet. male	name	42	X		X	X	X					
Viet. children		43	X		X	X	X					
Animals												
small pig			X	X								
chicken			X	X								
Stunts			X			X	X					

Fig. 3–13. Production board with movable strips, showing the transfer of information from the script breakdown sheets.

D-N/1-E:			D/1	D/1	D/1	D/E	D/E				
Scene:			70	72	72	79	71				
Page Count:			1/8	1/8	1/8	3/8	1/8				
Estimated Prod. Time/Hours:			12	24	24	8	3				
Title: *Endless Voyage* Producer: name/company Director: name Assistant Director: name Production Manager: name			Old Vietnam Bus	Old Vietnam Bus First Bus Day	Old Vietnam Bus Sec. Day	Vietnam Road/Bus	Vietnam Road				
Part	**Actor**	**No.**									
Melissa	name	1	1	1	1	1	1				
name	name	2									
name	name	3									
Chau	name	4				4					
name	name	5									
Extras / Silent Bits ⟶											
Viet. boy (7)	name	21	21								
Bus driver	name	22		22	22		22				
Viet. man	name	23				23					
Extras / Atmosphere ⟶											
Viet. female	name	41	X	X	X	X	X				
Viet. male	name	42	X	X	X	X	X				
Viet. children		43	X	X	X	X	X				
Animals ⟶											
small pig			X	X	X	X					
chicken			X	X	X	X					
Stunts ⟶			X		X	X					

Fig. 3–14. Production board with scheduling information.

Arranging the Shooting Schedule

Most shooting schedules are arranged in accordance with several principles. The overriding goal of all planning is to stay within both the schedule and the budget to avoid delays and cost overruns. For this reason, the organization of a shooting schedule almost always centers on the actual shooting sites, that is, where the scenes are actually being shot.

This basic principle is violated only in rare instances. For example, if a certain actor is available only on particular days, the producer is forced to make concessions. The shooting schedule then centers on the star, and certain scenes that would otherwise have been shot in a more economical order are grouped together to accommodate the needs of the star. In general, though, for independent films, the production schedule revolves around the shooting sites.

In determining the shooting schedule, two other considerations are of primary importance. First, must a scene be shot at a particular time, as described in the screenplay? For example, must interior night scenes be shot at night? In many cases, interior scenes that do not show anything of the outside or that take place in rooms without windows, such as stairways or offices, can be shot at any time of day. It is frequently possible to block windows and thus create a night atmosphere during the daytime. In most cases, shooting interior night scenes during the day is less stressful and expensive.

Would it be possible to shoot night exterior scenes during the day? Many years ago, under low-budget conditions, these scenes were shot during the day with appropriate camera filters. However, today's sophisticated audiences will not accept such obvious trickery. In most cases, night exterior scenes should be shot at night. The development of highly sensitive film stock or the use of video make night shots less complicated and cumbersome than they were previously.

Day interior scenes, of course, can be shot at night, if necessary, provided that the actual exterior is not seen. It is possible that the shooting schedule might require night filming for logistical reasons, or it might be more economical. For example, a location may be too expensive for the production to return another day.

Before any decisions can be made and implemented into the shooting schedule, actual locations for the shoot must be found and secured by contract. All of this back-and-forth may seem confusing, and indeed for quite a long time during preproduction final decisions cannot be made because many facts depend on one other.

The second priority in scheduling is the availability of actors and the arrangement of their scenes. As most productions deal with SAG members, it is necessary to adhere to the rules of the SAG. The organization provides, free of charge, extensive information and documentation on these rules to all producers who become signatories. It is also possible, though more cumbersome, to obtain this information without becoming a signatory.

To keep down production costs, day players (actors used for only one or a few days) should not become weekly players. For example, if an actor works in only a few scenes but these scenes are placed throughout the shooting schedule, that actor must be paid as a weekly player. The SAG stipulates that actors be paid higher fees when working as weekly players, even if they do not work more or longer than they would as daily players. Daily players become weekly players when their working days are fewer than 10 days apart. For example, if an actor works in a scene on shooting day 2 and again on day 9, he or she becomes a weekly player and must be paid for the interim time. If the scene on day 9 can be scheduled for day 13, the actor can be classified and paid as a daily player working on two days.

Other considerations come into play when designing the shooting schedule:

1.   It is desirable to schedule less complicated scenes during the first few shooting days, especially if the film's crew has not worked together previously and must find its specific rhythm and chemistry. Easy scenes that feature dialogue rather than special-effects-laden action also allow the director to establish a style of working and communicating with the crew.

2.   If the weather cooperates, exterior scenes should be scheduled before interior ones, which are independent of weather conditions and can be shot safely toward the end of the shooting period. If, on the contrary, all interior scenes are shot first and only exterior scenes remain, then uncooperative weather can lead to time overruns. Interior scenes should also be scheduled as backup scenes in case the weather does not allow exterior shooting. These so-called cover sets should ideally be available during all weather-dependent shoots.

Note that perfect conditions almost never exist throughout a production. The PM should be accustomed to quick improvisations and changes of schedule and locations. No production will serve perfectly all artistic, logistical, and financial considerations at the same time. Very rarely has it occurred that a film has been shot exactly within the schedule as planned on the production board—constant adjustments and changes are the rule.

3.   The PM should try to exploit the natural flow and order of operation at a location. For example, if one scene takes place on the front lawn of a house, another in the hallway of the same house, and a third in the kitchen, then the first scene shot should be on the lawn, the second in the hallway, and the third in the kitchen, even if the continuity

of the screenplay is destroyed. This assumes that the crew has just arrived on location. If, however, the crew already has set up inside the house and will stay there for several days, then of course interior scenes should be scheduled before exteriors. It is best to avoid any unnecessary movement of equipment and crew. If the lawn scene must be shot at sunset, the scene should be scheduled at the end of the location shoot, when the crew must move out anyway and wrap that particular location.

4.   As indicated earlier, on SAG productions, the use of actors may influence the shooting schedule. In addition, turnaround times must be observed. Turnaround time is the actors' minimum time off between consecutive shooting days. This time, also called the rest period, is 12 hours, and violators are penalized by the SAG. The turnaround period begins when actors are dismissed from the set and ends when they are required to reappear for makeup, wardrobe, and hair the next day.

After a six-day week at an overnight location, actors are entitled to a weekly rest period of 36 consecutive hours; this rest period extends to 56 hours on a local shoot. The SAG's "low-budget provisions" permit more flexibility in the latter case, as long as the actors waive the additional-pay provisions for work performed on weekends. Rest periods are, of course, desirable—though rarely kept—for the crew as well.

The structure of a single shooting day should also follow SAG guidelines; it is implemented by the AD on the set. The PM is usually not involved in scheduling lunch breaks. The SAG stipulates that a meal be called not later than six hours after the start of work (or after the 15 minute breakfast if work begins before 9 a.m.). A second meal must be called not more than six hours after the callback from the first meal break.

When these guidelines are followed, the shooting schedule comes into shape, and its requirements almost automatically fall into place. From here on, the production manager's full-time job is to have everything and everyone ready and available when they are needed.

Scheduling Software

Some IBM or Apple software programs on the market allow the PM and AD to perform on computers most breakdown and scheduling work discussed in this chapter. These programs usually permit the user to create customizable breakdown sheets, generate shooting schedules, and implement changes. In addition, they allow the user to view "what-if" previews. Although many of these software programs make the production manager's job easier, they cannot replace the

PM's knowledge and scheduling experience. Frequently, too, the PM must be in places where computer access or printouts are not available.

As much as it can be argued for the fastness and accuracy of the software programs, it remains true that by creating the first forms, breakdown sheets and schedules by hand the PM's knowledge of the production becomes much more ingrained and personal. It seems a wise procedure to go at it first the "old-fashioned" way (pencil and paper), then transferring to the software.

Now that the screenplay has been broken down and the shooting schedule designed, the PM has completed two vital steps in the process of creating an accurate production budget. The basic elements are known and can be calculated. These include the length of the shooting period, the number of day and night shoots, the number of weekend or overtime shoots, the number and sites of the locations, and the length and frequency of employment periods for actors and extras. Also known at this time are the requirements of the various departments (such as the art department), construction, props, equipment, and shooting ratio. As previously mentioned, the information contained in the screenplay, being transferred to the breakdown sheets and then automatically onto the production board's scheduling provide the basis for the next step of budgeting. Most software programs use industry standard budget forms, allow for individual specifications, may easily get transferred to foreign currencies, automatically provide re-budgeting whenever previous information has been changed and also implement flat and percentage fringe benefits, current taxes, current guild and union labor rates and "what if?" scenarios.

The next chapter discusses some tips for low-budget productions.

4

Special Tips for Low-Budget Productions

The term *low budget* means different things to different people. For a major studio or a large production company, a budget of $10 million is considered "low" and such films really are not worth the effort. It is not economically feasible to produce them within the studio system. For the independent filmmaker, on the other hand, a $10 million budget usually feels very comfortable. Nevertheless, today's independent producers and filmmakers can raise even such a "small" amount only with extreme difficulty.

This chapter offers suggestions for filmmakers who hope to make low-budget or "no-budget" movies with a professional look but costing as little as possible. These conditions apply to most student productions and to those of independent filmmakers who do not want to or cannot presell certain rights to raise financing. In most cases, these films also lack the elements that usually qualify for presales to foreign territories or market segments: stars and established directors. These tips also might be of interest to filmmakers who want to retain complete creative and business control of their projects and do not want to hustle for financing before actually going into production.

Despite the current market trend toward mega-budget movies with spectacular special effects and major box office stars, there always seems to be room for those special independent pictures—those with unique and fresh angles, dealing perhaps with relationships—that succeed in engaging audiences, and go on to commercial success. No one really knows what makes a picture a success, and there are no rules. The restrictions of a low budget actually give filmmakers the freedom to make the pictures they want without overriding consideration for a mass audience or mainstream story lines. Small films might be attractive enough to the general public to recoup the film's costs and become commercially successful, especially in domestic and foreign TV, cable, and video/DVD and online markets. Clearly, films with small budgets have much earlier break-even points than big-budget pictures, which must recoup worldwide to become commercially successful.

The chances of a low-budget production becoming a "surprise hit" are slim, though, considering the market and mechanisms of the film business; it is still possible, however, for a picture to be discovered at a festival, find an audience, and, if nothing else, gain enough critical praise to help the filmmaker or producer launch another project.

What Makes a Movie Expensive?

To identify areas in which low-budget productions can save money, it is prudent to consider the factors that make a production expensive. In general, most expensive movies involve expensive screenplays, actors, producers, and directors—the so-called above-the-line items. These elements are usually responsible for the major share of any budget. When it becomes common to buy screenplays for $1 million or more and to pay stars, executive producers, producers, associate producers, and directors several million dollars each, it quickly becomes clear how budgets of $35 million are reached. Add to this general studio overhead, contingencies, completion bonds, and finance charges, and the budget can easily reach far and beyond $50 million.

With advertising campaigns that cost more than $50 million, these pictures clearly must cater to a worldwide mass audience to turn a profit. Movies like these must follow certain formulas and meet audience expectations; hence the popularity of sequels, which have a "built-in" audience. It should never be forgotten that "Hollywood" is, first and foremost, about money and profits. The term *art* can usually be heard only on the night of Academy Award presentations.

The other costs of below-the-line items like crew, rentals, film, postproduction, and so on, are of course highly dependent on the nature of the screenplay and the production. Exotic locations, large crews, the destruction of massive amounts of hardware, historic settings, sophisticated special effects, and an overly long shooting period quickly raise any budget. Yet under "normal" circumstances, these below-the-line items remain more or less stable and predictable for most motion pictures.

This chapter examines the following elements, all of which contribute to the cost of a production: screenplay, locations, film format, crew, actors, equipment, insurance, postproduction, special effects. It also looks at ways to structure financial deals with cast and crew.

Screenplay

Elements of the screenplay help determine the production's cost. Producers of low-budget pictures must be aware that their screenplays cannot feature plot lines or situations that are expensive to realize. Foreign or exotic locations and multiple settings are out, as are scenes with dozens of actors and hundreds of extras. Sophisticated postproduction trickery only obtainable with expensive hardware and software should not be considered, nor should the destruction of costly items, such as cars, boats, planes, and houses. In general, then, this leaves us with screenplays that are less action-oriented, but that deal with human relationships, screenplays that focus more on dialogue and character or plot developments than on hair-raising stunts and special effects. Of course, it helps if the screenwriter is familiar with the process of shooting and general production. The writer should be able to judge how the scenes will be realized, how long it will take, and how expensive it will be. Well-seasoned writers are capable of writing according to budget, and they make sure their screenplays do not contain "impossible" items.

The following tips will help writers create screenplays appropriate for low-budget films:

1. If SAG actors will be involved in the film, avoid writing characters who have only one or two lines. For example, a waiter who says, "Yes, Ma'am," must be paid for a speaking part. If the same character remains silent and nods his head, the part can be played by an extra, who will be paid considerably less.

2. If minors will be involved, write for a 19-year-old rather than an 18-year-old. Employing a person over 18 saves the production company the cost of a studio teacher as well as time-consuming paperwork.

Locations

The screenplay should limit the story to scenes in locations that either are available or easily will be and that can be found locally without much expense. Local locations have the advantage of not requiring travel or an overnight stay. As a filmmaker, you should not hesitate to employ the help of relatives, friends, and acquaintances, but be frank about your intentions and the scope of the work you will do on location. Locations should be limited as much as possible to private properties and homes, and the use of mechanical special effects and explosives should be avoided. Make sure the location is available for the entire time you will need it, and be sure your equipment can remain safely at the site overnight to avoid wrapping every night and setting up again the next day.

Look for locations that offer the potential for multiple and widely different sets. For example, if the main shooting occurs in a residential house, check if the various rooms lend themselves to conversion into the sets the production needs. It is frequently much more cost-efficient to change an existing room with a little set dressing and a few props than it is to find and negotiate a new shooting site. Staying at one site also reduces rental fees and city permits, and, most of all, it saves time. The longer the cast, crew, and equipment can stay at one site, the more time available for artistic work and the less time spent packing, loading, and moving. Catering is easier, and the general mood of the shoot improves when the crew does not have to move every day or every other day. Transportation hazards, such as damage to equipment, are reduced as well.

If public locations, such as government buildings, streets, and parks, are needed, choose locations that do not require expensive permits and other fees, and try to stage the scenes during times of little public traffic (before or after office hours, on weekends, or at night). If you observe these rules, the production may not have to hire off-duty police officers for traffic and crowd control, and a fire marshal may not be required on the set. Although many items are negotiable, such as equipment rentals, cast and crew salaries and fees, lab charges, and postproduction services, the salaries of such public officials as city workers, off-duty police officers, and fire marshals are not. Their fees are quite substantial and add up quickly; also, they must be paid at the end of the shooting day or shooting period. Official shooting permits may be required, and with them comes the need for general liability insurance. Check with local state, county, or city offices on the procedures for obtaining filming permits.

Film Format

Careful thought should be given to the choice of film format for the production. It may not be necessary to shoot on 35 mm stock for later commercial theatrical exploitation. If production on 16 mm (or Super 16 mm) is carefully planned, the film can be enlarged to 35 mm later. This route can be technically satisfactory if carefully planned. Several films, including *Metropolitan* and *She's Gotta Have It*, used this technique and became successful. In general, an audience will not be interested in the technical look of a film if the story and the actors are involving and interesting. People do not go to a movie house to see a technically outstanding film that provides no emotional or other kind of involvement.

The producer and the director of photography (DP) must be aware of the particular needs of shooting in 16 mm for later 35 mm enlargement, such as different framing, lighting, and developing. Labs, such as DuArt in New York, specialize in this work, and they should be contacted before the shoot. They generally provide free materials and guidelines as well as personal consultation. Their experience is invaluable and should be utilized. A shoot in 16 mm can cut expenses for film stock, development, and dailies by up to 40 percent compared with 35 mm.

However, if it is possible to make a deal with the lab to defer payment for developing, processing, and supplying dailies and prints on 35 mm, then it is definitely preferable to shoot in 35 mm. Be aware that the lab practically owns your negative until all bills are paid, and you may be denied access to "your" film.

You might also consider shooting in 35 mm and continuing all postproduction work, such as dailies and festival or demo prints, in 16 mm. The whole postproduction process, including editing, accessories, and sound mixing, is less expensive in 16 mm than in 35 mm. Frequently, 16 mm prints can be shown at festivals or markets and will lead to sales of the film. (Be aware, though, that many "A" festivals like Cannes will accept only 35 mm prints for projection.) It has become customary to view films on video cassettes. Thus, it is a good idea to use the 16 mm format for the postproduction phase before the 35 mm negative cut. Transfers from 35 mm negative to video provide first-class quality.

For both 35 mm and 16 mm shoots, check out the use of the less expensive "recanned" stock. This is film stock purchased by another production company but not used on the production. You can frequently obtain unopened and complete cans, but sometimes only short ends are available. In any case, the company that sells the stock guarantees the quality of the material. The disadvantage, of course, is that you are dealing with stocks of different emulsion code numbers, which might result in slight color changes when spliced together and timed in the lab. Confer with your lab about this problem.

However, careful consideration should be given to the use of video nowadays, as the professional arrival of digital video (DV) has changed many of the previously set rules. With careful planning it is quite possible to shoot with low-cost-level DVD cameras or work with top-level Mini-DVs, DVCAM, Pro-DVCAM or HDCam. The advantages in terms of shooting materials—tapes *vs.* film stock, viewing the results on the site instead of waiting for dailies to come back from the lab, size of lighting equipment, handling and logistics, postproduction procedure and editing on your PC or Mac as well as further use in digital effects work—are seriously to be counterbalanced against the quality of the final release print. But the progress in transferring video tape to film stock for theatrical release is breathtaking. Thorough discussions and tests with a lab if a "film look" is to be desired should be made to finally determine which way to go. Eventually film projectors will be replaced by video beamers—eventually the film release print will disappear.

Preproduction costs little. Few of the crew have been hired at this point, perhaps just the director, the DP, and the producer or PM. Use this phase to get the screenplay into the best possible shape, find the right locations and the perfect cast and crew, have your screenplay analyzed and storyboarded, and make sure that the shoot is perfectly organized and that everyone knows what to do. Be certain that locations are secured, catering is arranged, props are on the set, permits are in place, equipment is available, and the schedule is firm.

The director should be thoroughly prepared to take charge and avoid confusion and indecisiveness on the set.

Crew

If you must shoot without much cash, use of union personnel or seasoned professionals generally is excluded—unless the project is unusually attractive. Although productions like these are not unheard of, the enthusiasm only lasts for a short period, and this is not a reliable way to organize a shoot.

On low-budget or no-budget productions, the PM must do many jobs. He or she scouts for locations, is involved in casting of extras, serves as assistant director, and handles accounts and payroll (whatever little there may be). The PM must be careful not to take on too many tasks, though. For example, the PM can only serve as AD when the shoot has been organized so perfectly that a production assistant or secretary can run the production office, and the PM's presence is not required throughout the day.

When hiring a crew, the producer or PM should take advantage of the fact that many film students and many professionals in the commercial or music-video field are eager to participate in feature film productions. The attraction of a possibly "glamorous" theatrical production and distribution motivates many people to work on productions for less money than they would demand for more "commercial" products, such as corporate videos. The crew is of utmost importance, and hiring the right crew—one that will harmonize and work enthusiastically—is one of the arts of the production manager. On the other hand, the PM must not be afraid to fire those who prove to be a poor choice and have a negative impact on the production. Personal friendships and considerations are no reason to tolerate someone who endangers the work of many others.

Hire the best people you can get or afford. The key personnel—director of photography, key grip, key gaffer, sound mixer, and first assistant director—should be professionals, preferably with feature film experience. Once these positions are filled by professionals—perhaps union personnel willing to work on a nonunion picture—it is often a rather minor risk to fill additional crew positions with responsible and determined film or theater students who have experience with college or university productions. Positions such as camera assistant, grip assistant, gaffer assistant, makeup, wardrobe, props, still photography, production assistant, catering, second assistant director, script, and positions in postproduction usually are not critical and can be handled by students with some experience.

Posting available positions on bulletin boards of film departments or in trade publications usually generates a flood of résumés from personnel available in all departments. However, be aware that students' commitments are often only good as long as they are not offered a paid job on another production. Filmmakers of no-budget productions should be prepared to have a flow of people accompanying the production, though not necessarily from start to end. It might be necessary to shoot only on weekends if that is when the talent and crew are available.

As a rule, try to limit the crew size to a minimum. Not only does this help keep costs down (for example, catering and transportation), but it also means a faster shoot. Just as the PM may be asked to wear different hats, so too other crew members can frequently serve in more than one capacity. The prop master might serve as art director and set dresser, the grip can double as gaffer, the DP might also be the camera operator, the makeup person might also handle hair and wardrobe, and the script supervisor might take stills or even be an assistant director (but not first AD).

Most important, treat everyone involved in the production with respect and consideration; serve good, large meals (no alcohol); and always have refreshments and snacks on the set. Money required for these items is well spent. Nothing destroys a good working relationship faster than inconsiderate treatment, inattentive service, and bad food.

Actors

Even a low-budget production should avoid "actors" who are not real actors—that is, friends, relatives, and amateurs. The success of the film largely depends on the audience's identification with the people on screen. Casting the right actors is an essential part of the director's and producer's art.

If the production has no need for a "name" actor, it may not have to be a SAG production at all. If the SAG does not participate in the production, all contract provisions, including overtime, night-time, and weekend work, are freely negotiable. Clearly, this can have a significant impact on the production's budget. Many exciting actors are not members of the SAG and are willing to work for minimum or deferred pay, point sharing, or even just "food and video" (meals on the set and a video copy of the finished film). Just because an up-and-coming actor is not a SAG member does not mean that he or she would not be right for the part and an inspiration to others. Production time and length of shoot become less of a factor when cast members, crew, and staff agree to work on a lower-than-usual or deferred-salary basis or agree to point-sharing arrangements.

Although most experienced actors are members of the SAG, many are willing (at their own risk) to work on non-SAG pictures for conditions to be negotiated individually. SAG members are frequently permitted to work on student productions. Special conditions and waivers apply, and it is worthwhile to check with the local SAG office, if appropriate (for further information see

Chapter 6). In this case, provisions must be made in case the film becomes a commercial success so that the actor who worked for nothing or next to nothing is entitled to retroactive compensation.

Actors can be found at local theaters, at university theater groups, at model agencies, and through casting calls in trade papers. These periodicals are published once a week. The ad should outline the essential requirements, including sex, age, particular features, and type of part to be played. In the production centers of Los Angeles and New York, an advertisement will cause an avalanche of 8 × 10 black-and-white photographs with professional résumés attached to the back.

When interviewing actors, have a few pages of the screenplay prepared so they will have time to go over the lines before you call them. The elusive "star quality" does in fact exist. When the right person for the part enters the room, you will know it, and you will also know very quickly when the wrong person enters. It is an additional thrill to cast an unknown and to see that person become a star because of your picture.

Again, treat everyone with the same respect and polite manners with which you expect people to treat you. Avoid division between above-the-line and below-the-line personnel. Have everyone eat the same food at the same place, and have everyone stay at the same hotel at an overnight location. Once some of the cast and crew feel as though they are being treated as workers while others (like key personnel or executives) are pampered and get special favors, the team quickly falls apart, especially on low-budget shoots where most work is voluntary.

You might encounter actors on the production accustomed to big-time star treatment. If you cannot afford an extra "honey wagon" for them, at least try to give them a room at the location where they can retire.

Equipment

If you are a student filmmaker, you might get some film or video equipment from your school. You might be able to borrow some lights, a Nagra, and a few microphones, and you might be able to use the school's postproduction facilities. Rarely, however, is 35 mm equipment available; you might be restricted if other students want the equipment or if it is booked for school productions during the semester.

In any case, you will need to rent at least some of your film or video equipment. If you are lucky, members of the crew might possess their own equipment. Sound mixers frequently do, and directors of photography sometimes do, as well. They will give you special deals when you hire them and their equipment as a package. Look for a rental house that will supply you with everything else you need.

Most rental houses make deals on the prices and packages offered in their catalogs. It is customary for them not to charge more than two-and-a-half, three, or four days' rent when you lease the equipment for a whole week or more. In other words, when you rent for 14 days, you pay for just six or eight days. You can sometimes negotiate special weekend rates, depending on your skills, the circumstances, and luck.

If you ask around, you might find an editor who owns his or her own Moviola, you may purchase the appropriate software to edit yourself on your PC or Mac, you may find a postproduction facility that will give you a good deal on the mix, and so on. Networking is the key. You might be surprised to discover, for example, that the clerk in the rental house is also a gifted composer and musician waiting for a break, and that he would love to do the soundtrack for you free.

Much has been said about product placement and the money it saves the production. With low-budget films, you might as well save the energy needed to go after these deals. Companies that pay to have their products placed are only interested when a wide distribution is in place. In addition, few financial rewards are gained for placing products of smaller companies. How much money will you actually save when a donut shop provides three dozen donuts free to be placed on a kitchen shelf? Most items you get free are small and inexpensive. If you buy them yourself, you will avoid any interference and all the hustling. Do not count on receiving cash when you place a product; small, low-budget films just are not in the right league for something like this.

Insurance

Save what you can in other areas, but do not skimp on insurance. Two basic types are policies required by law. The first is workers' compensation insurance. Check with the proper local authorities about procedures and requirements for this coverage. In addition, you should have general liability insurance. Most city or government offices will not give you a filming or location permit without this insurance; they will instruct you on details of the required coverage. These insurance premiums cannot be negotiated and must be paid up front. (For all types of insurance tailored to the needs of film production, see Chapter 10.)

Postproduction

Post-production concludes your project. Plan this phase as well as you did all the other phases, and do not take shortcuts. Take all the time you need to edit your picture, create or assemble sounds, and arrange for an effective soundtrack to be composed and performed. Sloppy editing and shoddy sound mixes will ruin any chances of success your picture might have and will certainly destroy all the work everyone has put into the picture.

Just like equipment rental houses, postproduction facilities might offer you special deals, particularly if you are willing to work during their slow hours (weekends and nights). Some facilities might donate their services or agree to deferred pay, and labs are known to offer discounts.

Try to strike a deal with the composer. Most have their own equipment, such as synthesizers. Let the composer keep all or some of the rights to the music so he or she will be able to collect fees from the American Society of Composers, Authors and Publishers (ASCAP) if the music gets airplay or the film finds distribution and is shown publicly.

In low-budget productions, it is extremely important that all money spent is visible on the screen: in the choice of sets, wardrobe, and props; time and skill invested in camera movements and lighting; time permitted for actors to perform; and time required in postproduction. The film will be judged by what is seen on the screen; the details of production difficulties or budget restraints are of no interest to audiences or potential buyers. Excuses will not be accepted.

Special Effects

Special effects have become a major component in today's filmmaking, be it mechanically, pyrotechnically, or digitally created, or, as in most cases, a combination of all three. Accordingly, it has become increasingly difficult to estimate the costs of such effects, and it is wise to be in close touch with a special effects company as early as the development phase. Special effects art directors can point the way to the most economical and artistically creditable way of creating effects, emphasizing digital imagery in combination with traditional crafts. The imagined and desired effects frequently can be achieved by a variety of different methods; generally, a modern screenwriter already knows how these digital effects are achieved. Frequently, however, the special effects budget is rather elusive, as the effects often can only be seen and judged once all the different components are put together in postproduction. Frequently enough, they don't match the vision the director had in mind, which then calls for additional shooting at extra expense. Be extremely precise, using storyboards and elaborate descriptions to evaluate the amount of work necessary to achieve a specific effect, a certain look. Clear and precise communication among production, art department, director and special effects house is of vital importance to avoid cost overruns.

Making Deals

Let's look at two different ways to structure financial deals with coworkers. First, everyone might work under the condition of "food and video", an offer frequently made in trade publications. It means that no one who agrees to work will be reimbursed for anything, not even expenses like gas or mileage, nor will they receive any compensation at any time during production or if the film becomes financially successful. All they get for their work is free meals on workdays and a videotape of the film after completion. In reality, they might never receive the tape, and practically no way exists to force the producer to adhere to the agreement. "Food and video" arrangements generally are possible in cities and production centers where competition is high and any work adds to a person's résumé, list of personal contacts, and working experience. No more is expected.

Second, everyone might work on a deferred basis and agree to be paid from the first funds earned. Individual fees might be negotiated separately, or they might be based on the minimum union salary scales. Sometimes, 10 percent is added to compensate for the risk of working "on spec"; no financial returns can be guaranteed when the work starts. In this case, the producer or PM must treat the production exactly as though it were a regular union production. Time sheets must be kept to record who worked and how long so that the accrued salaries can be computed later. This formula can be used for all actors and extras, using SAG and Screen Extras Guild (SEG) wage scales; for above-the-line personnel, using Writers Guild of America (WGA) and DGA wage scales; and for all below-the-line personnel, using National Association of Broadcast Employees & Technicians (NABET) wage scales. After completion of the production, everyone knows the precise amount due. Of course, this arrangement means extraordinary work for the production office.

If certain crew members have made equipment contributions, such as a Nagra lent by the sound mixer, these contributions should be computed according to their market rental value and added to the person's share. Contributions can extend beyond production equipment to cars, private wardrobe, catering services, postproduction, and general office equipment.

These arrangements become more complicated when cash contributions toward production expenses are made by third parties not directly involved in the production. Cash investors usually expect that they will be first in line for recoupment of their investment. In fairness to cast and crew, the producer should negotiate with cash investors to treat them on a 50/50 basis with service investors (personnel working for deferred pay). In this case, any money that comes in before production costs (or cash investments, whatever is negotiated) are recouped will be split 50/50, with half going to deferred salaries and half going back to the cash investors.

How income is split after service expenses and cash investments are recouped is a matter of negotiation. Generally, cash investors, the producer, and perhaps some above-the-line personnel will want to continue the profit participation. This may be the case if the writer, director, or PM opt to waive their minimum union-scale wages for a share in ownership of the picture. Such ownership options may be offered to cast and crew members, too. Thus, the arrangements become even more complex.

In such instances, the contracts must spell out very clearly at what point ownership shares translate into cash to be received. Terms such as *net*, *gross*, *first position*, *first dollar*, *adjusted gross*, *box office receipts or revenues*, *break-even point*, *overhead*, *interest*, *distribution and sub-distribution fees*, and *most favored nation* become vitally important, as are provisions to be able to inspect the books and records kept by the producer. It is highly advisable to employ the services of a legal professional when negotiating such agreements.

Unless gross participation is arranged (money to be shared from the very first dollar that comes in), all money received and distributable by the producer can only come out of the producer's share. From every dollar earned by a film, part goes to sales agents, distributors, and exhibitors before the producer receives a share. The producer's share generally amounts to perhaps 20–30 percent of all revenues, depending on markets and media, but individual situations may vary considerably.

Any agreements with cash investors and service investors must spell out clearly all applicable conditions of recoupment. It is obvious that all such agreements involve a high degree of risk and trust. It is a sad fact that often these agreements are not kept, and litigation proves to be a time-consuming, expensive, nerve-racking, hopeless attempt to receive any money.

5

Locations

Location Survey

After the screenplay is broken down, and discussions with the producer and director establish a clearer picture of how they envision the movie, it is time to find appropriate location sites. Although it would be ideal to have all locations secured before the start of principal photography, in reality the location search may continue from preproduction through the beginning of the shoot, depending on the individual circumstances of the production. On a short shoot with many different locations, most locations must be secured before the start of production; on a long shoot with ordinary, easy-to-find locations, the location research may continue while the shooting is in progress.

Normally, this is the task of the location manager, who first must find the "right" location in terms of "look" as the Director envisions it. Usually he must consider the seasons during the year, the times of sunrise and sunset if the location search takes place quite ahead of the shoot, he usually takes pictures or videos to take back to the director and to the production manager, who sees any location from a different point of view—the one which means organization, access and costs. Then the location manager must also negotiate the site, draw up contracts, obtain all necessary private and government permits, and maintain contact with police and fire departments. However, it is the production manager's task to supervise and make sure all arrangements are made on time and within budget. On low-budget productions, the PM traditionally does the work of the location manager in addition to his or her regular duties.

Not only must the prospective location site suit the artistic demands of the director, but it must also fit within the budgetary and logistical framework of the production. For example, a "perfect" location from the director's and art director's points of view might be impossible if extensive travel to and from the site is required and the shooting time per day is reduced to an unacceptable level. A "perfect" location from a logistical standpoint might be impossible from the art director's point of view if extensive remodeling outside the production's schedule or budget is required. An otherwise perfect location might be impossible if the director of photography finds it too difficult to light or if the site is in an area prohibitively expensive for film production. The PM should know which areas of a city fall under specific jurisdictions and have different location fees. In Los Angeles, for example, the area of Beverly Hills has elevated its permit fees to heights that make it prohibitive for small companies to shoot there—exactly the purpose of the regulation. The location manager must consider all these different aspects when looking for a location.

Once prospective locations are found and photos taken of them, location manager, production manager, director, art director, and director of photography visit them together. Each checks the location in accordance with his or her individual requirements. After all agree on a particular location, the PM begins negotiations with the owner or another person with the right to negotiate about the property. It is important that the PM locates the real owners of the property or their legal assignees; renters or leasing partners often rent out properties without actually having the right to do so. If the proper permissions are not obtained, whether from private or official parties, the shooting could be closed down on the spot, and lawsuits could follow.

Frequently, negotiating with just the owner is not good enough. When the shooting affects neighbors or adjacent business owners, these people also must give their permission. Permission should be secured in writing with the property release form (see Chapter 8 for appropriate documents). Some owners insist on reading the screenplay to ensure that their property will not appear in a dubious light; this is especially true of places like hospitals, government facilities, train stations, airports and schools. In light of the "Home Security Act" some locations may not be available at all.

All this takes time, so the PM should clear the location as early as possible before actual production. This guarantees that the PM will not be held hostage when time runs out and a location is desperately needed, regardless of the asking price. Some property owners try to raise the location fees immediately before the shoot, so it is necessary to have all agreements in writing. No rules exist about what a private person can charge; it is a matter of negotiation. Official sites and properties, on the other hand, have set fees (discussed later in this chapter).

When negotiating for a site, the PM should deal in a straightforward manner, disclosing all details of the prospective shoot to avoid canceled agreements and even lawsuits. The PM should be prepared to provide the following information:

- Type of production (commercial, TV, feature film, music video, corporate production);

- Number of shooting days;
- Day or night shooting, or both;
- Daily preparation schedule, shooting and wrap hours;
- Set dressing and prep days;
- Type of activity to occur;
- Number of people and vehicles involved;
- Pyrotechnics or stunts planned.

The PM should also be prepared to provide proof of insurance and references.

The production manager should point out to the owner that daily shooting schedules can change at any time due to weather, cast illness, script rewrites, and equipment breakdown or failure to arrive. During the negotiations, the PM should ask these questions:

- Can the production company use the building's electrical power?
- Should a building electrician be present?
- Will there be a charge for usage?
- Do any regularly scheduled activities interfere with the shooting, such as gardening, watering, or window washing?
- Can the crew use the building's trash receptacles?
- Can the production company park its vehicles on the premises?
- Who will provide access to the property after hours?
- Does the production company use public or private telephones at the site?
- Are the tenants amenable to the filming?
- Can the facility be accessed easily, via freight elevators or loading docks, for example?
- If the "look" of the location does not meet the script's needs, to what extent will set dressings and changes be possible, and will the property be available for set building, dressing, and striking?

For the actual shoot, vehicle logistics must be considered. The space closest to the location should be reserved for the following vehicles: electrical truck, generator, production truck, and camera van so that the heaviest equipment can be moved with as little effort as possible.

The following vehicles should be parked as close as possible, the following being a rule of thumb as to the general distance: 5 or 10 ton electrical truck containing lighting equipment—35 ft; generator (power supply for lights and cameras)—35 ft; 10 ton production truck—60 ft; camera van—20 ft; 5 ton set dresser's truck, with props etc.—30 ft; 5 ton special effects truck (if special effects are used in the shoot)—30 ft; crane (if camera crane is required for the shoot)—30 ft.

The following are usually parked nearby: dressing room/toilet unit (commonly called "honey wagon")—65 ft; pick-up truck with wardrobe trailer—30 ft; catering truck, motor-homes, typically 8×25 ft (two or more) for actors and director—30 ft; maxi-van for shuttling crews and cast—15 ft; production cars for errands or local trips, "picture vehicles" (cars or trucks used within the shot).

Until actual location sites are negotiated, pinned down, and put in writing, a realistic and definite shooting schedule (and budget) cannot always be made. In large urban areas or on locations that require long travel times to and from a hotel, these times must be known to schedule shooting realistically. Schedules affect overtime payments and other costs. These considerations are unnecessary, of course, if the shooting takes place in the controlled environment of a soundstage, studio, or studio backlot.

Film Commissions

Film commissions are of great assistance in finding locations and planning a production, whether it involves a local, overnight, or distant location shoot. Film commissions are created and run by individual states, counties, and even cities. They can be found in almost every state in the United States, and in many other countries and usually maintain very informative websites, even detailing individual location sites available.

In the past, film commissions were hardly more than offices that mailed out materials collected from local chambers of commerce and tourist offices, but now most are separate entities that publish and advertise their services regularly in the trade papers or at film festivals and other appropriate markets. Their efforts are geared toward attracting film productions to their area. Commissioners understand that much money is spent during preproduction and production. Even if few local residents are hired on a production, out-of-town companies still need accommodations, transportation, food, and hundreds of other items that boost the local economy.

As a general rule, film commissions never get involved in the negotiations of permits or releases between private property owners and the production company. Nor do they get involved in contracts between production personnel and production companies.

Today, the materials that film commissions mail free of charge to interested companies and individuals are very sophisticated. These production manuals, or production guides, are tailored to meet the needs of production companies on distant location shoots. Mostly this information can be obtained on-line, too.

Film-commission staffers often go out of their way to assist filmmakers during preproduction, and their efforts go far beyond just mailing production manuals. The film commission might break down the screenplay and photograph possible locations or assemble photos from the commission's location resource library. The library is generally organized into different categories, such as hospitals, schools, industrial sites, parks and recreational areas, ranches, farms, and beaches. Figure 5.1 shows the subject categories of one film commission's library.

The location manager or PM and director should visit every possible location site themselves before making any decisions. What looks wonderful to an enthusiastic film commission staff member might look quite different to a production person. When the PM and others arrive for a first-hand survey of the site, film commission staffers usually take them around and discuss individual needs, sometimes supplying transportation and accommodations.

Before spending money on a research trip, though, the PM should check the overall production conditions of the area under consideration. Most production manuals provide sufficient specific information to enable the PM to decide in advance whether a shoot in a particular distant location would be possible and economically worthwhile. Production manuals generally contain information on preproduction services, production services, historical background and locations, and the area's infrastructure.

Preproduction Services

The best production manuals contain the names, addresses, and professional backgrounds of local residents and companies that can assist with preproduction, including casting directors, extras agencies, graphic designers, professional guilds, payroll companies, prop builders, set painters, vehicle rental services, and wardrobe personnel. The PM can use this information to assess whether most of the crew can be hired locally and to determine who must be brought in from elsewhere. Clearly, this has an effect on the budget: If most personnel are hired locally, travel, accommodations, and per diem expenses are cut. Customarily, a production company brings to a location its own key people in the camera department and other important departments and hires locally for all positions below department heads. However, individual production circumstances and requirements vary. The PM can also determine what equipment and services are available locally and what must be shipped from other locations.

It is desirable to hire as many people locally as possible. Aside from the savings, their private connections and knowledge might prove invaluable. Local residents find locations easily because they already know their way around, they can meet the production's logistical needs, and they can mobilize the support of the whole community. Casting of local extras also is of great advantage. Conversely, if the support of local residents vanishes, the production may find

LOCATION RESOURCE LIBRARY SUBJECT CATEGORIES
California Film Commission
California Trade & Commerce Agency

Pete Wilson, *Governor*	Julie Meier Wright, *Secretary*

101 **TOWNS AND COMMUNITIES**
    101 General\Cities (aerials, rooftops and urban landscape)

    101.1 Los Angeles County
    101.2 Southern California (This system for each number)
    101.3 Central California
    101.4 Northern California

  102 Small Towns and Environments
  103 Western, Mining and Ghost Towns
  104 "Matches" and Foreign Looks (by type,
      i.e., NY looks, Vietnam, etc.)
  105 Backlots, Studios and Stages

200 **RESIDENTIAL**
  201 Castles and Mansions (filed by city within each country)
  202 Houses (filed by city within each county)
  203 Apartments, Townhouses and Condos
  204 Residential Neighborhoods
  205 Mobile Homes and Trailer Parks
  206 Log Cabins

300 **COMMERCIAL AND RETAIL**
  301 Banks and Office Buildings
  302 Ballrooms, Dance Halls and Nightclubs
  303 Theaters, Stages and Auditoriums
  304 Hotels, Motels and Inns
  305 Stores and Retail Districts
  306 Restaurants and Bars
  307 Dance Studios and Lofts
  308 Beauty Salons, Barbershops and Beauty Schools

400 **PUBLIC/GOVERNMENT/MUNICIPAL**
  401 Government Buildings
  402 Courthouses and Courtrooms
  403 Prisons and Jails
  404 Observatories
  405 Museums and Galleries
  406 Hospitals and Medical Facilities
  407 Military Bases and Forts
  408 Police and Fire Stations

500 **EDUCATIONAL AND RELIGIOUS**
  501 Elementary and Secondary Schools
  502 Colleges and Universities
  503 Seminaries and Convents
  504 Libraries
  505 Churches, Temples and Synagogues
  506 Missions
  507 Cemeteries and Funeral Homes

600 **INDUSTRIAL**
  601 Plants, Factories and Boiler Rooms
  602 Dams, Pumping Plants and Water Treatment Fac.
  603 Warehouses and Industrial Districts
  604 Windmills and Turbines
  605 Abandoned Structures and Vacant Lots
  606 Junkyard and Container Yards

700 **RANCHES AND FARMS; AGRICULTURE**
  701 Ranches and Farms
  702 Wineries and Vineyards
  703 Crops/Orchards
  704 Livestock

800 **PARKS AND RECREATION AREAS**
  801 State Parks and Forests
  802 National Parks, Forests and Monuments
  803 City and County Parks
  804 Jungles and Gardens
  805 Sports Facilities (Stadia, Racetracks, Pools-by type)
  806 Amusement Parks, Zoos, Attractions and Carnivals
  807 Ski Areas and Tramway
  808 Summer Camps, Resorts and Spas
  809 Fairgrounds, Rodeos and Exhibit Halls
  810 Town Squares, Plazas, Fountains and Statues

900 **TRANSPORTATION**
  901 Roads
  902 Bridges
  903 Rail Transportation and Depots
  904 Airports and Heliports
  905 Boats and Ships
  906 Aircraft
  907 Gas Stations and Auto Repair Shops
  908 Freeways and Freeway Look-A-Likes
  909 Alleys
  910 Tunnels
  911 Parking Lots and Structures

1000 **WATER AND COASTAL AREAS**
  1001 Beaches and Coastline
  1002 Lighthouses
  1003 Rivers, Streams, Whitewater and Waterfalls
  1004 Lakes, Ponds and Reservoirs
  1005 Harbors, Ports and Marinas
  1006 Piers and Boardwalks
  1007 Swamps and Marshes

1100 **GEOGRAPHY/GEOLOGY**
  1101 General Terrain
  1102 Mountains and Rocks
  1103 Desert Areas
  1104 Dry Lakes
  1105 Caves, Caverns and Mines
  1106 Sand Dunes

Fig. 5–1. Subject categories of the California Film Commission's location resource library.

itself in real difficulty. As noted previously, it pays to treat everyone involved in the production with respect and politeness.

Production Services

No established format exists for production manuals, but one section usually provides an overview of the production services available, from labs to rentals. You frequently may encounter multiple listings of names. Many people list their qualifications in different areas. A production guide that looks impressive because of its size might be reduced to a booklet once the multiple listings are deleted. The same section might contain postproduction services and facilities for video and film, from composers to sound mixing to screenings.

Historical Background and Varying Locations

This section of the production manual describes locations in the area, especially those that can look like somewhere else: hills in Kansas that resemble Salinas, California; downtown areas that can double for a New York street corner. The aim is to describe the variety of locations available, from rural sites to small-town neighborhoods to industrial sites to historical landmarks, all of which are found within short distances. Maps are usually part of this section.

Accommodations and Infrastructure

Another section of the production manual might deal with the accommodations and infrastructure of the area, including hotels, restaurants, vehicle rentals, airports, carriers, trains, highways, and ports. It might describe the general topography of the surrounding area and provide weather charts giving average sunshine, rain, and temperature statistics and sunrise/sunset data.

Permits

Once location scouting is concluded, contracts are drawn up, and tentative shooting dates are set, then location sites must be green-lighted by official county or city permits. The PM must hire a location manager, if one is not in place already. Even when a location manager is on staff, the PM is ultimately responsible for ensuring that all permits are in order. Failure to obtain the proper permits might result in the immediate closing down of the shoot, a costly and potentially devastating occurrence.

This section deals with the official permits that must be obtained from the appropriate government agencies. The process of filing for and issuing permits can take anywhere from 24 hours to four weeks, depending on the agency involved and its familiarity with the procedure. Production centers like Los Angeles have streamlined the permit process, but small towns might be a different story. The location issue should be addressed early so that locations are secured and permit procedures are begun as soon as possible.

As an example, a short overview of the permit process for Los Angeles follows. (The extracts are adapted from its publications.) Many counties and cities use similar processes. In some areas hoping to attract film productions, official permit fees are waived or are nonexistent. This can translate into significant savings for a production company. While the authorities in big production centers such as Los Angeles and New York City insist on following all the rules and regulations to the point, the situation outside of the cities may be quite different and less regulated.

Although permits are required for all commercial filming and taping (including still photography) done outside a studio, the permit fees may be waived if (1) a production is undertaken by non-profit organizations, or (2) a production is non-commercial, educational, or public-service-oriented. Permit fees are not required for news crews and non-commercial still photographers.

The L.A. Motion Picture/TV Office assists in making arrangements with the more than 20 municipal departments wherever applicable. Although these departments try to accommodate the production company, their primary concern and responsibility is the provision of good service to the public. They cannot permit the public to be exposed to unhealthy or dangerous conditions; thus they may limit access to certain neighborhoods or may limit the times in which particular scenes can be shot. For example, simulated gunfire may be permitted only during regular office hours or may be prohibited after 9 p.m. Discuss your requirements with a staff member of the film commission well in advance. Applications may be made by telephone or in person but must be made no later than 48 hours before the shoot. Permits cannot be obtained on the day of the shoot.

The office seeks the required approvals from and makes arrangements with other city departments, such as police or fire. A filming permit is issued that details exact locations, date, and time of day required. It includes remarks on equipment, personnel, and any special conditions, as well as a list of scenes to be shot, noting any special effects, special actions, or stunts. Minor changes may be obtained by telephone for a rider, but extensions and alterations of effective permit periods must be approved in writing by the Motion Picture/ TV Office. This permit and the rider (if applicable) must be carried by the production manager, the first assistant director, or another production person on the location in case an official wants to inspect it.

In addition to a one-time application fee (which lists one or all locations), user charges are added for filming and preparation/dressing of and on municipal property (not including streets and sidewalks), as well as charges whenever a municipal department is required to provide services. These charges usually include direct labor costs for city workers as well as a general overhead fee. These charges are to be prepaid but will be adjusted later to match the actual costs incurred.

If a street or part of a street must be closed for more than a few minutes, the production company must apply for a street or lane closure permit 7–10 days in advance. Off-duty police officers are required for traffic and crowd control. The producer should abide by the following guidelines when shooting in public:

1.   All advance signs and any other traffic control devices must be furnished and installed in conformance with the "Manual of Traffic Controls".

2.   Traffic may be reduced to one 12 ft lane of traffic and/or stopped intermittently, not to exceed three minutes at any time.

3.   The activities should be conducted in such a manner that the attention of motorists is not diverted from their driving so as to cause deceleration of travel or stopping on the highway.

4.   Traffic must not be detoured across a double line without prior approval of the road department.

5.   The camera car must be driven in the direction of traffic, must observe all traffic laws, and must not in any way interfere with the flow of traffic.

6.   The stationary camera must be mounted off the roadway.

7.   The producer's equipment, such as buses, trucks, cars, and catering service equipment, must be parked off the traveled way so that equipment and employees do not interfere with the free flow of traffic.

8.   Any road work or construction by county crews and/or private contractors, under permit or contract to the road department will have priority over filming activities.

Generally, permits do not grant production personnel the right to disregard existing parking rules and regulations. However, minor exemptions to such regulations as no-parking hours or special neighborhood permits are possible and must be applied for 72 hours prior to use. It is important to give the exact number of crew cars as well as trucks, motor homes, and so on.

No permits will be issued without proof of adequate insurance. (For liability minimums, see Chapter 10.) An official permit is always necessary when the shoot takes place on private property, even with full consent of the owner.

In Los Angeles, permit applications usually are routed through the police department, which advises the production on the use of appropriate off-duty police personnel for traffic and crowd control, when applicable. These police officers (in uniform, armed, and with their police motorcycles) are booked through private agencies and paid on an hourly basis, with overtime provisions. It is advisable to establish a good working relationship with individual police officers; the agency will try to provide specific officers on request, subject to their availability. The appropriate local police station must be notified whenever scenes involving gunfire, simulated police action, or other activities that might confuse the public are scheduled.

Additionally, all permits are routinely forwarded to the Los Angeles Fire Department, which may require a fire safety officer to be on duty, usually on locations such as buildings used by the general public, schools, mountain fire districts, and whenever combustible materials are used. The pay schedule resembles that of police officers, and the officials are provided through the fire department. The special effects person (pyrotechnician) must carry a special effects permit valid for Los Angeles and California, issued by the Engineering Unit of the Los Angeles Fire Department.

If animals are used on the shoot, an animal act exhibition permit must be obtained from the Los Angeles Department of Animal Regulation five days prior to the shooting date.

All firms doing business in the City of Los Angeles are subject to the business tax and must have a business tax registration certificate.

Failure to comply with any requirements is unlawful and may result in the suspension of the filming permit and immediate shutdown of the production.

Because relations between a filming crew and the neighborhoods impacted have to be friendly and professional, behavioral codes (Filmmaker's Code of Professional Responsibility) have been established, which will help everyone involved to deal with such the exceptional situations that quite frequently disrupt a daily routine. These rules are (cited from the Entertainment Industry Development Corporation):

1. When filming in a neighborhood or business district, proper notification is to be provided each merchant or resident who is directly affected by production activities (includes parking, base camps and meal areas). The Filmmaker's Code of Professional Responsibility should be attached to the filming notification that is distributed to the neighborhood.

2. Production companies arriving on location in or near a residential neighborhood should enter the area no earlier than the time stipulated on the permit and park one by one, turning engines off as soon as possible. Cast and crew should observe designated parking areas.

3. When production passes, identifying employees, are issued, every crew member should wear it while at the location.

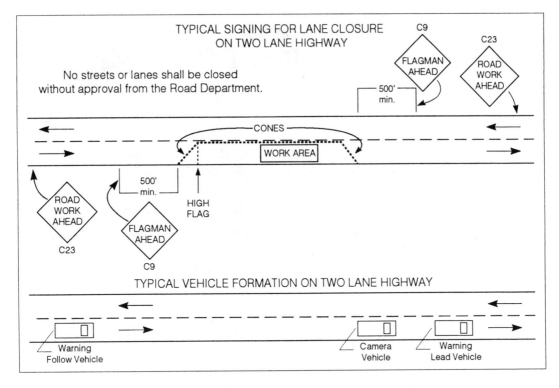

Fig. 5–2. Permit attachment detailing regulations for filming on two-lane highways.

4. Moving or towing vehicles is prohibited without the express permission of the municipal jurisdiction or the vehicle's owner.

5. Production vehicles may not block driveways without the express permission of the municipal jurisdiction or the driveway owner.

6. Meals should be confined to the area designated in the location agreement or permit. Individuals must eat within the designated meal areas. All trash must be disposed of properly upon completion of the meal.

7. Removing, trimming and/or cutting of vegetation or trees is prohibited unless approved by the owner, or in the case of parkway trees, the local municipality and the property owner.

8. All catering, crafts services, construction, strike and personal trash must be removed from the location.

9. All signs erected or removed for filming purposes must be removed or replaced upon completion of the use of the location, unless stipulated otherwise by the location agreement or the permit.

FILM OFFICE

ATTACHMENT IV

NOTIFICATION OF FILMING/PARKING

SAMPLE

Dear Resident:

We will be filming scenes of _____
in your area which require posting of temporary "No Parking" signs. Your signature below
confirms that you have no objection to the filming activity.

We are applying for the necessary County filming permit and maintain all legally required
liability insurance. Additionally, all County personnel required to ensure public safety will
be on location. We will abide by all County filming rules and specific conditions applicable
in your neighborhood.

We will make every effort not to disturb you and will treat your neighborhood with the
respect you deserve.

Location of Filming:_____

Dates and Times:_____

Scenes:_____

_____

Thank you in advance for your cooperation. If you have any further questions or
concerns, we are available 24-hours a day by pager and please don't hesitate to call.

Production Company   L.A. County Film Office

_____   Office: (213) 957-1000

_____   Pager: (310) 885-0241

I do not object to filming/parking activity.
(Name)   (Address)   (Phone)

_____

_____

_____

_____

| ECONOMIC DEVELOPMENT CORPORATION | L.A. MEANS BUSINESS! | 6922 Hollywood Boulevard, Suite 606 | Los Angeles California 90028-6124 | 213-957-1000 Telephone | 213-463-0613 Facsimile |

Fig. 5–3. Notification letter for residents regarding parking.

FILM OFFICE

ATTACHMENT V

REQUEST TO FILM - EXTENDED HOURS

SAMPLE

Dear Resident:

We will be filming scenes of _____
in your neighborhood.

Normal filming hours are between 7:00 a.m. and 10:00 p.m. Your signature below confirms that you have no objection to the extended hours of filming.

We are applying for the necessary County filming permit and maintain all legally required liability insurance. Additionally, all County personnel required to ensure public safety will be on location. We will abide by all County filming rules and specific conditions applicable in your neighborhood.

We will make every effort not to disturb you and will treat your neighborhood with the respect you deserve.

Location of Filming:_____

Dates and Times:_____

Scenes:_____

_____

Thank you in advance for your cooperation. If you have any further questions or concerns, we are available 24-hours a day by pager and please don't hesitate to call.

Production Company   L.A. County Film Office

_____   Office: **(213) 957-1000**

_____   Pager: **(310) 885-0241**

____ I do not object to the extended filming hours.
____ I do not object, but will not sign my name.
____ I do object to the requested extended hours filming.

_____
Signature   Print Name   Address

_____
Phone (For verification purposes only)

| ECONOMIC DEVELOPMENT CORPORATION | L.A. MEANS BUSINESS' | 6922 Hollywood Boulevard, Suite 606 | Los Angeles California 90028-6124 | 213-957-1000 Telephone | 213-463-0613 Facsimile |

Fig. 5–4. Notification letter for residents regarding extended hours for filming.

Fig. 5–5. Notification letter for residents regarding filming.

10.   All signs posted to direct the company to the location must be removed.

11.   Noise levels should be kept as low as possible. Generators should be placed as far as practical from residential buildings. Do not let engines run unnecessarily.

12.   All members of the production company should wear clothing that conforms to good taste and common sense. Shoes and shirts must be worn at all times.

13.   Crew members must not display signs, posters or pictures that do not reflect common sense and good taste (i.e., pin-up-posters).

14.   Cast and crew should remain on or near the area that has been permitted. Do not trespass on to another neighbor's or merchant's property.

15.   The cast and crew should not bring guests or pets to the location, unless expressly authorized in advance by the production company.

16.   Observe the designated smoking areas and always extinguish cigarettes in butt cans.

17.   Cast and crew should refrain from using lewd or offensive language within earshot of the general public.

18.   Cast and crew vehicles parked on City streets must adhere to all legal requirements unless authorized by the film permit.

19.   Parking is prohibited on both sides of City streets unless specifically authorized by the film permit.

20.   The company must comply with the provisions of the permit at all times.

Los Angeles has designated some neighborhoods and areas as special filming areas, where certain restrictions and guidelines are applicable. If filming is planned on county, state, or federal property, the PM must contact the appropriate government agencies (in addition to the city agency) for the permits to be cleared.

Filming in national parks is subject to many of the procedures described earlier. National parks frequently have additional, unique requirements—for example, restrictions on the use of helicopters and planes, traffic regulations, and environmental concerns. (For contacts for filming in national parks, refer to the appropriate state film commission in Appendix 1.)

Private "one-stop" companies and agencies specialize in location scouting and clearing of permit and release requirements. These companies often have their own location photo or video libraries and list individuals interested in renting their properties for filming. No general guidelines have been established on fees paid to private owners.

Foreign Shoots

Increasingly, foreign countries are setting up their own film commissions in an attempt to lure big production companies to their shores. With the changing political situation in Europe and former Eastern bloc countries, even more opportunities will develop, especially if coproduction and below-the-line arrangements can be negotiated. Many big Hollywood-productions have made use of former Eastern bloc studio facilities, such as in Prague, in Romania and the Baltic States—and they keep coming back. For example, some countries offer to supply below-the-line personnel and facilities in exchange for certain exploitation rights. When planning to shoot outside the United States, explore the different, ever-changing areas of production, joint ventures, and bartering of rights, and discuss them with official or private parties.

Frequently additional special tax or rebate incentives are offered; these measures, however, are also offered by some states within the U.S. (currently Alabama, Arizona Arkansas, California, Connecticut, Florida, Georgia, Hawaii, Idaho, Illinois, Louisiana, Maryland, Michigan, Minnesota, Mississippi, Missouri, New Jersey, New Mexico, North Carolina, Oklahoma, Oregon, Tennessee, Texas, Vermont, Virginia, Washington, Wyoming). These incentives include wage-based rebates providing credit back to the production company for paying a certain amount in salaries to state residents and/or investment tax credits that allow a resident investor to earn substantial tax credits for investing in a motion picture that will be produced in that state.

Financial and coproduction conditions in one country sometimes are more favorable than in others. As long as the look of the film is maintained and the production is safely conducted, countries might be interchangeable. Malaysia, Thailand, and Vietnam, for example, might offer the same types of locations, yet the production conditions might vary greatly from one country to the next. Such negotiations are usually conducted by the executive producer or the producer, but the PM is frequently asked to assess production conditions during a survey trip.

If an official film commission is not set up in a country of interest, a call to the embassy or official travel bureau might be a helpful first step to establish contacts with authorities or foreign production companies and services. For a foreign shoot, it is virtually impossible to obtain all required information and proper permits without a knowledgeable local production person. During a pre-production location survey (a must for any foreign shoot), a local production coordinator must be found prior to the company's arrival to organize location site surveys and contact the authorities, if applicable. A production coordinator should be put in charge of obtaining all proper permits. In many developing countries, the road to permits might be long, winding, and labyrinthine; cash might be required; and receipts might not be issued. In other words, no rules exist there for production companies to follow.

6

Unions

This chapter takes a closer look at those unions the production manager must deal with most often. It also discusses the process by which the PM may become a union member.

Screen Actors Guild and Screen Extras Guild

As mentioned previously, the below-the-line personnel involved in most low- to medium-budget independent film productions rarely belong to unions. In production centers like Los Angeles, plenty of nonunion personnel are available, and qualified workers are virtually guaranteed. The one union, though, that production companies usually deal with is the Screen Actors Guild (SAG). Members of the Screen Extras Guild (SEG) are represented through the SAG. No law requires production companies to work with union actors, but, in practice, almost all actors are members of the SAG, especially those in the business for some time. Union members are not permitted to work under nonunion conditions, and are fined by the union when they do so. If a production company requires the participation of a "name" actor—whether for "marquee value" or to improve the film's chances for distribution—it will have to become a SAG signatory and adhere to SAG regulations.

Communication between the production company and the SAG is usually handled by the production manager. The PM is responsible for providing any information and paperwork that the SAG requires, as detailed later in this chapter. Failure to do so in a complete and timely manner will result in monetary fines against the production company.

Exceptions do exist to the rule of SAG participation. In low-budget films, films with limited exhibition, student films, experimental works, music videos, educational films, and sometimes films for public television, union members are permitted to work on the basis of deferred compensation. Payment becomes due or negotiations become necessary if the film is commercially exploited and makes money. (The SAG Low-Budget Agreements are mentioned at the end of this chapter and form part of Appendix 2.) Close communication with a SAG representative is highly advisable at all stages of production.

Once a production company uses a SAG actor and becomes a signatory to the SAG Basic Agreement, all actors and extras employed on that particular production must be SAG and SEG members. An exception is permitted in the so-called Taft/Hartley cases (described later in this chapter). A production company becomes a SAG signatory on a picture-by-picture basis. In other words, a production company that uses SAG actors for one film need not use them for the next. Adhering to SAG regulations does not mean the production company must use members of any other union (with the exception of the SEG). SAG members who work without a SAG contract will lose pension and health benefits, residual payments, work safety, and other protections from the SAG.

The Basic Agreement applies to all areas in the United States in which the guild has a branch—virtually the entire country. (For addresses, refer to Appendix 1.) Moreover, if a production company based in the U.S. shoots in Canada with Canadian actors, the Basic Agreement still applies. When an American producer hires and transports an American actor for work anywhere outside the United States, the Basic Agreement again applies. When an American producer hires a non-American actor for a SAG production, the actor is treated as if he or she were a SAG member, too, and all union dues and fringe benefits apply even if the actor never actually becomes a beneficiary of those benefits. However, when a non-American production company hires an American actor for a film to be shot entirely outside the United States, the actor and the production company may not have to comply with SAG regulations. Since May 1, 2002 the "Global Rule One" covering television, theatrical, commercial and industrial, applies which means that whenever SAG members are employed—also outside the U.S.— foreign producers are also requested to become SAG signatories. Waivers will be decided on a case-by-case basis by the SAG and only after careful analysis of a particular production. Global Rule One does not apply to non-English productions that are shot within the jurisdiction of another country's performer's union. Non-English productions shot anywhere in the U.S. are under SAG Rule One.

Because the SAG also represents SEG members, a producer who shoots a SAG picture must hire SEG members. A SAG production may employ nonunion extras only under certain conditions. On a SAG picture with a budget of more than $2 million, the first 100 extras on any day must be SEG members; after that, nonunion extras may be employed. On a SAG picture with a budget of up to $2 million, the first 40 extras on any day must be union; thereafter, nonunion extras may be employed. The producer must follow the SEG's pay schedule and pay an additional 13.8 percent of gross payments for union benefits (health and pension).

Participation of these unions to a large degree shapes the form of the production. The Basic Agreement spells out in great detail obligatory guidelines for the producer–actor relationship. These guidelines determine the form of the shooting day as well as the shooting week. They structure all aspects of the production, including casting call, wardrobe fitting, rehearsal times, meal periods, and travel arrangements, as well as compensation, overtime, night pay, and weekend and holiday provisions.

The SAG requires extensive paperwork from the production company to ensure that all its rules and regulations are being observed. Of prime importance, for example, are the Production Time Report and Performer's Overtime Records, which note the following information: date worked, first time called, time arrived at location, meal (lunch, dinner), time dismissed, studio location, miles, time for makeup, and wardrobe removal. Even more paperwork is required for the so-called low-budget productions, defined as those with a variety of budgets (discussed later in the chapter) different from regular productions. SAG representatives have the right to visit the set or location site of any SAG-regulated picture, regardless of budget, to observe the production.

The following is a step-by-step description of the communication process between the production company and the SAG, as required by the SAG. Certain extracts are quoted from SAG documents, such as the Television/Theatrical Production Checklist, which the SAG sends to the signatory production company.

Preproduction

1. A principal of the production company has to complete and sign the Information Sheet, Theatrical or Television Adherence Letters (whichever applies), Extras Adherence Letters, Pension and Health Adherence Letters and Security Agreements and UCC-1 Financing Statement for each production and return it to the Guild fifteen (15) working days prior to the production (principal photography) start date.

    The SAG information sheet asks for basic information on the production, including title, start and completion dates, legal status of production company, budget figures (total, performers, extras), licensing agreements (if any), distribution agreements (if any), payroll company, bank, staff information, number of performers (weekly, daily, extras), studio, locations, number of shooting days, insurance carrier, corporate structure, and information on partnerships and joint ventures.

    The Security Agreement gives the SAG the right to hold the film negative as collateral against unpaid fines, late fees, or payments due to actors or the SAG that exceed the deposit given the guild at the beginning of production. The UCC-1 form is also necessary in this context.

2. The guild requests the following information as applicable:

    a. Corporation—articles of incorporation and corporation resolution;

    b. Partnership or joint ventures—fictitious business name statements and partnership agreements;

    c. Sole owner—fictitious business name statement;

    d. Individual—Social Security number and copy of driver's license or I.D.

3. Financial assurances are (as defined below) to be provided no later than fifteen (15) working days prior to production (principal photography) start date. The producer must also submit all chain-of-title documents relating to the picture, a copy of the PA Form application relating to the screenplay upon which the picture is based, and proof of receipt by the US Copyright Office of the PA Form, a completed Pre-Production Cast List, a copy of the script and day-out-of-days for a SAG representative to calculate the amount of the security deposit. The minimum financial security required is $10,000.

"Financial Assurances" include, but are not limited to the following:

Security deposit and related agreements;

Security agreement;

Financing statements;

Assumption statements;

Subordination agreement (if applicable).

The security deposit must be deposited as a certificate of deposit at a bank designated by the SAG, and only a SAG officer is permitted to withdraw any funds. The size of the deposit, beyond the $10,000 minimum, is determined by various factors, including the overall actors' and extras' payroll and the track record of the production company and individuals involved. The deposit money (or the balance thereof) is returned to the producer with accrued interest after the postproduction period.

The Pre-Production Cast List names all actors employed and gives their film-role names, their agents' names and telephone numbers, length of their employment, and their base salary and total earnings.

The day-out-of-days sheet shows which actors worked on which shooting days. On the basis of this form, which really is a condensed shooting schedule, the SAG computes salaries due to the talent.

If the producer asks to be regulated under the Low-Budget Theatrical Pictures Agreement, additional paperwork is involved. The producer must provide the top sheet of the film's budget, which should show that the picture's total above-the-line and below-the-line costs are less than $2 million (may be increased to $3 million if the producer meets certain criteria demonstrating diversity in casting) or whatever may apply (discussed later in the chapter). For low-budget productions, an actor's compensation may be about 10 percent less than it would be on a regular picture. However, most other provisions (such as overtime, premium pay, and penalties) remain the same, but are based on the lower compensation. Health and pension benefits, which currently run at about 13 percent of gross payment, remain intact. The producer must sign a special form called the Letter Agreement for Low-Budget Theatrical Picture. Upon completion of the film, the producer must give the SAG a detailed report of actual expenditures that shows the final cost of the production. In the event that the actual production cost for the picture exceeds $2 million (or whatever may apply), the producer must make full payment of any additional sums to bring each performer's rate of pay into compliance with the minimum rates specified in the latest Basic Agreement. The producer also must make upgraded health and pension contributions.

Production

1. Station 12

    a. All performers (excluding extras) must be cleared with the Guild at least one (1) week prior to commencement of employment. The SAG suggests that the producer designates a member of the production staff to be responsible for all clearances. In order to clear, call the department at the Guild known as "Station 12" . . . and supply performer's name, Social Security number and work date. Station 12 will advise verbally of the performer's Screen Actors Guild membership status. Written confirmation will be mailed to the production company. Clearance will not be issued unless all preproduction obligations of the producer have been satisfied.

    b. If the performer's membership is in current good standing, the producer will be advised that the performer is "OK".

       If the producer is advised that the performer is a "Station 12", it is the production company's responsibility to advise the performer to contact the Guild's Station 12 Department immediately in order to bring his/her membership status up to date.

("Station 12" usually means that the performer has failed to pay union contributions and fees. The performer must immediately pay any money due to the Guild before he or she can be employed by the producer.)

       Note: Employing a member not in good standing can result in a Union Security Violation with liquidated damages assessed against the production company.

    c. Notification that the performer has performed previously under the Guild's jurisdiction through the Taft/Hartley provisions (often referred to as a "must-pay") indicates that in those States where the Union Security provisions of SAG's contract are applicable, the performer must join immediately or within 48 hours of his/her employment or, failing to do so, a Union Security Violation claim could be filed against the producer.

d.   Notification of "no-record, non-Guild" means that the performer has never worked under the Guild's jurisdiction. The producer, therefore, must file a Taft/Hartley report.

2.   Taft/Hartley

Filing a report of the first engagement of all non-members must be made in writing to the Guild within fifteen (15) days of the first date of employment or within twenty-five (25) days when on an overnight location. It is very important that the producer be very specific as to the reason for hiring each non-member.

Note: Non-compliance with the provision can result in liquidated damages assessed against the production company.

3.   Tender individual performer's contracts and all necessary tax forms to performers prior to their employment, but no later than the first day they appear on the set. Copies of the contracts should be distributed as follows: one each to performer, agent, Guild and Producer.

4.   Payment to performer shall be made as follows: Day Players shall be paid no later than five (5) working days after each day of work. Three-Day and Weekly Players shall be paid no later than the Thursday of the week following the work week.

Note: There is a late payment penalty for each day late.

5.   Individual payment vouchers must indicate: production title or number, employment period and a breakdown of overtime, meal penalties and any deductions.

6.   Producer shall submit to the Guild Production Time Reports . . . signed by each performer no later than Friday of the week following each work week.

Note: Liquidated damages can be assessed for substantial breaches.

7.   The producer's casting office must provide a Sign-In Sheet for all interviews and auditions conducted and make it available to the Guild. Each Sign-In Sheet must indicate whether parking was provided. The casting office must also make the latest version of the screenplay accessible to each performer twenty-four (24) hours in advance of a scheduled reading or immediately after the scheduling of the interview, whichever is later.

8.   Affirmative Action . . .

9.   Safety

. . . A qualified first-aid person, visually identifiable, shall be present on all sets where hazardous work is planned. The producer (production manager) shall properly equip this person, establish the capabilities of nearby medical facilities, and provide transportation and communication with these facilities.

The Producer (Production Manager) must always get the performer's consent before asking him/her to engage in a stunt or hazardous activity. Performers may always request a double or refuse to do the stunt.

When stunts are required, a person qualified in planning, setting up or performing the stunt must be present on the set, the Stunt Coordinator.

Table 6–1. Maximum working time for minors, in hours

Age	Time at workplace	Work time	Rest and/or education
<6 years	4	2	2
6–9 years	8	4/6	1/3
9–16 years	9	5/7	1/3
16–18 years	10	6/8	1/3

Strict rules are in place for the employment of minors. Persons up to 18 years of age are considered a minor unless (a) the performer has satisfied the compulsory education laws of the state governing employment, (b) the performer is married, (c) the performer is a member of the Armed Forces, or (d) the performer is legally emancipated. The current regulations are as follows. A parent or guardian must be within sight or sound of all minors under the age of 16 years. A studio teacher must be present for minors up to 16 years of age. A studio teacher and a nurse are required for every three minors aged 15 days to 6 weeks and for every ten minors aged 6 weeks to 6 months. Besides providing for the education of the minor, the studio teacher is responsible for caring for and attending to the health, safety, and morals of children under 16 years.

If the minor and employer are residents of California and if the contractual agreements between the two parties are made in California, these regulations also apply for out-of-state shoots. Travel time to the studio or location is considered part of the minor's workday. On overnight locations, however, company-provided travel of up to 45 minutes is not considered work time.

The time that a minor can actually be on a set or location and in front of the camera is sharply regulated. The maximum time, in hours, is shown in Table 6.1. The workday usually runs between 5:00 a.m. and 10:00 p.m. All exceptions must be confirmed in writing by the appropriate authorities. The production company must provide a 12-hour turnaround for all minors. In other words, 12 hours must elapse between the minor's dismissal and his or her time of call on the following day.

Postproduction

1. A Final Cast List must be submitted to the Guild no later than one-hundred-twenty (120) days after completion of principal photography or ninety (90) days after completion of the picture, whichever comes first.

   When the Final Cast List is received at the Guild, a business representative will confirm that all required payments have been made to the performers, that there are no outstanding claims and verify with the Pension and Health Office that all Pension and Health contributions have been made.

As soon as the business representative has verified that everything is in order, the Security Deposit shall be returned to the production company along with any interest that has accrued.

Note: If the producer submits the Final Cast List prior to completion of all postproduction work, then an amended Cast List must be submitted, which includes all performers' postproduction services such as ADR (automated dialogue replacement), looping, singing, etc.

Music Cue Sheets must be submitted to the Guild upon completion of postproduction.

2. A Casting Data Report must be submitted for each production upon completion of principal photography and filed with the Guild no later than twenty (20) days following the calendar quarter in which principal photography was completed. There are separate Casting Data Report Forms: one for performers, one for stunt performers. Failure to comply may result in liquidated damages.

    The Producer or the Guild, upon ten (10) days' notice, may request a meeting to discuss any matter relating to discrimination, fair employment, data submitted, or any matter relevant to equal opportunity employment for performers.

The minimum rates for performers are subject to yearly increases. Up-to-date summaries can be obtained free of charge at SAG headquarters or local offices, or via the Internet. (More detailed information on payment, residuals, and special provisions, such as overtime regulation, is presented in Chapter 9.) The current rates as of July 1, 2003 for theatrical are as follows:

Day performers (per day): regular budget, $678; low budget, $466;

Stunt performers (per day): regular budget, $678; low budget, $3,750 (weekly);

Weekly performers (per week): regular budget, $2,352; low budget, $1,620;

Stunt performers (per week): regular budget, $4,118; low budget, $4,118.

For SEG members, the following daily rates apply:

General extra: $115;

Special ability extra: $125;

Stand-in: $130;

Silent bit: $150.

Professional dancers are employed as principal performers. A general extra is defined as a performer of ordinary business, including normal action, gestures, and facial expressions, portraying the functions of the extra player's assignment. A special ability extra is assigned to perform work requiring a special ability, including riding or handling horses, camels, or elephants or handling livestock; nonprofessional singing or mouthing to playback in groups of 16 or fewer; playing professional or organized athletic sports or officiating at a sports event; doing stand-in work; skating, swimming, or skateboarding; driving a vehicle that requires a special license; and playing a musical instrument. A silent bit player is an extra directed to perform a silent part of such significance that it portrays a point essential to the staging of the scene.

The SAG defines the following as the primary violations for which fines or penalties may be assessed against the production company and deducted from the security deposit:

> Union Security Violation: failure to report the first time employment of a SAG non-member within 15 days after employment begins (25 days for performers hired on overnight locations).
>
> *Fine*: $500
>
> Union Security Violation: employing a non-member who had been Taft/Hartley-ed on a previous production and has failed to become a "must join" member of the union before completion of the current production.
>
> *Fine*: $500
>
> Union Security Violation: employing a SAG member performer who is not in good standing with the union.
>
> *Fine*: $500
>
> Preference of Employment: failure to give preference to "qualified professional performers" or failure to employ a non-professional who meets one of the following exceptions (also called Taft/Hartley Report):
>
> a. Employment of a freelance Weekly or 3-Day Player at a salary equal to or greater than double scale;
>
> b. Member of a "name" specialty group;
>
> c. Person portraying himself (famous, well-known, unique);
>
> d. Extras adjusted for non-script lines;
>
> e. Military or government personnel who must be used due to overriding government regulations;
>
> f. Persons with special skills and ability, unusual physical appearance for whom no qualified professionals are available;
>
> g. First employment of a non-professional who pursues an acting career.
>
> *Fine*: $400, $500, $700

Employment of a member of the production staff: producers are not allowed to employ anyone from the casting or production staff to work as performers in the film.

Fine: $400, $500, $700

Safety violation: failure to provide safe conditions for performers when working under dangerous conditions such as explosives, animals, stunts, etc.

Fine: $900

Reuse of film from another production without negotiating for the right to such use.

Fine: equal to three times player's original salary for the number of days' work used, or damages may also be awarded by judgment.

Failure to honor contractual billing agreement.

Fine: up to $3,500 and possibly recall and correction of prints.

Rest period violation: if the turnaround time of 12 hours or the extended rest period between consecutive workweeks (36, 54, or 56 hours) is not observed.

Fine: 1 day's salary up to $950

Meal period violations: performers are entitled to a meal period no less often than every six hours.

Fine: in increments of 1/2 hour of violation or fractions thereof and cumulative.

Late payment of salary: Day Players are to be paid within 5 working days. Other performers must be paid no later than Thursday for work performed in the week ending the preceding Saturday. *Fine:* min. $10 to $200

Doubling performers in violation of the SAG BA: applies to performers earning more than $475/day and all other players.

Fine: to be assessed per arbitration

Adjustment of an extra player for a script stunt.

Fine: from $250 to $375

Failure to deliver a written contract to a freelance Weekly Player: a written contract has to be delivered to the performer by the first day of employment or no later than 4 days after agreement has been reached.

Fine: min. $10 to $200 or to be assessed

Disputes between the producer and the guild may be arbitrated if they involve day players, three-day players, stunt players, freelance players, and multiple-picture players with compensation of up to $20,000 provided that the disputed amount does not exceed $30,000.

The workweek is the basis for overtime computation and is defined differently, depending on whether the work takes place within the studio zone. In Los Angeles, the studio zone is defined as a circle of 30 miles in radius from Beverly Boulevard and La Cienega Boulevard. The studio workweek consists of any five days out of seven consecutive days as designated by the producer. The sixth and seventh days of each workweek are the regular days off. The overnight location workweek consists of any six days out of seven consecutive days, as designated by the producer. The seventh day of each workweek is the regular day off.

It is advisable to work closely with a professional payroll service when computing performers' salaries and benefits and when reporting to the SAG. Payroll services can compute the salaries, fines, and so on, on the basis of the SAG's actor's production time reports, which contain all the relevant information, such as the time the actor reported on the set, the time he or she was dismissed from the set, time taken for meals, when the actor left for the location, arrived on the location, and was dismissed from the location. This information is usually kept by the assistant director. The performers must sign off on the timesheet before dismissal.

In an effort to reach the large independent filmmaking community limited by smaller budgets, the SAG, on October 1, 1996, started a new program especially tailored to those needs. In short, these agreements are as follows:

- "Low-Budget Agreement" is applicable when shooting a low-budget feature (budget to be under $2 million) for initial theatrical release being shot entirely in the United States.

- "Modified Low-Budget Agreement" for budgets under $500,000 shot entirely in the United States.

- "Limited Exhibition Agreement" for very-low-budget films under $200,000 made in workshops or training settings, shot entirely in the United States (Day Player $100), to be shown at/on Film Festivals, PBS and Basic Cable, Art Houses.

- "Experimental Film Agreement" for films with budgets under $75,000 made for the experience, in workshops or training settings, and shot entirely in the United States (entirely deferred salaries) to be shown at Film Festivals.

- "Student Film Agreement" (performers may defer all of their salaries).

In each case, the local SAG office should be contacted by sending a copy of the script, the shooting schedule, and a detailed budget not later than 30 days prior to the start date. Rates above as of October 1997.

Because of the rapid development of interactive/multimedia technologies using top-level performers, the SAG has issued the "Special Internet/Online Agreement", applicable to all producers creating especially for CD-ROM or the Internet. Again, in case of doubt, contact the local SAG office. Minimum scale for principal performers is as follows:

Full-budget productions

On-camera performers: $636

Weekly performers: $2,206.

Low-budget agreements
Under $2,000,000   Day performer: $466
      Weekly performer: $1,620
Under $500,000   Day performer: $248
      Weekly performer: $864
Under $200,000   Day performer: $100
      3 days $225 plus $75 for each day beyond 3

Directors Guild of America

The Directors Guild of America (DGA) represents production managers, assistant directors, and technical coordinators. A 2-week window of opportunity to become a member of the DGA is provided annually when hundreds of applicants are tested to become DGA trainees. This is a very rigid process, and applicants have only a very marginal chance of being accepted. Union shoots must employ at least one DGA trainee on the production. Trainees work under the supervision of the UPM and AD and are to become familiar with all tasks managerial, administrative, communication and facilitation support to all cast, crew, and production personnel working on a production. This includes at least complete detailed paperwork, communication of the on-going status of all elements of the production to everyone associated with the production, organization of the movement of actors and background, planning ahead and problem solving, set operations as well as facilitation of all tasks involved in communication with all departments.

Most applicants to become a DGA member find themselves in the classic "catch-22" situation: to become a member of the DGA, they must have experience working on motion picture productions, but to get this work, it helps to be a member of the DGA. The DGA issues the following guidelines for applicants, quoted from the Los Angeles County Qualification List:

Composition

The respective Los Angeles Qualification List for 1st ADs, 2nd ADs, and UPMs shall be composed of those qualified and available persons who, as of July 1, 1984, were on the respective Qualification List as 1st ADs, 2nd ADs, and UPMs, or who satisfy thereafter the eligibility provisions hereunder.

Requirements for Placement

The following requirements shall determine eligibility of individuals applying for placement on the Los Angeles County Qualification List. . . .

Any individual who has been employed 260 days in work as a 1st AD in the production of motion pictures of the type covered hereunder shall be eligible to be placed on the First Assistant Director Los Angeles County Qualification List. . . .

Also, an individual who has completed 400 days in work as a Unit Production Manager (UPM) in the production of motion pictures of the type covered hereunder shall be eligible for placement on the Los Angeles County Unit Production Manager Qualification List. Of such working days, not more than 25% may be spent in preparation or postproduction and at least 75% must have occurred during production (principal photography). Of the 75%, 10% must be on location (distant or local). An individual's workdays on motion pictures on which someone else was employed as Unit Production Manager shall not be counted as qualifying workdays for any purpose under this Article 14 by virtue of the individual performing UPM functions delegated to him or her pursuant to Paragraph 1-302 of this Basic Agreement [quoted at the beginning of Chapter 1].

The forms that must be used to apply for membership in the DGA are available free of charge from the union. (For addresses, see Appendix 1.) The following is the procedure for applying:

Within six months following completion of applicant's last work assignment, complete forms must be submitted with appropriate documentation.

Please note that all persons who consider themselves eligible shall be required to prove their claim with documentation, which includes a combination of:

1. A letter from the employer stating exact working days (prep, shoot, wrap), production name(s), and a clear statement of actual duties performed and title of position held;

2. Production reports (minimum of 6 per production, reflecting start, middle, and end dates);

3. Call sheets (minimum of 6 per production, reflecting start, middle, and end dates);

4. Start slips;

5. Cast and crew lists;

6. Payment documentation (payroll records, check stubs, or tax forms);

7. Credit lists (evidence of screen credit);

8. Other business records which will prove that applicant has worked in the category for which he [or she] is applying;

9.   Deal memos;

10. Pension, health, and welfare reports.

Please note that applicant's documentation must reflect: (1) job title, (2) exact number of work days, (3) whom he [or she] was directly supervised by (name and title), and (4) in the case where job title is not the norm used by the industry, applicant must include documentation describing applicant's exact duties. When Saturday and Sunday work days (6–7 days per week) are claimed, documentation must be provided to substantiate days worked.

Simple arithmetic shows that, to accumulate 300 days (75 percent of the required 400 days) in production—assuming that many of those days will come from low-budget productions with tight shooting schedules of about 20 days—a successful applicant must have worked on about 15 motion pictures. In a competitive industry such as the motion picture business, it may take several years to achieve this, especially since many film projects that reach pre-production never actually go into production. In this case, the applicant accumulates an enormous (and ultimately worthless) number of days in pre-production. All in all, these requirements make it extremely difficult, if not impossible, to become a member of the DGA.

For more detail see the following pages on the DGA website:

http://www.dgaca.org/dgaca/placementprocess.htm

http://www.dgca.org/dgca/instruct_sc.htm

http://www.dgaca.org.dgaca/sc_genreqs.htm

Nonunion PMs asked to work on DGA productions may be able to do so without joining the union. The executive producer or producer of the motion picture may grant the PM above-the-line status, such as associate producer, producer, supervising producer, or production supervisor. However, in this case, a union production manager must also be hired. As associate producer, the nonunion person may execute the same duties as the union PM.

The Union/Nonunion Debate

It is quite possible and legal to work on a picture that has no union involvement at all. No laws force producers to hire union personnel or union actors for a production. In reality, however, a production almost always must deal with the Screen Actors Guild.

As noted at the beginning of the chapter, involvement of one union does not mean the entire production must be staffed with union personnel. For example, you can have a DGA director, SAG actors, and a nonunion technical crew working on the same production. However, once a union is involved, all the positions that can be filled through that particular union must be filled with union personnel. In the case of the DGA, when the director is union, the ADs and the PM must also be union.

Whether a nonunion shoot is appropriate for a particular production depends on a number of factors. The most important of these is the financial situation.

A secondary element is the location of the shooting. In large metropolitan areas like Los Angeles, San Francisco, New York, and Chicago, enough experienced nonunion production personnel can be found, so union members need not be hired. In less active production centers, almost all qualified personnel are union members. However, union personnel sometimes work on nonunion projects and under nonunion conditions. In this case, the producer is not held liable for any penalties levied by the union against the union member. It is the union person's decision to work on a nonunion production, and he or she alone faces possible fines and penalties.

The producer can sometimes negotiate with a union for more favorable conditions—for example, the easing of requirements regarding minimum staff or fringe benefits. However, no rules have been established, and each case is considered unique and without precedent.

What are the implications of going union? First, the production company must become a signatory of the union and its basic agreements. These agreements, which can be obtained free of charge from the unions, spell out in great detail almost every aspect of the production, including the following:

- Minimum wages;
- Compensation for overtime, night-time, and weekend work;
- Meal times and minimum length of meal periods;
- Job descriptions and minimum staffing requirements;
- Travel obligations and distant-location wage scales;
- Allowances for hazardous work;
- Union dues and fringe benefits;
- Insurances;
- Subcontracting;
- Arbitration procedures.

Second, any failure to observe these provisions leads to financial penalties levied against the producer. Before the start of principal photography, the producer is required to deposit a certain amount of the anticipated overall accumulated union salary payments in an escrow account on behalf of the union. All fines are subtracted from this fund. The remaining money is returned to the producer after principal photography is completed and after the union verifies that all union members have received the final paychecks due them.

Although individual philosophies of course vary, most independent producers view these requirements as a hindrance. From a financial point of view, union involvement in a shoot greatly increases production costs, even if no fines are ever levied. The minimum staffing requirements might force the producer to hire more personnel than are actually needed, and fringe benefits, overtime, night-time, and weekend surcharges, per diems, and meal regulations represent additional costs the producer might have been able to negotiate or avoid. These costs make it practically prohibitive for low-budget productions to go union.

The unions' answer to these "complaints" is that producers actually save money by hiring experienced union personnel and can thus finish the production in much less time than with a nonunion crew. The unions claim that membership guarantees a high standard of professional competence and a strong work ethic and thus guarantees filmmakers a trouble-free, fast, professional production. It is my experience, however, that nonunion crews in large production centers are certainly not less experienced or less motivated than their union counterparts.

For all individuals working in the entertainment business, it is highly desirable to become a union member and work under union conditions. All major theatrical motion picture production and much of network TV production is done exclusively by union crews. This means that nonunion personnel will never be allowed to work on those productions. In addition, union members take more money home than do nonunion members, and the protection that a strong union offers in case of arbitration or lawsuits is certainly an advantage.

In large production centers where nonunion shoots are common, the worst working conditions can be found. Competition is so fierce that almost anything is possible. It is not unheard of that crew people are hired for a low flat fee, including all overtime and work performed at night, on weekends, and holidays, perhaps even for seven-day workweeks for several weeks. They receive no additional compensation for irregular meal periods or travel and no per diems. These shoots often have nonunion actors or union actors who need or want the work. These productions, often set up on a deferred-payment or points-owned basis, clearly can be done for very little cash, especially if some crew members agree to double for certain positions (see Chapter 4).

Clearly, nonunion productions leave the door wide open for all sorts of abuse. This is not to say that nonunion shoots should be avoided. Generally, for the sake of self-respect and decency, independent filmmakers maintain the standards of a union production. However, one must be aware of the industry's many black sheep. It is usually a good sign if at least the SAG is involved in a production. Many of the below-the-line unions' provisions are adhered to through the SAG Basic Agreement. SAG guidelines give structure to the shooting day, which is of benefit to everyone involved in principal photography. At least the actual working conditions will be tolerable. This, of course, does not affect compensation issues for below-the-line personnel.

7

Cast and Crew

Hiring Procedures

It is generally part of the production manager's duties to hire some personnel for a production and to supervise the execution of contract agreements and related formalities. Figures 7.1 and 7.2 provide an overview of the personnel involved during principal photography and postproduction. These figures also depict the lines of communication and command.

If the PM does not know enough personnel through previous productions or personal connections, he or she can place a "wanted" ad in trade papers (*Daily Variety* or *Hollywood Reporter*) or weekly casting magazines or make use of the Internet where a wide variety of websites deal with job openings and casting wishes. In large metropolitan areas where frequent production activities take place, an advertisement is likely to draw many résumés for each position to be filled. If the advertisement does not attract sufficient applicants, the PM should consult the local film commission's production manual. As a last resort, the PM can contact the local unions; however it might become impossible to have a nonunion production.

Applicants' résumés usually list types and titles of the productions on which they have worked and sometimes include additional information on producer, director, or cast. If a résumé does not include references, the PM should request them. It is a good idea to contact references before hiring an applicant. It is customary that applicants for key creative positions, such as art director, makeup person, director of photography, still photographer, and script supervisor bring a portfolio or tape of their work to interviews.

Next to his or her professional qualifications, the personality of the applicant is the deciding factor in hiring. Obviously, a neat, clean, energetic, and articulate person is preferable to a lazy, uncaring, and disorganized one.

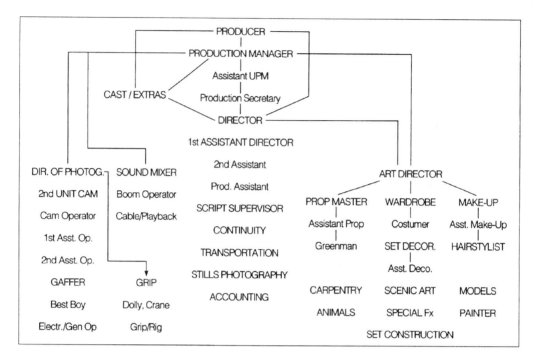

Fig. 7–1. Organization and lines of communication for personnel involved in principal photography.

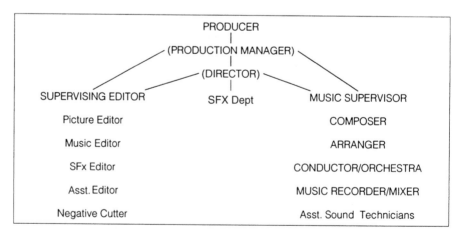

Fig. 7–2. Organization and lines of communication for the personnel involved in postproduction.

Attention should be given to whether an applicant would rather have a position other than the one for which he or she is applying. For example, does the AD secretly want to direct? Does the second camera assistant believe him- or herself to be more competent than the director of photography? Such people can create great stress in a production and should be avoided.

When interior shots are prevalent, the director sometimes requests that all personnel be nonsmokers. Drugs and alcohol are never permitted on the set or location during the workday. However, it is customary to provide "crew beer" at the end of the shooting day.

A full feature film production (which generally runs a minimum of six weeks for preproduction, four to six weeks for principal photography, and up to 10 weeks for editing and postproduction) places different demands on the crew and cast than a commercial or a music video, which usually only involves a few days of principal photography. Frequent location site changes, alternation between day and night shoots, and the generally long hours of feature film production require that the crew be picked with great care. If the shoot takes place outside the home-base, virtually all of the crew and cast has to be together 24 hours a day for weeks on end. Part of the PM's art is exhibited in putting together a good crew, ensuring a smooth and trouble-free production.

For teamwork and cooperation on a production, the PM must select personnel who can work together in an easy manner without conflicts. Because no one should be dismissed except for professional incompetence, the choice of personnel must be made very carefully. If someone must be fired for a reason other than professional incompetence, severance pay is expected. The method for determining severance pay should be negotiated and spelled out in the deal memo before employment to avoid arbitration or litigation.

Usually, the production manager pre-interviews prospective personnel and leaves the final decision—at least for the key positions—to the director or producer. The PM processes all contracts and agreements with personnel after the director and producer make their selections. The first key personnel to be hired (other than those needed to run the production office) are director of photography, art director (and more and more so: the SFX supervisor), and, if necessary, location manager. These three people usually start their work well in advance of principal photography. They are involved in many creative decisions and preparatory work; they will discuss the film's look and needs with the director and producer during preproduction.

Depending on the nature of the screenplay, the art department may go into full operation—designing and building sets—several weeks before principal photography is scheduled to begin and as soon as the location manager finalizes the location agreements. The art director and director of photography frequently are able to bring to the project staff members with whom they have worked during previous productions. The PM should check whether the production will employ these people on the basis of the art director's or DP's previous experience with them. Depending on the work to be done and the budget, the art department will be staffed during preproduction with an assistant art director, a set-construction coordinator, a set designer and drafter, a sketch and storyboard artist, model makers, carpenters, and painters.

As soon as the sets are available or several weeks before commencement of principal photography—again depending on the production's requirements— the set dresser, prop master, and their assistants are hired. At about the same time, the wardrobe person begins work designing or purchasing the necessary clothes and making rental arrangements after having discussed any artistic suggestions with the director. Toward the end of the preproduction phase, the first assistant director is hired to help the PM prepare logistical and organizational aspects of the shoot. The script supervisor is usually hired several days before the start of photography.

If no special effects makeup or masks are required, the makeup person generally does not start work much before production begins. At the beginning of principal photography—unless the director requests otherwise—most other personnel begin work. The following positions are filled at this time: grip crew, lighting crew, camera crew, sound crew, drivers, still photographer, caterer, set guards, special effects crew and stunt coordinators, and production assistants.

The PM usually tries to finalize deal memos with all personnel as soon as the director and producer reach a decision but late enough so that any delays in the production schedule do not oblige the production company to pay compensation. An appropriate passage in the deal memo may free the production company from any obligations in case of delay, but this of course opens the possibility that personnel might leave the production if other opportunities arise.

For independent and low- to medium-budget nonunion productions, the following below-the-line crew members are generally sufficient (bear in mind that a crew member might fill more than one position). The actual crew requirements for any film are of course dependent on the nature of the screenplay and the activities involved in the production:

- Production manager;
- Production coordinator/production secretary;
- First assistant director;
- Second assistant director;
- Script supervisor;
- Director of photography/camera operator;
- First assistant camera operator/driver of camera van;
- Second assistant camera operator/driver of camera van;

- Key grip/driver of grip truck;
- Key gaffer;
- Dolly grip;
- Electrician/grip/driver of electrical truck;
- Costume designer/wardrobe supervisor;
- Assistant wardrobe/driver of wardrobe van;
- Makeup/hair;
- Assistant makeup/hair;
- Sound recorder;
- Boom operator;
- Art director;
- Prop master;
- Set dresser;
- Assistant art/prop department/driver of prop truck;
- Assistant art/prop department;
- Production assistant/craft service;
- Production assistant;
- Still photographer;
- Production accountant;
- Painter;
- Carpenter;
- Operator of "honey wagon";
- Editor;
- Assistant editor;
- Sound editor.

The following personnel are hired as needed:

- Casting director for principals and extras;
- Location manager;
- Technical advisers/experts;
- Teacher/nurse;
- Dance director;
- First aid specialist;
- Second unit crew;

- Special effects teams;
- SFX-supervisor;
- Seamstress;
- Nursery person/greenery;
- Animal handlers;
- Music coordinator;
- Publicist.

Crew Duties

The actual duties of many crew positions are self-explanatory, but others might need a more detailed description. The responsibilities of various positions are described in this section.

Production Coordinator or Production Secretary

The production coordinator or production secretary assists the PM in the organizational tasks of the production office; follows up on telephone conversations, appointments, and agreements; and facilitates the flow of production documents and information to the appropriate departments.

First and Second Assistant Directors

During preproduction, the first assistant director assists the PM in organizing the crew, breaking down the script, and preparing the production board and shooting schedule. During production, the first AD assists the director with on-set production details and coordinates and supervises activities of cast and crew. If necessary, this person is involved in location research and negotiations, checks weather reports, prepares day-out-of-days schedules, determines cast and crew calls, supervises preparation of daily call sheets for cast and crew, directs background action, and supervises crowd control. The first AD might also be required to secure minor contracts and extra releases and generally supervise the functioning of the shooting set and crew.

The second assistant director serves as helper to the first AD. This person is in charge of preparing daily call sheets, handling extras requisitions and other required documents for approval by the first AD or the PM, preparing the daily production report at the end of each shooting day, distributing scripts and changes to cast and crew, distributing and collecting extras' vouchers, communicating advance scheduling to cast and crew, aiding in scouting and managing locations, and facilitating transportation of equipment and personnel. The second AD may also be required to handle extras' contracts and releases; coordinate with production staff so that everyone, including cast, crew, and extras, is ready at the beginning of the day; supervise the wrap; schedule food, lodging, and other facilities; sign cast members in and out; assist the first AD in crowd control and background action; and assist in proper distribution and documentation of mileage money.

Script Supervisor

The script supervisor takes notes on all relevant details of each shot: number of takes to be printed, length of each shot, type of lens used, information on slates, whether actors said the lines as written in the screenplay, and if not, what changes were made. The script supervisor is also responsible for continuity from scene to scene. The person in this position might point out that a scene is not covered sufficiently for editing and might help prepare the production report at the end of the shooting day. The script supervisor's notes are part of the daily production report and continue to be used during the editing process because they contain information on each take and whether it will be printed in the lab.

Director of Photography

The director of photography is in charge of the camera department. In addition to supervising the camera crew, the DP also gives instructions to the grip and gaffer. During preproduction, the DP usually breaks down the screenplay in cooperation with the director and designs individual scenes, including setups, lighting, and camera requirements at the set or on location. Some DPs operate the camera themselves; others prefer to have a camera operator for this task. The DP sets the lights and gives instructions accordingly to create the visual mood the director envisions. A good DP proposes ideas and creative solutions to the director but is versatile enough to give the director any style desired.

Assistant Camera Operator

Assistant camera operators are responsible for handling all camera equipment and the camera van, properly storing film, loading film into magazines and the camera, making sure the camera is in perfect working condition, filling out the slate with the correct information (in cooperation with script supervisor and AD), and transporting exposed film safely to the lab. They are also responsible for filing correct camera reports that detail consumption of film, markings on film cans, sequence of takes shot, and results of each take.

These camera reports are incorporated into the daily production report at the end of the shooting day.

Grip Personnel

Grip personnel work under the instructions of the DP and under the supervision of the key grip. They are responsible for the grip truck and for the rigging, mounting, and construction of all camera and lighting support equipment, including stands, boxes, and flags. The dolly grip is in charge of the tracks, dolly, and supporting equipment.

Gaffer and Electricians

The gaffer and electricians are in charge of all electrical equipment, the lights and generator, and the electrical truck. They work under the instructions of the DP, who sets the priorities of each scene. Once the director and actors (or stand-ins) block a scene and determine how the actors and the camera will move, the DP instructs the grip and gaffer on how to set up their equipment to achieve the appropriate mood. During final rehearsals, some of these elements may change as the DP continually tries to achieve the best effects and strives for technical perfection. After several run-throughs, the optimum solution will be found. During these rehearsals, members of the grip and gaffer departments, with the exception of the dolly grip, who moves the camera, are generally resting, waiting to take down the equipment and prepare for a new set or location.

Sound Crew

The sound crew generally consists of two individuals. The *sound recordist* operates the tape recorder and helps the *boom operator* set up microphones. The latter operates the boom and continually tries to move the microphones into the best possible position: close enough to actors to ensure optimal sound, but far enough away to ensure that they are not in the picture.

Art Director

The art director heads the art department and is responsible for the overall look of sets and locations. He or she supervises the carpenter and painters and frequently oversees the set-dressing and prop departments as well. The art director designs the sets in accordance with the director's instructions and ensures that the required camera movements are possible—for example, that walls can be taken out if necessary—and that tracks can be laid and lights installed. Designing a set for filming is quite different from designing an ordinary room or house; the needs of the production cannot be compared to those of a normal living environment.

The SFX-Supervisor

The SFX-Supervisor is hired when digital or optical special effects work will have to be implemented—almost a given on any production today. He or she is involved in the storyboard-process and in all matters related to the camera and art direction and set-building departments. As much of the visuals which once might have been built are now created through digital imagery, pre-planning has changed considerably. Which special effects will have to be used—also a serious budgetary consideration—can only be decided in close communication with the director, DP, and producer.

Property Master

The property master is in charge of all props needed during the production. He or she is generally in contact with rental houses or is responsible for purchasing and handling props and picture vehicles. Generally, more than one of each prop is rented or purchased to ensure that damage or loss does not affect the shooting.

Set Dresser

The set dresser is responsible for renting or purchasing all materials needed to dress a set or location to give it the required look. Set-dressing props are usually stationary and include furniture, books, and background materials. They are different from props supplied by the prop master, which are handled and used by an actor.

Wardrobe

Besides designing and sewing the wardrobe for cast members, the wardrobe person is in charge of all wardrobe rentals and purchases. He or she is responsible for properly storing wardrobe items and making them available during shooting. Wardrobe pieces are frequently doubled to avoid delays in the event of destruction or damage.

Production Accountant

All funds needed for rentals or purchases, once approved by the PM, are processed by the production accountant, who is authorized to release funds or issue checks. All production departments are required to keep track of their expenses by collecting and listing receipts, agreements, and contracts with rental houses. The production accountant examines all expenses and evaluates their appropriateness. The production accountant is also in charge of issuing the crew's and perhaps the actors' paychecks, generally due on Fridays. The SAG, the insurance company, and the completion bond company (if applicable) require regular payroll reports. The production accountant also keeps track of expenses incurred and how they relate to the production budget; he or she must determine whether the production is still operating within budget or has gone over budget—and if so, to what extent.

Each department is responsible for wrapping and properly returning rented equipment, props, and wardrobe after production. The accountant pays outstanding balances, which are invoiced after completion of principal photography. In general, a production company establishes long-term working relationships with rental houses and other companies and goes through a credit check before production.

Still Photographer

The still photographer takes still photos of the production used for publicity. He or she usually works with the actors during rehearsals or right after a scene has been shot, recreating the action on the set or location, but almost never takes photos during an actual take. The still photographer also documents the production work itself, taking behind-the-scenes pictures. The photographer usually carries at least two cameras, one loaded with color film and the other with black-and-white film. Lower-budget pictures might employ a still photographer only on certain days to cover important scenes.

Actors and Agents

Besides being responsible for communications and relations with the crew, the production manager is also responsible for supervising the formalities of all matters regarding actors, their agents, and the SAG, when applicable. The PM generally has very little to do with the process of casting actors. Scheduling of interviews and preparations for auditions are handled by the production secretary, the producer's assistant, or the casting agent.

If a casting agent is involved in the production, he or she presents a list of first-choice actors to the producer and the director. The casting agent—or the producer or someone in the producer's office—arranges for casting interviews and conducts negotiations with the actor's representative (the personal manager, agent, or whomever the actor has designated as the contact) in accordance

casting sheet

PROD*

DATE

_____ PHOTO _____

NAME:				
HOME ADDRESS:				
HOME PHONE:				
SOCIAL SECURITY NO.:				
AGENT:				
SAG		AFM	
SEG		AGVA	
AFTRA		WORK PERMIT	

AGE		HEIGHT		HAIR	
EYES		WEIGHT		HANDS	

MEASUREMENTS

SUIT		DRESS		SHIRT	
WAIST		HAT		SHOES	
GLOVE					

REMARKS:

ENTERPRISE PRINTERS Telephone: 876-3530

120

Fig. 7–3. Casting sheet.

with guidelines set by the producer. These negotiations eventually lead to a deal memo, which serves as a blueprint for the later contract. The deal memo contains information about pay, length of work, credits, availability for looping and publicity, and more. (For a detailed actor's contract, see Chapter 8.)

Some casting agents work only with actors; others focus solely on extras. Generally, the casting of extras happens more or less automatically along the lines of the character descriptions provided by the production office. Often, no extras' photos or résumés are required. Casting agencies often take care of all payroll requirements. The PM need only make sure that the casting of extras goes as planned and occurs on schedule. He or she should supervise the agencies' activities when it comes to organizing the extras' appearance on the location and on the set and should also be certain that the extras appear on time and where needed.

A low-budget production might not be able to afford the services of a casting agent or casting service. In that case, talent can be found in other ways, and the PM may get involved in this process to some degree. In major production centers, publications print casting notices weekly or biweekly. These notices as well as a wide array of specific websites are free of charge to producers. The producer must give the magazine a short synopsis of the film and short characterizations of the parts to be cast. This is an effective method of casting a film. Within a week, the production office is flooded with actors' photos and résumés, usually sent out by their management agencies. It is with these management agencies or the actors' personal agents that the PM sets up interviews; almost never does the PM or even the producer talk directly with an actor. All business matters are discussed with the manager or agent, not with the talent directly.

The Screen Actors Guild also offers a casting service. The producer provides the SAG with a list of characters to be cast, and the guild publishes or posts it on its casting boards, which are frequented regularly by many actors.

The SAG each year publishes voluminous books containing small black-and-white photos of all its members, including their managers' names and telephone numbers. By going through these books, which are divided into categories for men, women, and children, a variety of casting possibilities will come to mind. The SAG also provides a telephone service that gives out the numbers for the representatives of their members. This is convenient if you are looking for someone specific, but do not know how to get in touch with that person.

8

Contracts, Agreements, and Working Permits

In an industry such as the film business, known for using lawsuits and litigation as an accepted way of doing business, and in a country like the United States, where the legal system allows lawsuits to be filed for all the right and wrong reasons and where obtaining justice depends to a large degree on the financial resources of litigants, it is vitally important that everyone involved in motion picture production is protected every step of the way by deal memos, agreements, and contracts that spell out in complete detail all elements involved. Although production managers are not commonly targets of lawsuits, when things go wrong, when money is lost and egos are hurt, anyone can become a defendant, regardless of whether the plaintiff has a valid case. Even an unjustified lawsuit costs the defendant a sizable amount of money—an expense usually unrecoverable even if the defendant wins. Lawsuits sometimes are filed as a means of blackmail and intimidation. The only protection from possible litigation is to keep records of all transactions, memos, and activities.

When negotiating contracts or other legal agreements, the services of a lawyer are certainly desirable; however, they are also expensive. Producers and PMs can use the boilerplate contracts contained in this chapter, modifying them to suit their particular needs, to understand the solid legal foundation required for their productions. Bear in mind that these documents are only informational in nature, and, in providing them, the author is not rendering legal advice. If legal advice is required, the services of a competent professional should be sought.

Generally, contracts with actors are handled by the producer and casting agent, both of whom deal with the artist's representative, perhaps a manager or an agent. No law requires a casting agent or even an artist's agent to be involved in negotiations. It is perfectly legal for a producer and an actor to agree to a deal between themselves.

The PM's duty is to discuss and conclude negotiations with the crew and staff in accordance with guidelines established by the producer. The PM must also arrange or oversee equipment rentals and appropriate agreements and contracts generally supplied by rental companies. His or her duties also include overseeing or negotiating and arranging for location agreements, permits, and contracts.

As a rule of thumb, producers avoid agreeing to contracts that lock them into fixed starting dates for as long as possible. Thus, contracts are frequently made just before the beginning of employment. Legally binding deal memos often serve as guidelines throughout the production before the sometimes-extensive contracts are finalized. In addition to the contracts that follow, which are of main concern to the PM, the producer or executive producer must also negotiate contracts and agreements, beginning with the purchase of a treatment or screenplay all the way through music rights and postproduction, distribution, and flat-out sales.

For productions operating within union guidelines, most contract and employment details are regulated by the union's basic agreement. Nonunion productions must negotiate most terms of employment on an individual, case-by-case basis. The following contracts can serve as guidelines for nonunion situations.

Staff, Crew, and Actor Agreements

Independent Contractor Agreement

Sometimes a production manager wishes to be employed as an independent contractor. Most crew members do not qualify for this status, but PMs who might be elevated to the position of line producer can qualify. A bona fide independent contractor works for a company (which must be legally constituted with a business license and so on) hired to provide certain services.

Basically, an independent contractor is responsible to another person (in this case, the producer) for the completion of a project but not for the manner in which the project is completed. In contrast, an employee is responsible not only for the completion of the project but also for the manner in which it is completed. If the employer has complete control over the activities of the employee, usually the case during film production, the employee does not qualify as an independent contractor.

Independent Contractor Agreement

This Agreement is entered into on this ＿＿＿＿ day of ＿＿＿＿, ＿＿＿＿[year] by and between ＿＿＿＿ (Contractor) and ＿＿＿＿ (Client), and the Contractor and Client hereby agree to the following:

1. Contractor agrees to perform the following services on behalf of the client on the film project tentatively titled: ＿＿＿＿＿＿＿＿＿＿.

2. Contractor shall begin work on or before ＿＿＿＿ and he/she will continue to perform above-mentioned services on a daily/weekly/monthly basis. The services shall continue until ＿＿＿＿, which shall constitute termination.

3. Client shall pay the contractor the following amount on a periodic basis as follows:＿＿＿＿＿＿＿＿＿＿＿＿＿.

4. Contractor and Client intend this Agreement to be one of independent contractor relation; therefore Contractor retains the sole right to control or direct the manner in which the services described herein are to be performed. Subject to the aforementioned, Client shall retain the right to inspect, to stop work, to recommend alterations, and generally supervise the work to insure its conformity with that specified in this Agreement. Contractor and Client understand that it is the Contractor's sole responsibility to obtain and maintain a business license, to provide for all employment taxes, including estimated withholding taxes. Contractor shall be liable for his own liability insurance, including workers' compensation coverage.

5. Other express provisions:＿＿＿＿＿＿＿＿＿＿＿＿＿.

6. This agreement shall be subject to termination in the event of any incapacity or default of the Client or in the case of any suspension or postponement of production by reason of strikes, acts of God, governmental action, regulations or decrees, or for any other customary "force majeure" reason.

Signed this ＿＿＿＿ day of ＿＿＿＿, ＿＿＿＿[year]

City ＿＿＿＿＿＿

＿＿＿＿＿＿＿＿＿＿＿＿   ＿＿＿＿＿＿＿＿＿＿＿＿

Contractor   Client

For the PM, the other express provisions mentioned in section 5 might include the following:

1. *Billing/credit*: For example, the PM might insist on a single card, equal in size to the largest other credit in the last and first places in the front and end titles, to appear in all paid advertising, including newspaper ads, posters, and billboards;

2. *Travel arrangements*: first, business, coach class; hotel accommodations required;

3.   *Living/transportation expenses*: per diems, mileage allowance;

4.   *Pay-or-play clause*: the client might reserve the right to terminate the contractor's employment at any time, subject only to the obligation to pay the balance of any compensation due;

5.   *Bonus provisions.*

Crew Deal Memo

This confirms our agreement to employ you _____ [name], Address _____, S.S. no./employer ID no. _____, Union/guild [if applicable] _____ on our film project tentatively titled _____ in the position of _____ under the following conditions:

_____.

Accepted by: Approved by:

_____   _____

Employee   Executive in Charge of Production

In a nonunion situation, practically any deal can be made regarding the length of daily work, minimum fees, and other arrangements. The conditions to be agreed on generally include the following:

1.   Beginning and ending dates and duration of employment;

2.   Flat fee or daily hours, overtime provisions, terms of payment;

3.   Remuneration for work on weekends or holidays;

4.   Per diems, mileage allowance;

5.   Paid preparation time allowed and at what fee;

6.   Travel arrangements;

7.   Billing/credit;

8.   Termination provisions;

9.   Bonus provisions.

Agreement Between Casting Agent and Producer

This Agreement is entered into on this day _____ of _____ [year] between the Casting Agent _____ [name] and Producer _____ [name] _____ [company] on the film project tentatively titled _____.

1.   Casting Agent will be supplying all leading/weekly/daily actors and/or all Extras needed for the film at rates and conditions to be negotiated according to Producer's guidelines and/or in accordance with SAG/SEG minimum salary schedules.

2. Casting Agent will receive a flat/weekly fee of $ _____ payable at time of or in accordance with the schedule as follows: _____.

3. Casting Agent will receive credit as follows: _____.

4. Producer will provide a check of the total amount of all Extras used for that week with an overpayment for use to pay overtime at the beginning of each week.

5. A coordinator from the Casting Agency will be provided if there are ten (10) or more Extras requested by the Producer at a particular location site. The coordinator will be responsible for signing in, paying, and making sure that Extras are in proper attire.

6. A 12-hour notice of call time, location, and cancellation is necessary so that the Extras will be guaranteed at no extra cost to Producer.

7. Producer will be responsible for all insurance and workers' compensation.

8. Producer will supply hot meals on the location site for Extras.

All terms agreed upon and accepted by:

_____   _____

Producer   Date

_____   _____

Casting Agent   Date

Actor's Deal Memo

This deal memo is entered into on this _____ day of _____, _____ [year] between _____ [player's name and address], S.S. no./employer ID no. _____, _____, [Agent's name and address], and _____ [Producer's name/], _____ [Company], for the film project tentatively titled _____, for the part of _____.

Deal: _____.

Daily/weekly: _____.

Guarantee: _____.

Detail: _____.

Billing: _____.

Player must keep Producer's office or the Assistant Director advised as to where Player may be reached by telephone without unreasonable delay. The compensation stated above is payment in full for all services rendered during the period of employment and for all rights granted to Producer. In witness whereof the parties hereto have executed and delivered this Memo as of the date first written above.

_____   _____

Player/Agent   Executive in Charge of Production

The "guarantee" spells out the duration, start, and finish of employment as well as the salary, which might be nonunion scale, union scale, or union low-budget scale, or might be freely negotiated. If this information is given under "Deal" it is not repeated here. "Detail" describes all arrangements, such as work on weekends or holidays, dubbing or looping obligations, advertising and personal appearance obligations, and special provisions. "Billing" refers to the actor's credit, size of card, and position of card, and the producer's obligation in regard to advertisements.

A deal memo, although a legally binding document, usually only serves as a reminder of the elements that later will be transferred to a regular and highly detailed contract. Parts of this contract that do not conform with SAG guidelines will be renegotiated and amended by the actor or agent to adhere to SAG regulations or to meet the actor's special wishes or demands. If SAG actors perform exclusively outside the United States, SAG agreements do not necessarily apply; the SAG's jurisdiction is limited to the United States, as described in Chapter 6.

Although this contract may seem unexciting, it is actually a fascinating distillation of years of producer–actor relationships, arguments on sets and locations, battling egos, hurt pride, power-hungry individuals, and sheer madness. The PM almost always stands in the middle of these battles, trying to protect the interests of the producer. Although it is the PM's job to keep the production moving, on schedule, and within budget, he or she must also consider the artists' egos and vulnerabilities and, especially in lower-budget productions, must make sure that hostile parties find a sensible way of working together and finishing the picture.

Actor's Motion Picture Agreement

This Contract executed on the _____ day of _____ [year] between _____ (Employer) and _____ (Artist) witnesseth:

In consideration of the covenants and conditions herein contained, and other good and valuable consideration, the parties agree as follows:

1. Employment: Employer hereby employs Artist to render his services as an actor to portray the role of _____ in the motion picture tentatively titled _____. Artist hereby accepts such employment on the terms and condition herein provided and agrees that throughout the term hereof he will render his services solely and exclusively for the Employer. Artist's services hereunder shall be rendered at such studios and other places and on such locations as may be designated by Employer from time to time.

2. Term of Employment: Term of Artist's employment hereunder shall commence on or about _____ on which date Artist agrees to report

to the Employer at _____ or such other place Employer may designate, for the rendition of his services, and shall continue thereafter for such time as the Employer may require his services in connection with the production of the Picture. Subject to the obligation of Employer to pay Artist compensation for the minimum period of employment hereinafter provided for, which obligation in turn is subject to the provisions of Sections 11, 12, 13 hereof, Employer may terminate Artist's employment hereunder at any time.

3. Compensation: On condition that Artist is not in default hereunder and as full consideration for all services rendered and all rights granted and agreed to be granted by Artist to Employer hereunder, and subject to all of Employer's rights under this Contract, Employer agrees to pay Artist and Artist agrees to accept compensation at the rate of _____ per _____ during the term hereof during which Artist renders his services hereunder; provided that subject to Employer's right of suspension and termination as hereinafter provided, Employer shall pay such compensation to Artist for not less than _____ consecutive weeks/days (Minimum Period). Employer shall have first call on the Artist's services during the period of _____ (Free Period) immediately following expiry of Minimum Period. Artist agrees further on to inform Employer before assigning any new commitment before _____.

    If the term hereof during which Artist renders services hereunder as required by Employer is longer than the Minimum Period plus the Free Period, compensation shall be payable at the rate of per week. Artist's compensation hereunder shall commence when Artist reports to Employer at the place and on the date specified in Section 2 for the commencement of the term hereof. Compensation for any period of less than a week shall be pro-rated and for this purpose the rate per day shall be one-sixth (1/6) of the said weekly rate. No increase or additional compensation shall accrue or be payable to Artist by reason of the fact that any of his services are rendered at night or on Saturdays, Sundays, or holidays, or after the expiration of any particular number of hours of service in any period.

    Compensation accruing to Artist hereunder during each calendar week of the term hereof shall be paid to Artist on Employer's regular weekly payday during the following week. All of Artist's compensation hereunder shall be paid by check made payable to Artist and forwarded to Artist at c/o _____ whose receipts therefore shall be binding upon Artist.

4. General Services: Throughout the term hereof Artist shall advise the Employer of his whereabouts so that he may be reached at any reasonable hour of the day or night; render his services solely and exclusively for the Employer and at all times required by the Employer, including nights, Saturday, Sunday, and holidays; promptly and faithfully comply with all reasonable instructions, directions, requests, rules, and regulations

made or issued by Employer; perform and render his services conscientiously and to the full limit of his ability at all times when and wherever required or desired by Employer and as instructed by Employer in all matters, including those involving artistic taste and judgment. Without limiting the generality of the foregoing, Artist shall, if, as, and to the extent requested by Employer, perform and render services as an actor in the said role; record his voice and other sound effects, and in addition, render his services in the making of electrical and electronic transcriptions for radio broadcasting purposes and in the making of films and other devices for television purposes, for use in connection with the advertising publicity and exploitation of the Picture; sing and play such musical instruments as Artist is capable of playing in connection with the rendition of any of his services; and render any other services incidental to the rendition of the services enumerated in Sections 5 and 6 hereof.

5. Preliminary Services, Publicity: In addition to Artist's services in the portrayal of his role in the Picture, Artist shall, throughout the period of eight (8) days immediately preceding commencement of the term hereof and throughout the term hereof, report to such studios or other places as Employer may designate for the rendition of Artist's services in connection with rehearsals, consultations and discussions, tests, wardrobe fittings, publicity interviews, publicity stills, electrical and electronic transcriptions for advertising purposes, prerecordings, and other preliminary and preparatory activities in connection with Artist's services hereunder. Such services shall be rendered without any additional compensation in as much as the compensation payable to Artist pursuant to the provisions of Section 3 shall be deemed to include payment for such services. If Artist's services in connection with the principal photography of the Picture are completed prior to the expiration of the minimum period for which compensation is payable to Artist hereunder, Artist shall be available to the Employer for the rendition of the foregoing services herein above required by Employer during the unexpired balance of said minimum period. If Employer shall require Artist's services after the expiration of the term hereof in connection with publicity interviews and/or making still photographs for advertising and/or publicity purposes, Artist shall, subject to his availability by reason of other actual commitments in the entertainment industry, render such services as and when required by Employer at such place or places as the Employer may require, without payment to Artist of any additional compensation, as aforesaid. If Employer shall require Artist to return from a point outside of the place of Artist's permanent residence in order to render the services provided in the foregoing sentence, then Employer shall furnish Artist with or reimburse Artist for the cost of transportation (first class, if available) to the place designated by Employer and return to the place from which Artist came if Artist returns within one (1) week after the completion of such services, and living accommodations and meals (first

class, if available) during the period that Artist is rendering such services. If Artist is unable to render foregoing services by reason of other employment as herein specified, Artist agrees to cooperate with Employer to the fullest extent in making Artist's services available to Employer for the purposes herein specified as and when required by Employer.

6. Retakes: If Employer requires Artist's services in connection with the Picture after the expiration of the term hereof for additional photography and/or recording including, but not limited to, retakes, changes, added scenes, process shots, transparencies, trick shots, sound track, wild lines, trailers, and/or foreign versions, Artist shall render such services as required by Employer from time to time. Artist shall be obligated to render such services herein above so requested, unless Artist is unavailable due to other actual commitments in the entertainment industry, in which event, however, Artist shall cooperate with Employer to the fullest extent in making his services available for such purpose. Compensation shall be payable for such additional services at the rate specified in Section 3 hereof and in the same manner as therein specified.

7. Transportation, etc.: In addition to Artist's compensation hereunder, Employer agrees to furnish or pay the cost of round-trip transportation (first class, if available) for Artist from the place where Artist is when required to depart to render services hereunder, to such place or places in which Employer may require Artist to render his services hereunder. Employer shall also pay Artist a living expense allowance at the rate of _____ per week (pro-rated for any period of less than a week at a daily rate equal to one-seventh (1/7) of said weekly rate). Notwithstanding anything to the contrary contained in this section, Employer shall have no obligation to furnish or pay for Artist's return transportation if, prior to Artist's return, Artist shall render services in the entertainment industry for any other person, firm, or corporation. Artist shall use the method, means, and kinds of transportation furnished or designated by Employer in connection with any travel that Artist is required to undertake pursuant to the terms of this Contract.

8. Credit: On condition that Artist is not in default hereunder and on the further condition that the Picture is released and Artist's role is retained in the Picture as finally released, and Artist appears recognizably in such role, Employer shall give to Artist the following billing:

_____.

9. Wardrobe: Employer will be responsible for any damages to wardrobe furnished by Artist at the request of Employer. Employer shall supply all other wardrobe and costumes required for the portrayal of Artist's role. Any wardrobe or costumes furnished by Employer shall be furnished solely for the purpose of enabling Artist to perform his role in the Picture and the same shall remain Employer's property and be returned by Artist on or before the completion of Artist's services hereunder.

10.   Rights Granted: Artist grants to Employer all rights of every kind what-
       soever, whether now known or unknown, exclusively and perpetually,
       in and to his services performed pursuant to this agreement, and in and
       to all the results and proceeds thereof. Without limiting the generality of
       the foregoing, and in part in addition thereto, Artist makes the follow-
       ing additional grant of rights to the Employer:

   a.   *Photography and Recordation and Their Use*: Artist grants to
         Employer the sole and exclusive right to photograph or otherwise
         reproduce all or any part of Artist's performances, acts, poses,
         plays, and appearances of every kind and nature made or done by
         Artist in connection with Picture; to record or otherwise reproduce,
         by any present or future methods or means, his voice and all musi-
         cal, instrumental, or other sound effects produced by him in
         connection with the Picture; to produce, record, and transmit the
         same either separately or in conjunction with such performances,
         acts, poses, plays, and appearances as Employer may desire, in and
         in connection with the Picture; and perpetually to exhibit, transmit,
         and reproduce, and license others to exhibit, transmit, and repro-
         duce (whether by means of printing, motion pictures, radio,
         television, televised motion pictures, whether theatrically or non-
         theatrically, and including all forms of commercially sponsored,
         sustaining pay-as-you-go, or other kinds of television, and in con-
         junction with the advertising of any commodity, service or product,
         or otherwise, as Employer may determine in his sole discretion, or
         any other means now known or unknown) any such reproduc-
         tions, recordings, and transmissions in connection with the Picture
         or the advertising or exploitation of the Picture.

   b.   *Advertising and Exploitation*: Artist grants to Employer, in addi-
         tion to and apart from the use of Artist's name, likeness, and voice
         in said Picture, the perpetual right to use, and to allow others to
         use, Artist's name and pictures, photographs, and other reproduc-
         tions of Artist's voice and of instrumental, musical, and other
         sound effects produced by Artist, in and in connection with the
         advertising and exploitation, also in and in connection with the
         advertising and exploitation of any other products, commodities,
         or services in so-called commercial tie-ups (as that term is known
         and used in the motion picture industry) relating to the Picture, but
         Employer will not, without Artist's written consent, permit the
         advertiser to advertise or announce that Artist endorsed or uses the
         advertiser's product. Without limiting the generality of any rights
         herein elsewhere granted, Employer shall have the right to televise
         portions of the Picture, including those in which Artist appears, for
         the purposes of advertising and exploiting the Picture, and to utilize
         otherwise excerpts or portions of the Picture in connection with the

exploitation thereof. Excerpts from the Picture used for advertising and exploitation purposes, as aforesaid, may be utilized in or in connection with, or as part of, television programs produced and/or paid for by Employer or by its assignees or licensees, or in commercially sponsored or sustained television programs of others. Employer may broadcast by radio portions of the Picture, condensations thereof, or radio dramatizations thereof, for the purpose of advertising and exploiting the Picture.

c. *Double or Dub*: Employer shall have the right to use a double in lieu of the Artist and shall have the right to dub Artist's voice in any language at the Employer's discretion.

d. *Literary Material*: Artist agrees that all material, works given, ideas, gags, or dialogue composed, submitted, or interpolated by him in connection with the preparation or production of the Picture shall automatically become the property of Employer, which shall for this purpose be deemed to be the author thereof. Artist shall, at the request of Employer, execute such assignments, certificates, or other instruments as Employer may from time to time deem necessary or desirable to evidence, establish, maintain, protect, enforce, or defend its right or title in or to any such material.

e. *Control of Production*: Employer shall have complete control of production of the photoplay, including but not limited to all artistic controls and the right to cut, edit, add to, subtract from, arrange, rearrange, and revise the Picture in any manner.

All rights granted or agreed to be granted to Employer hereunder shall vest Employer immediately and shall remain vested in Employer, its successors and assigns, whether this Contract expires in normal course or is terminated or whether Artist's employment hereunder is terminated for any cause or reason.

11. Incapacity or Change: If Artist shall become incapacitated or prevented from fully performing in accordance with the terms hereof by reason of illness, accident, disfigurement, impairment of voice or mental or physical disability, or any other cause rendering such non-performance excusable at law (all of the foregoing being herein referred to as "incapacity") or if the facial or physical appearance or the voice of Artist shall be materially changed (all of the foregoing being herein referred to as "change"), then Employer shall have the right, at its option, to suspend Artist's employment hereunder during the period of such incapacity or change by oral or written notice to Artist. If any such incapacity or change continues for a period of five (5) consecutive days or an aggregate of periods often (10) days, during a period of time that Artist is rendering or is obligated to render his services for Employer hereunder, Employer shall have the right, at its option, to terminate this Contract and Artist's employment

hereunder by giving Artist written notice thereof at any time during the continuance of such incapacity or change or within three (3) days after the cessation thereof. During any period of suspension based on any such incapacity or change Artist shall not render services of any kind to or for any person, firm, or corporation or on his own behalf. In the event of such termination Employer shall be released from all further obligations to Artist whatsoever, except that Artist shall be entitled to receive such compensation, if any, as may have become due and unpaid prior to such termination. If Artist, at any time during the term hereof, alleges that he is incapacitated from performing his services hereunder, Employer shall have the right at its election, to have medical examinations made of Artist by such physician or physicians as Employer may designate, and Artist shall submit to such examinations and tests as such physician or physicians may deem desirable. If, at any time prior to the commencement of the term hereof, Employer obtains an opinion from a doctor designated by Employer and from a doctor designated by Artist to the effect that Artist will be incapacitated from rendering his services hereunder on the commencement of the term hereof and/or from completing the rendition of his services as required hereunder, then Employer may at its option cancel this Contract in its entirety and make it of no effect by giving Artist written notice thereof. If the opinion of the doctor designated by Artist does not concur with the opinion of Employer's doctor, with respect to such an availability of Artist, then each of such doctors shall forthwith agree upon and appoint a third doctor whose opinion shall be controlling.

12. Failure, Refusal, Neglect: If Artist fails, or neglects, other than because of incapacity or change as defined in Section 11 hereof, to perform *any* of his required services hereunder to the full limit of his ability as, when and where required by Employer, or to keep and perform any of his obligations and agreements hereunder (such failure, refusal, and neglect being hereafter referred to as "default"), then Employer shall have the right, at its option, to suspend Artist's employment hereunder during the period of such default and thereafter until Artist personally reports to Employer in good faith, ready, willing, and able to resume the rendition of his services and obligations hereunder and for such additional period, not exceeding three (3) weeks, as may be necessary to prepare for the actual utilization of Artist's services, by oral or written notice to Artist. In the event of such suspension based on default, Employer shall have the right, at its option, to reduce the minimum period during which it is obligated under the terms of this Contract to employ or pay compensation to Artist by a period of time equal to the aggregate of such period or periods of suspension. Employer shall have the right, at its option, to terminate this Contract and Artist's employment hereunder by giving Artist written notice thereof at any time during the continuance of such default or at any time during the period of

seven (7) days after the cessation thereof. During any period of suspension based on any such default Artist shall not render services of any kind to or for any person, firm, or corporation or on his own behalf. In the event of such termination, Employer shall be released from further obligations to Artist whatsoever, and the compensation, if any, which has theretofore accrued to and been earned by Artist hereunder shall be payment in full to Artist under this Contract, but the Artist shall be liable to Employer for the actual damage (which damage shall include as an item thereof, but not limited to, compensation theretofore paid to Artist hereunder) caused to Employer by any such default, and in addition to any other rights or remedies, Employer may deduct the amount of such damage from any compensation payable to Artist hereunder. Any reference or statement by Artist or by his agent that Artist will refuse to complete or perform any of his obligations or agreements hereunder may be treated by Employer as an anticipatory breach of this Contract and as an event of default hereunder.

13. Force Majeure: If during the time when Artist is rendering or is obligated to render his services for Employer hereunder Employer is prevented from or hampered or interrupted or interfered with in any manner whatever in preparing or producing the Picture by reason of any present or future statute, law, ordinance, regulation, order judgment, or decree, whether legislative, executive, or judicial (whether or not constitutional), act of God, earthquake, flood, fire, epidemic, accident, explosion, casualty, lockouts, boycott, strike, labor controversy (including but not limited to threat of lockout, boycott, or strike), riot, civil disturbance, war or armed conflict (whether or not there has been an official declaration of war or official statement as to the existence of a state of war), act of a public enemy, embargo, delay of a common carrier, inability without fault on Employer's part to obtain sufficient material, labor, transportation, power, or other essential condition required in the conduct of its business, or by reason of any other cause or causes of any similar nature; or if the production of the Picture is suspended, interrupted, or postponed by reason of any such cause or similar cause, or the death, illness, disfigurement, or incapacity of the director or a principal member of the cast of the Picture, or if for any reason whatsoever a majority of the exhibitors of motion pictures in the United States shall cease exhibition for a period of one (1) week or more (all of the foregoing being hereby referred to as an event of force majeure), then as a result of any such event Employer shall have the right, at its option, to suspend Artist's employment hereunder as often as any such event occurs and during such periods of time as such events exist, by oral or written notice to Artist. If any such event of force majeure continues for a period or periods of eight (8) weeks in the aggregate during the term hereof, either Artist or Employer may elect to terminate this Contract and Artist's employment hereunder by giving written notice of

such election to the other, provided, however, that such termination by Artist shall not become effective if Employer, within one (1) week after the actual receipt of such notice, from Artist, gives Artist written notice that Employer elects to resume the accrual of compensation to Artist and that Artist's employment hereunder has been resumed, effective on or before the expiration of the said one-week period, and in such event this Contract shall not be terminated by Artist but shall continue in full force and effect, subject, however, to the right of Employer to suspend or terminate Artist's employment thereafter for other proper cause, including but not limited to the occurrence of a different event of force majeure, in accordance with the provisions of this Contract.

If, between the date of this Contract and the date designated in Section 2 hereof for the commencement of Artist's employment, the preparation of the Picture is prevented, hampered, or interrupted by any of the events for force majeure so that Employer cannot practically commence Picture on such starting date, Employer may postpone such starting date for such period as may be reasonably necessary to prepare for the commencement of Picture, not in excess of fourteen (14) days. Artist shall not be entitled to receive any compensation for or during any period of suspension provided for in this section. The term of Artist's employment hereunder shall be automatically extended for a period of time equal to the aggregate of the period or periods during which Artist's employment hereunder is suspended pursuant to any of the provisions of this Contract. Artist shall not at any time revoke any of the rights granted hereunder by him to Employer.

14. General Covenants and Warranties: Artist will indemnify Employer, its successors, and assigns, against and hold them harmless from all damage, liability, or expense, including reasonable attorney's fees, resulting from any breach of any warranty of agreement made by Artist in this Contract.

15. Negative Covenants, Publicity, Air Transportation: Artist will not, without Employer's prior written approval, issue or authorize the publication of any news stories or publicity relating primarily to the Picture, or to his employment hereunder, or to Employer, as distinguished from personal publicity relating primarily to Artist; from the date hereof until the completion of all services required of Artist in connection with the production of the Picture, travel in an airplane or any other vehicle that travels in the air, other than as a passenger on a recognized scheduled airline. In the event of a breach of the terms of this section, Employer, in addition to any other right or remedy, may within ten (10) days after receiving knowledge thereof, terminate this Contract.

16. Insurance: Employer may secure in its own name or otherwise and its own expense, life, accident, health, cast, and other insurance covering Artist, either independently or together with others, and Artist shall have no right, title, or interest in and to such insurance. Artist shall

assist Employer to procure such insurance by submitting to the usual and customary medical and other examinations and by signing such applications and other instruments in writing as may be required by the insurance company involved. If Employer is unable to obtain, at ordinary rates, cast insurance on Artist, Employer shall have the right to terminate this Contract without liability by giving Artist written notice of termination within ten (10) days after the Employer acquires knowledge that Artist failed to pass a physical examination for cast insurance, or otherwise qualify for such cast insurance.

17. General Provisions: Each and all of the several rights and remedies provided for in this Contract shall be construed as being cumulative, and no one of them as being exclusive of the other or of any right or remedy allowed by law or in equity. Time for performance by Artist hereunder is of the essence hereof. Nothing in this Contract contained shall be construed so as to require the commission of any act contrary to law, and whenever there is any conflict between any provision of this Contract and any present or future statute, law, ordinance, or regulation contrary to which the parties have no legal right to contract, the latter shall prevail, but in such event the provision of this Contract affected shall be curtailed and limited only to the extent necessary to bring it within the requirements of the law. This Contract in all respects shall be subject to the laws of California relating to agreements executed and wholly performed within the territorial limits of such state.

18. Assignment and Lending: Employer may transfer or assign this Contract or all or any part of its rights hereunder to any person, firm or corporation, and this Contract shall incur to the benefit of Employer, its successors, and assigns. Employer shall have the right, at its discretion, to lend Artist's services hereunder to any person, firm, or corporation that may produce the Picture, and in such event Artist shall render his services to such other person, firm, or corporation to the best of his ability and Employer may grant to any such person, firm, or corporation any and all rights and services to which it is entitled during the period of such lending.

19. No Obligation to Produce or Release Picture: Employer shall not be obligated actually to utilize the services of Artist, or to include all or any of his performances in the Picture, or to produce or to release or to continue the distribution or release of the Picture once released. Nothing contained in this section shall be deemed to relieve Employer of its obligation to pay Artist the compensation payable to him pursuant to this Contract (and subject to all provisions hereof) for the minimum term of his employment as herein provided.

20. Notices: All notices that Employer is required or may desire to serve upon Artist under or in connection with this Contract may be served in lieu of delivering them personally to c/o: _____ or at such address as Artist may designate in writing from time to time.

All notices that Artist is required or may desire to serve upon Employer under or in connection with this Contract may be served by mail or telegraph or fax addressed to Employer at: or at such other address as Employer may designate in writing from time to time.

21. Entire Contract: This Contract constitutes the entire Contract between the parties and shall supersede any and all prior written or oral agreements between the parties relating to the subject matter hereof and cannot be modified or amended except by written instrument signed by Artist and by Employer. Artist acknowledges that he has not executed this Contract in reliance on any representation or promise made by Employer or any of its representatives other than those expressly contained in this Contract.

22. Withholdings: Employer may, as the employer of Artist, deduct and withhold from the compensation payable to Artist hereunder any amounts of money required to be deducted or withheld by Employer as Artist's employer under the provisions of any statute, regulation, ordinance, or order, and any and all amendments thereto now or hereafter enacted requiring the withholding of or deduction of compensation.

23. Section Headings: Table of Contents (if such is used in connection herewith) headings and sections, and other subdivisions of this Contract are for convenient reference only. They shall not be used in any way to govern, limit, modify, construe, or otherwise be given legal effect.

24. Gender and Number: Terms used herein in the masculine gender include the feminine and neuter genders, and terms used in the singular number include the plural number, if the context may require.

In Witness hereof, the parties hereto have executed this Contract, which consists of pages exclusive of Exhibits, if any, attached hereto, the day and year first above written.

By _____   _____

    Employer   Artist's Signature

                                     _____

                                     Agent's Signature

Other Agreements

In addition to the actor's contract, a production usually requires contracts or releases of a simpler nature from extras, minors, and others employed in an ad-hoc situation (for example, when shooting on a public street, the director wants a particular person or passerby to be featured in the background). Also needed are releases for properties used as location sites. Sample contracts and releases are given in this section.

Screen Extras and Minor Agreement and Release

Employee _____, Address _____, S.S. no. _____,
Home phone _____, Union affiliation [if any] _____, Title
of picture _____, Producer/company _____.
Guaranteed compensation: _____.
Days worked: _____.

Employee is hereby hired as a Screen Extra as the term is understood in the entertainment industry. Employee shall report at the time and location site specified by Producer. Employee shall provide his/her own wardrobe as specified by Producer.

Employee shall render all of Employee's services as Producer's employee for hire, and Producer shall own all of the results and proceeds of Employee's services hereunder, as well as the right to use Employee's name and likeness in connection with the exhibition, promotion, and exploitation of the Picture. Employee hereby releases and discharges Producer from any and all claims, demands, or causes of action arising from anything contained in the Picture or in the publicity or advertising pertaining hereto. This Agreement and Release shall inure to the benefit of the legal representatives, licensees, successors, and assigns of Producer.

To be completed if Party is under 21 years of age:
I represent that I am the parent/guardian of the above-mentioned person. I hereby consent to the foregoing on his/her behalf.

I/we further agree and warrant that [name of minor] will not disaffirm or disavow said agreement and permission on the ground that he/she was a minor on the date of execution thereof or any similar grounds whatsoever, or endeavor to recover from you personally or through any guardian, any sums for participating in the above-entitled Picture. This Agreement is the entire agreement between the parties and shall be governed by the laws of the State of California.

I have read the foregoing and fully understand and agree to the contents thereof.

_____   _____
Producer/Company   Parent/Guardian

_____   _____
Date   Employee

Personal Release

To (Production Company) _____
From (Releasing Party) _____

In consideration of your filming or otherwise recording me, my performance, or voice in the tentatively titled Picture _____, I hereby grant to you and to your employees, agents, successors, licensees, and assigns the perpetual right and license to use, simulate, and impersonate my name, face, likeness, voice, appearance, actions, activities, career, and experiences either actually or fictionally, under my name or under any name, in and/or in connection with the production, distribution, exhibition, advertising, and other exploitation of the above Picture in perpetuity throughout the world. The rights herein granted to you shall include the right to depict and/or portray me to such extent and in such manner as you in your discretion may determine, and to edit any of my statements or comments and/or to juxtapose my face, likeness, appearances, actions, activities, career, experiences, and/or statements or comments, or any simulation and/or impersonation thereof with any film clips and/or other material at your sole discretion.

You shall have the right to distribute, exhibit, or otherwise exploit any such production, in whole or parts thereof, by any method known and unknown in any medium in connection with the above Picture or separate and apart from above Picture.

I warrant that I have not been induced to execute this Release by any agreements or statements made by you and/or your representatives as to the nature or extent of your proposed exercise of any of the rights hereby granted, and I understand that you are under no obligation to exercise any of your rights, licenses and privileges herein granted to you.

The above permission is granted for the sum of $ _____.

I hereby release and discharge you from any and all liability, loss, costs, damages, or claims of any nature, including but not limited to attorney's fees, arising from, growing out of, or concerning a breach of the above warranty.

I have read and understood the foregoing and agree to the contents thereof.

_____   _____
Name   Address

                                                _____
                                                Date

To be completed if Party is under 21 years of age:
I represent that I am the parent/guardian of the minor who has signed above release, and I hereby agree that I and said minor will be bound thereby.

_____   _____
Parent/Guardian   Address

_____   _____
[Print name]   Date

Location Agreement and Property Release

I _____, Address _____, hereby grant permission to _____ [Producer], _____ [Company] and its successors and assigns to use the Property and adjacent area located at [address] and consisting of _____ [a yard, living room, cellar, garage, and so on] to enter upon, to photograph by motion picture, video tape, still photography, or otherwise, and to make sound recordings and to otherwise use for so-called "location" purposes (the results of which are hereafter collectively referred to as "Photographs") with the right and all the ancillary and subsidiary rights to exhibit, distribute, and exploit all or any part of said Photographs perpetually throughout the world in any media known or unknown at the Producer's sole discretion. Said permission shall include the right to bring personnel and equipment onto said property and to remove the same therefrom after completion of work.

The above permission is granted for _____ [tentative title of picture] for _____ days/weeks beginning on or about _____ and ending on or about _____ for the amount of $ _____ payable in installments on _____. The Producer agrees to pay the sum of $ _____ for each day of dressing or striking.

The Property will be under the complete control of Producer who will have exclusive use of that site from the commencement of construction (if any) to completion of principal photography and removal of construction (if any). If such photography is prevented or hampered by weather or occurrence beyond Producer's control, it will be postponed to or completed on such date as Producer may reasonably require.

The rights herein granted include the right to photograph all structures and signs located on Property, including the exterior and interior, and the names, logos, and verbiage contained on such signs; the right to refer to the Property by its correct or any fictitious name, and the right to attribute fictitious events as occurring on the Property and to fictionalize the Property itself. It is agreed and acknowledged that any or all Photographs made or to be made by Producer shall be Producer's sole and exclusive property and the undersigned shall have no claims thereto or rights herein or to the proceeds thereof.

Producer agrees to use reasonable care to prevent damage to the Property and to restore the Property as nearly as possible to its original condition at the time of Producer's taking possession thereof, reasonable use thereof, damage not caused by Producer use excepted.

Producer hereby agrees to indemnify and hold the undersigned harmless from any claims and demands of any person or persons arising out of or based upon personal injuries and/or death suffered by such person or persons resulting directly from any act of negligence on Producer's part while Producer is engaged in photographing of said Picture upon the Property.

The undersigned hereby warrants and represents that he is the owner/ lessee/agent for the owner of said Property and has the full right and authority to enter into this Agreement concerning the above-described Property, and that the consent or permission of no other person, firm, or corporation is necessary in order to enable Producer to enjoy full rights to the use of said Property, hereinabove mentioned, and that the Undersigned, its heirs, successors, or assigns do hereby indemnify and agree to hold Producer and its licensees, successors, assigns, all networks, stations, sponsors, advertising agencies, exhibitors, cable operators, and all other persons or entities free and harmless from and against any and all claims, demands, or causes of action and any and all losses, costs, liability, damages, or claims of any nature, including but not limited to attorney's fees, arising from, going out of, or concerning a breach of the above permission.

Agreed to and accepted: _____ [property owner's name]

Address: _____

Date: _____

Agreed to and accepted: _____[Producer]

Executive in charge of production: _____

Location Manager: _____

The production company should be prepared to furnish, at the property owner's request, the following General Provisions to the Location Agreement:

Activities, areas of use, dates, and times of filming, will not be modified without express written approval of the manager, owner, or designee;

All areas of the property not specifically included in this Agreement are off-limits to all cast and crew;

Tenants, public, staff, and visitors will not be restricted except during actual filming unless otherwise agreed;

Areas of production company use are to be kept continually free of trash, litter, etc. and are to be maintained in a safe manner. Cables, dolly track, and other potential hazards are to be shielded.

If interiors are permitted, floors and walkways will be protected from excessive dirt or water. Landscaped areas are to be undisturbed unless otherwise agreed. No personal animals are to be brought on the property.

_____ Circle and initial the items below which apply to this Agreement:

Production company is to furnish own: electricity _____ trash receptacles _____ sanitary facilities _____ phones _____.

_____ Locations are to be cleared of all equipment, props, and trash and returned to original condition within _____ hours after completion of filming. Cleaning will be to the owner and/or agent's satisfaction.

_____ Areas of filming will be cleared of hazards at the end of each day's filming or a set guard will be provided by production company. The set guard will follow the guidelines set by owner and/or agent.

_____ No overnight storage of equipment or vehicles.

_____ No smoking permitted.

_____ Smoking permitted only in designated areas properly equipped with butt cans.

_____ No activity, including arrival of vehicles and/or personnel, will occur before _____ a.m. or after _____ p.m.

_____ Crew meals will be set up as follows: _____

_____ Except as otherwise designated, no food or drink is permitted in the interior of the property.

_____ Parking of vehicles and equipment is as follows:

Generator location: _____;

Production vehicles, number and type: _____;

Location: _____;

Other vehicles, number and type: _____;

Location: _____.

_____ Any set construction, removal or covering of signs, painting, nailing, taping, or any other alteration to the property is prohibited unless specifically described below: _____.

Agreed to: _____ [name]   Date _____

Producer/Production Company _____

Owner/Agent _____

Immigration Laws and Working Permits

Since motion pictures have ventured outside sound stages and studios to "real" locations all over the country and the world, the problems and procedures for temporary or permanent working permits have become more prevalent. Not only are increasingly more American crews shooting outside the United States, but more non-American production companies are coming to the U.S. to shoot part, if not all of, their motion pictures. In addition, American productions are employing more residents of other countries, not only as actors, but also as members of creative crews and as directors, directors of photography, art directors, and other positions. The employment of non-Americans requires working permits for theatrical productions or commercials, but not for documentary shoots or news crews. Although foreigners can enter the U.S. on tourist and business visas, it is hardly advisable to hire anyone to work on a domestic or foreign shoot in the U.S. without the proper visa. The production could be shut down immediately, and the production company could face severe penalties.

The production manager must handle three different types of problems:

1.   Obtaining working permits for American personnel on shoots outside the U.S.;

2.   Obtaining temporary working permits for non-American personnel for foreign productions in the U.S.;

3.   Obtaining permanent or temporary working permits for non-American personnel for domestic productions in the U.S.

Working Permits for Americans for Productions outside the United States

Initial contacts can be made through foreign embassies or consulates to obtain information on the legal and procedural requirements of a specific country. Another source is the foreign film commissions that maintain offices in the U.S. or that direct contacts to film commissions overseas. If the production is working with a foreign production company, it should be able to obtain the appropriate visas or at least offer advice on how to obtain them. No general rules exist; each country handles these matters differently. It usually takes several weeks to gather all the required information and paperwork, as described later, and more time for the applications to be processed. Sometimes work may begin in the foreign country (on preproduction) while the applications are processed, but all the visas must be in order by the time the crew arrives for production.

Temporary Working Permits for Non-Americans for Foreign Productions in the United States

Because motion pictures shot in the U.S. find their worldwide market much easier than films shot in foreign countries, and because only foreign films shot in the U.S. in English starring American leads have a fair shot at distribution in the U.S., increasingly more foreign production companies are shooting some or all of their pictures, TV series, or mini-series on American locations.

Of course, these foreign production companies want to bring their own key personnel, if not all their crew. This is in part because of language and communication reasons, in part because of the need to maintain proper continuity, especially if parts of the picture have been shot or will be shot outside the U.S., and in part because of financial reasons. The unfamiliarity and uncertainty of foreign producers about American crews, unions, and practices lead to the desire to retain as many of their own crew members as possible, despite very good reasons not to do so.

Few American film commissions are in a position to expedite the application process. However, due to fortunate personal ties between immigration authorities and local film commission personnel, and the general understanding that even having a foreign crew shooting in town is better than having no production at all, most local film commissions successfully make referrals to appropriate lawyers and write letters in support of the application process. However, the immigration authorities are completely independent, and even the strong recommendation and desire of a local film commission, mayor's office, or governor's office to host a production in town is no guarantee that the visas will be granted.

No law requires the employment of a lawyer to handle the applications, but due to the intricacy and complexity of the process, it is advisable to employ a law office that regularly handles such matters. A law firm in the city where the production will take place might not be the best one to employ. The immigration bureaucracy is set up in regions that do not necessarily reflect ports of entry or centers of production activity.

In my dealings with various overseas productions shooting in the U.S. and with various law offices in different parts of the country, I have frequently received conflicting advice, and I recommend exhaustive research into the requirements unique to each individual production. "Deals" can frequently be made: So many foreigners are permitted if so many Americans are employed. These deals depend on whether the foreigners' salaries are paid by an American company or by their foreign employer, whether the production is designed for domestic distribution or for foreign use only, and so on.

The following excerpts are quoted from correspondence with various law firms on different projects. The first case involves a television series for broadcast in a foreign country only, with 100 percent foreign staff, crew, and cast, and financed completely by a foreign production company:

> Proceeding on the assumption that the actors and actresses will not be paid by anyone in the United States for the services performed here, they should apply for individual B-I "business visitor" visas in the most convenient United States Consulate in [their respective countries].
>
> Technicians and other ancillary personnel, such as cameramen, should also be paid from overseas, in which event they should qualify for B-I visas. Generally, when entering the United States, the Immigration Inspector at the airport may grant a stay of six months subject to the filing of a request, if necessary, for an extension of an addition six months.

As a matter of procedure, we [the law office] often telephone the United States Consulate in a foreign country in order to obtain, if possible, informal assurance that the recommended procedure is acceptable.

The second case involves a theatrical motion picture for international release, financed solely by a foreign production company, using key foreign personnel and actors and additional domestic staff, crew, and actors (this situation is also applicable to coproductions with partial American financing):

Basically, as we discussed, while U.S. immigration laws are relatively generous as far as permitting individuals to visit the United States, they are highly restrictive as far as those individuals who can legally be employed in the U.S.A. This is especially true in the entertainment industry, where the SAG and other unions that represent various component parts of the production of a film periodically lobby the U.S. Immigration and Naturalization Service (I.N.S) to increase their standards in order to protect employment opportunities in the film industry in the United States for U.S. citizens.

The primary basis for qualifying such individuals would be under Subsection (H) of Section 214 of the Immigration and Naturalization Act, as H-1 aliens of "distinguished merit and ability". While this classification, by its very nature, is somewhat subjective, at the very least we would need detailed information and evidence to attest to the exceptional nature of the individuals, and the project, such as:

a. Whether the alien has performed and will perform as a star or featured entertainer, as evidenced by playbills, critical reviews, advertisements, publicity releases, contracts, a.s.o. [and so on];

b. Reviews in newspapers, trade journals, magazines;

c. Evidence of the reputation of theaters, concert halls, repertory companies, a.s.o., in which these individuals have performed;

d. The extent and number of commercial successes of their performances, as evidenced by such indicia as box office grosses, record sales, trade journal reports, a.s.o.;

e. The salary and other remuneration each alien has commanded and will command for the performance/production (contracts);

f. Evidence of national, international, or other significant awards for performances;

g. Opinions (such as letters of reference) from recognized critics in the field;

h. Evidence of previous H-1 nonimmigrant status for similar positions to any of the participants (such evidence consists of a copy of form I-171C and a copy of the H-I visa stamp);

i. Detailed curriculum vitae, including a complete list of works or credits, for all participants;

j.   Any additional information regarding the other participants in the production (including the Americans) who might be preeminent, including producer, author of screenplay, a.s.o.;

k.   Brochures and/or background information regarding the production company, including a list of previous productions (international or domestic). Also include date established, number of employees, and gross annual revenue;

l.   As available, details about the specific qualifications needed to perform these services;

m.   Specific dates that these individuals will be required, proposed salary and benefits (such as per diem expenses, a.s.o.), port of entry into the U.S.A.;

n.   As much detail as possible about the Production, including names of participants, estimated budget, and percentage of same to be spent during production in the U.S.A.;

o.   In case the visa needs to be obtained instantly: proof of why the visa is needed immediately, such as Production schedules, estimated sums of money that may be lost if there is a delay in coming to the U.S.A., other losses that may occur (such as scheduling conflicts for principal actors, a.s.o.).

Also, even if some individuals do not appear to qualify under the H-1 criteria listed above, it may also be possible to classify them as "accompanying aliens" whose services are "essential" to the success of the performance or production. Therefore, it is of advantage to have as much background as possible on the production and all participants to select the most advantageous facts to work with in preparation of the petitions.

Normally, once such information is gathered, an appropriate petition is prepared (the petitioner cannot be a foreign company; a U.S. company or film board can be used as a substitute), along with the required supporting documentation (copies of supporting documents must be certified and can only be certified by an I.N.S. attorney or clerk of the court, not a notary public; originals will be accepted, newspaper articles need not be certified; a consulate can also certify copies) and legal arguments under applicable statutes, regulations, and case provisions. Then this petition is filed at the appropriate Immigration Service's Regional Service Center. A regional immigration examiner then reviews the petition and makes a determination as to the individual's eligibility. Under certain circumstances the individual is required to check with unions or other appropriate organizations for their opinion as to the individual's eligibility as an alien of distinguished merit and ability.

The I.N.S. usually takes a minimum of six to eight weeks to make a decision and, in difficult cases, could take much longer.

Permanent or Temporary Working Permits for Non-Americans for Domestic Productions in the United States

Most of the documentation just described is also required for obtaining a permanent working permit for a foreigner—in this case, the foreigner's services. Additionally, further procedures and publications are necessary to show that no American citizen qualifies for the employment sought by the foreigner. This process can take up to a year or longer. However, exceptions have been made for high-powered stars, and the process is shortened considerably when a powerful studio is behind the application.

It should be clear that the process of applying for working permits is cumbersome and unpredictable, and decisions cannot be appealed. It is important to start this process as soon as possible to allow enough time to provide and process the required paperwork (which must also be translated into English). Unfortunately, due to risks and costs involved in this process, many foreign companies decide not to bring their production to the U.S. once they understand the scope of the efforts needed to obtain visas. Efforts are under way to substantially facilitate this process. These have mainly been initiated by film commissions, which understand that all productions benefit the area in which they are shot, regardless of how many domestic actors, extras, staff members, and crew personnel are employed.

Requirements of the Immigration Reform and Control Act of 1986 make it mandatory that producers seek proof from the cast and crew employed that they have a right to work in the U.S. Employment of illegally working personnel can result in fines levied against the employer. Although no such inquiries can be made during interviews, they must be conducted after an applicant has been offered employment. The extent to which the PM might become involved in this process depends on the specific situation. Clearly, in a union production, this is not part of the PM's duties; in a nonunion production, it very well might be.

Following is a list of documents acceptable for establishing identity and employment eligibility:

- U.S. passport;
- Certificate of U.S. citizenship;
- Unexpired foreign passport that either (1) contains an unexpired stamp that reads "Processed for I-551. Temporary Evidence of Lawful Admission for permanent residence. Valid until Employment authorized" or (2) has attached to it Form I-94, bearing the same name as the passport and having a current employment

authorization stamp, as long as the proposed employment is not in conflict with any restrictions or limitations identified on Form I-94;

- Alien Registration Card or Resident Alien Card with photograph;
- Temporary Resident Card;
- Employment Authorization Card;
- Native American tribal documents.

The following documents establish identity:

- State-issued driver's license or state-issued ID card with photograph;
- Voter's registration card;
- U.S. military card or draft record;
- Identification card issued by federal, state, or local government agencies;
- Military dependent's identification card;
- Canadian driver's license.

The following documents establish employment eligibility:

- Social Security card;
- Birth certificate bearing an official seal issued by a state, county, or municipal authority;
- Unexpired I.N.S. employment authorization;
- Unexpired reentry permit;
- Unexpired Refugee Travel Document;
- U.S. citizen identification card;
- U.S. resident citizen identification card.

It should be noted that since the September 11, 2001 attacks the State Department has installed a new policy in an effort to tighten border controls. This means that foreigners working in the United States will have to go to U.S. embassies abroad—not necessarily to their home countries—to be interviewed and fingerprinted when they need to renew their visas. Previously these people—including entertainers, investors, executives or journalists— were allowed to renew their visas by mail.

9

The Budget and Production Budget Forms

The production manager must oversee all aspects of the budget. He or she should be capable of judging from experience when a particular item or department is going over budget, and should be able to determine whether these overruns can be covered by savings in other departments.

The whole budget process usually is in a state of flux during preproduction and principal photography. Requirements change, expenses go up in some areas, savings develop in others. It is important that the PM, with the help of the production accountant, keeps on top of these developments and makes quick decisions, if necessary. Any decisions that have artistic repercussions should be discussed with the producer and director if they will affect the look of the picture. Some of the PM's main tasks are to spot trouble areas and fix them early on, and to be flexible when necessary and decisive when required. It is important to understand that budgets must be handled with great flexibility, because almost never does a theatrical motion picture shoot go according the first schedule—which of course makes the task and responsibility to maintain a balanced budget even more difficult. Savings in one department may be countered by cost overruns in others—a budget should be as up-to-date as possible, on a daily routine.

However, the production manager should avoid getting involved in tasks that are traditionally the responsibility of the production accountant. For the sake of the production, even on low-budget projects, the PM should insist that an accountant be hired to take care of the actual dispensing of cash, location payroll, cost control, and bookkeeping on a daily basis. When dealing with outside financiers or with banks and completion guarantees it is mandatory to be able to present up-to-date accounting at any given moment.

The Production Budget Process

After the producer and director outline the scope of the production and agree to the shooting schedule (described in Chapter 3), the PM can go ahead and draw up a preliminary budget. Only after all the details are discussed and agreed on—including the probable locations to be used, length of employment of actors, number of extras in each scene, type and number of vehicles and props required, and shooting ratio—is the PM in a position to estimate the film's production costs.

Until all the details of the production are negotiated and contractually secured, the preliminary budget is just an estimate, and the word "allow" is used in the budget. Preliminary figures are usually padded to cover potential cost overruns. The costs of such details as location site rentals or complicated special effects (mechanical, makeup, digital or optical) are determined as the work progresses. When new ground is broken and technical hardware or software must be developed, it is especially difficult to estimate the precise costs in advance. This is one reason why the production accountant must keep track of daily and weekly expenses and must state in a daily or weekly report whether the film is within the budget and, if not, to what extent it is over.

Creating a Preliminary Budget

The budget process remains the same whether done on paper in the traditional manner or with the assistance of a computer and appropriate software—which has become the absolute standard by now. Price lists from rental houses, labs, and other services must be obtained; prices and costs must be researched, negotiated, computed, and listed in the appropriate departments; individual accounts must be subtotaled and totaled; contingency and corporate overhead must be added; and the top sheet, which provides a one-glance look at the expenses of each production department, must be finalized.

It is important to establish a realistic budget. Insurance and bonding companies and the SAG (under its Low-Budget Agreement) request a copy of the budget or its top sheet. If personnel defer all or part of their salaries, the appropriate and full amount, whether deferred or not, should be included in the budget. Production managers do themselves a disservice when they try to cut corners and come up with a low budget to please the producer. Frequently, costs can be cut, favors cashed in, and deals made during a production, but these anticipated gains should not be included in the budget before they are contractually agreed upon.

All budgets are set up in such a way that all personnel, with the exception of above-the-line personnel who frequently work for a flat fee, are computed on a daily or weekly basis. Preproduction fees are generally lower than production fees for such personnel, such as the director of photography and the PM. These positions might be adjusted upward during production through an added production fee.

Up-to-date rates set by various unions and subject to regular increases, reviews, and negotiations can be obtained by consulting the "rate books", which list the various union wages and are available in specialized bookstores, or they can be obtained free of charge directly from the various guilds and unions. Smart software programs have these rates implemented and updates can be obtained when necessary. Guild and union fees can serve as a general guideline, but they are in no way obligatory for nonunion productions. Although key people might be paid more than the union rate, many other positions are generally paid less than the union rate. This, of course, depends on the production situation and on the availability of competent personnel.

Also regulated are travel and living expenses of SAG members. For example, if six or fewer actors are used, they must be transported first class if available (business class is permitted for more than six), and meal allowances currently run $11 for breakfast, $16 for lunch, and $29 for dinner, unless meals are provided by the producer. Equally precise are the SAG's regulations regarding overtime, night-time, and weekend work. Because these schedules are highly complex and definitions are adjusted to suit the different types of production (theatrical, TV, commercials, low-budget, regular-budget), it is advisable to consult the voluminous SAG documentation.

SAG documentation also specifies the union dues that producers must pay in addition to actors' salaries (dues are currently running at 13 percent of all gross payments), residual payments, and compensation schedules for various types of production. The documentation also gives the scales for residuals, which are of more interest to the producer than the PM.

It is not unusual to leave the responsibility of paying SAG and SEG members to payroll companies, which compute the money due based on the daily SAG production time reports. The PM can budget 0.45 percent of the total budget or $10 per check written for such a service. In addition to handling the payroll, these services usually calculate union, health, and welfare payments; compute, report, and pay all federal, state, and local taxes; prepare and file all necessary federal, state, and local reports, including W-2s and 941s; administer and process all claims for workers' compensation and disability; and keep complete and accurate records for the producer.

If the services of a payroll company will not be used, a personal accountant may be hired. He or she should be familiar with the current rates for FICA (Federal Insurance Contribution Act), FUI (federal unemployment insurance), and SUI (state unemployment insurance) contributions, which the employer pays on the employee's behalf. The use of specialized software programs facilitates this process.

When budgeting a film, the PM should keep in mind that almost all items—including personnel, equipment rentals and purchases, and preproduction, principal photography, and post-production services—are generally negotiable. (One exception is wages of union members.) For example, most rental houses charge only a three- or four-day rental fee per week if the equipment is rented for a prolonged period. Frequently, package deals can be obtained, not only at rental houses but also at labs and postproduction facilities and with personnel who own their own equipment.

It is customary to detail travel and living expenses in the budget at great length, listing type of transportation, number of overnight stays and cost, meal allowances, and per diems, which are negotiable. Extras and stand-ins are usually listed in great detail also, including how many will be used, on which set or location, and for which scene. This allows the PM to calculate precise cost overruns for individual scenes or locations, if necessary.

For productions that employ personnel in foreign countries, separate listings are recommended because their wage rates are generally different from those in the U.S. So are their fringe benefits and union dues, if applicable. Foreign shoots also involve different meal allowances, travel expenses, overnight expenses, and taxes than in the U.S. These differences must be clearly marked in the budget. If the expenses are converted from a foreign currency, the exchange rate and the date the exchange rate was given should be indicated.

Complicated sets, mechanical or digital special effects, or other extraordinary requirements of the art department are usually budgeted in cooperation with the art director and SFX-supervisor, who provides his or her own budget calculations. If possible, rented and purchased items are listed separately. Details of any set construction are provided. In fact, details of all expenses and purchases, no matter what department, should be given.

The budget should note which items will be resold after production, including leftover film stock, props, or wardrobe. It should also note any discounts that might be obtained on any services or items, unless already indicated.

A corporate overhead fee is frequently included in the production budget. This fee covers expenses that the production company incurs in the course of its day-to-day business and that are not shown in detail in any other category. Overhead fees vary, but 7.5 percent is a reasonable amount for low-budget nonunion productions. This amount is generally considered to compensate the production company for development of the project and the risk and time involved, and it usually need not be accounted for with specific receipts.

Finance charges should be added to the budget as they apply. These figures are generally supplied by the executive producer.

A contingency amount of 10 percent is usually added to the production cost; the percentage may be calculated before or after the corporate overhead fee is added to the budget. If the budget is required by a completion bond company, the direct production costs, excluding the 10 percent contingency fee, must be shown.

Revising and Finalizing the Budget

Software programs are very convenient for budgeting, a process generally involving several revisions and adjustments during the preproduction phase. Software is available that facilitates many processes employed; implements changes, such as to the shooting schedule; contains databases of union rates; sets, displays, and totals fringe benefits; offers subgroups for different eventualities, such as different production locations; performs foreign currency conversions; instantly recalculates changes made; permits custom-designed budget forms; and supports interfacing with accounting software.

If the budget is done on paper, calculations and estimates should be done on scrap paper before they are actually typed into the production form. This is not necessary if the budget is done with a computer program that permits changes to be implemented easily. Depending on the screenplay and production involved, the process of finalizing a budget can take anywhere from a few days to a week or two. The PM and eventually the director and producer must sign off on the final budget.

Production Budget Forms

A production budget form can be quite extensive, up to 30 pages or more in length. However, different budget forms are available for different needs. The sample production budget form shown in Figure 9.1 is widely used in the industry. It is also available as part of a computer software package.

The sample budget form in Figure 9.1 is designed for a low-budget theatrical motion picture but can serve as a blueprint for other types of production. Budget forms for productions of other sizes are available at specialized stores.

Cash-Flow Sheet

Once the production manager has established the final budget, he or she may be asked to work out a cash-flow chart, particularly in low-budget productions in which a production accountant will not be hired until the shooting actually begins. No established form exists for the cash-flow chart; the PM is free to design one to meet the production's specific needs.

The cash-flow chart details the expenses and financial requirements of the entire production period, usually on a weekly basis. It is required to determine

BLANK BUDGET (PARAMOUNT FORM)

PRODUCTION NUMBER: DATE:
PRODUCER: LOCATIONS:
DIRECTOR: DAYS:
SCRIPT DATE: WEEKS:
START DATE:
FINISH DATE: NOTE:

Acct#	Category Title	Page	Total	
600-00	STORY	1		$0
610-00	PRODUCER	1		$0
620-00	DIRECTOR	1		$0
630-00	CAST	1		$0
640-00	FRINGES	2		$0
650-00	TRAVEL & LIVING	2		$0
	Total Above-The-Line			**$0**
700-00	EXTRA TALENT	2		$0
705-00	PRODUCTION STAFF	2		$0
710-00	CAMERA	2		$0
715-00	SET DESIGN	3		$0
720-00	SET CONSTRUCTION	3		$0
721-00	SET STRIKING	3		$0
722-00	MINIATURES	3		$0
725-00	SET OPERATIONS	3		$0
730-00	ELECTRICAL	4		$0
735-00	SPECIAL EFFECTS	4		$0
740-00	SPECIAL SHOOTING UNITS	4		$0
745-00	SET DRESSING	4		$0
750-00	PROPERTIES	5		$0
755-00	WARDROBE	5		$0
760-00	MAKEUP & HAIRSTYLISTS	6		$0
765-00	PRODUCTION SOUND	6		$0
770-00	TRANSPORTATION	6		$0
775-00	LOCATION EXPENSE	7		$0
780-00	PROCESS PHOTOGRAPHY	7		$0
785-00	PRODUCTION DAILIES	7		$0
790-00	LIVING EXPENSE	8		$0
795-00	FRINGES	8		$0
797-00	TESTS	8		$0
798-00	FACILITIES FEES	8		$0
	Total Production			**$0**

Fig. 9–1. Movie Magic Budgeting software's Paramount budget form (courtesy IFP/Los Angeles Independent Filmmaker's Manual).

800-00	EDITING	8		$0
810-00	MUSIC	9		$0
820-00	POSTPRODUCTION SOUND	9		$0
830-00	STOCK SHOTS	10		$0
840-00	TITLES	10		$0
850-00	OPTICALS, MATTES, INSERTS	10		$0
860-00	LABORATORY PROCESSING	10		$0
870-00	FRINGES	10		$0
	Total Post Production			**$0**
910-00	ADMINISTRATIVE EXPENSES	10		$0
912-00	PPC INTERNAL	11		$0
920-00	PUBLICITY	11		$0
	Total Other			**$0**
	TOTAL ABOVE-THE-LINE			**$0**
	TOTAL BELOW-THE-LINE			**$0**
	TOTAL ABOVE & BELOW-THE-LINE			**$0**
	GRAND TOTAL			**$0**

Fig. 9–1. (continued)

BLANK BUDGET (PARAMOUNT FORM)

PRODUCTION NUMBER: DATE:
PRODUCER: LOCATIONS:
DIRECTOR: DAYS:
SCRIPT DATE: WEEKS:
START DATE:
FINISH DATE: NOTE:

Acct#	Description	Amount	Units	X	Rate	Subtotal	Total
600-00	**STORY**						
600-01	RIGHTS PURCHASED						$0
600-03	WRITERS						$0
600-04	SCREENPLAY PURCHASE						$0
600-05	RESEARCH						$0
600-06	SECRETARIAL						$0
600-11	SCRIPT COPYING						$0
						Total For 600-00	$0
610-00	**PRODUCER**						
610-01	EXECUTIVE PRODUCER						$0
610-02	PRODUCER						$0
610-06	PRODUCER'S ASSISTANT						$0
						Total For 610-00	$0
620-00	**DIRECTOR**						
620-01	DIRECTOR						$0
620-02	STORYBOARD ARTIST						$0
620-03	TECHNICAL ADVISOR						$0
620-04	RESEARCH CONSULTANT						$0
620-05	CASTING DIRECTOR						$0
620-08	CASTING EXPENSES/FEES						$0
						Total For 620-00	$0
630-00	**CAST**						
630-01	PRINCIPAL PLAYERS						$0
630-02	DAY PLAYERS						$0
630-03	REHEARSAL						$0
630-04	STUNT PERFORMERS						$0
630-05	SAG RESIDUALS						$0
630-06	LOOPING/ADR						$0
630-07	MEAL PENALTIES						$0
630-08	OVERTIME						$0
630-09	MEDICAL EXAMS						$0
630-10	CHILDREN'S TUTOR						$0
						Total For 630-00	$0

Fig. 9–1. (continued)

Acct#	Description	Amount	Units	X	Rate	Subtotal	Total
640-00	**FRINGES**						
						Total For 640-00	**$0**
650-00	**TRAVEL & LIVING**						
650-01	PRODUCERS						$0
650-02	DIRECTOR						$0
650-03	WRITER						$0
650-04	FOCUS PULLER						$0
650-05	STORYBOARD ARTIST						$0
650-06	CAST TRAVEL, LIVING & P...						$0
650-07	CHAPERONES						$0
						Total For 650-00	**$0**
	Total Above-The-Line						**$0**
700-00	**EXTRA TALENT**						
700-01	SIDELINE MUSICIANS						$0
700-02	EXTRAS AND STAND-INS						$0
700-03	WELFARE WORKERS						$0
700-04	PAYROLL FRINGES						$0
700-05	EXTRAS CASTING						$0
						Total For 700-00	**$0**
705-00	**PRODUCTION STAFF**						
705-01	LINE PRODUCER/UPM						$0
705-02	PRODUCTION COORDINAT...						$0
705-03	1ST ASSISTANT DIRECTOR						$0
705-04	2ND ASSISTANT DIRECTOR						$0
705-05	3RD ASSISTANT DIRECTOR						$0
705-06	SCRIPT SUPERVISOR						$0
705-08	PRODUCTION ACCOUNTANT						$0
705-09	ASST. DIRECTOR TRAINEE						$0
705-10	PRODUCTION ASSISTANTS						$0
705-11	PREPRODUCTION EXPEN...						$0
						Total For 705-00	**$0**
710-00	**CAMERA**						
710-01	DIRECTOR OF PHOTOGRA...						$0
710-02	OPERATOR						$0
710-03	1ST ASSISTANT CAMERA...						$0
710-04	2ND ASSISTANT CAMERA...						$0
710-05	FILM LOADERS						$0
710-06	STILL PHOTOGRAPHER						$0
710-08	CAMERA RENTALS						$0
710-09	CAMERA SUPPLIES						$0
710-11	CAMERA ACCES./VIDEO E...						$0

Fig. 9–1. (continued)

Acct#	Description	Amount	Units	X	Rate	Subtotal	Total
710-00	**CAMERA (CONT'D)**						
710-20	LOSS, DAMAGE, AND REP...						$0
						Total For 710-00	**$0**
715-00	**SET DESIGN**						
715-01	PRODUCTION DESIGNER						$0
715-02	ART DIRECTOR						$0
715-03	SET DESIGNER/LEADMAN						$0
715-04	SWING GANG						$0
715-05	ART RENTALS						$0
715-06	PURCHASES/SUPPLIES						$0
715-07	RESEARCH						$0
715-10	BOX RENTAL						$0
						Total For 715-00	**$0**
720-00	**SET CONSTRUCTION**						
720-01	CONSTRUCTION LABOR						$0
720-02	CONSTRUCTION MATERIALS						$0
						Total For 720-00	**$0**
721-00	**SET STRIKING**						
						Total For 721-00	**$0**
722-00	**MINIATURES**						
						Total For 722-00	**$0**
725-00	**SET OPERATIONS**						
725-01	KEY GRIP						$0
725-02	BEST BOY GRIP						$0
725-03	CRANE/DOLLY GRIP						$0
725-04	EXTRA GRIPS/COMPANY...						$0
725-05	CAMERA DOLLIES						$0
725-06	CAMERA CRANES						$0
725-07	TARPING AND DIFFUSION						$0
725-08	GRIP EQUIPMENT RENTALS						$0
725-09	GRIP EQUIPMENT PURCH...						$0
725-10	GRIP BOX RENTALS						$0
725-11	CRAFT SERVICEMAN						$0
725-12	CLEANUP AND TRASH						$0
725-13	STANDBY NURSERYMEN						$0
725-14	STANDBY PAINTERS						$0
725-15	STANDBY SECURITY						$0
725-19	FIRST AID						$0
725-21	ELECTRICAL HOOKUPS						$0
725-22	HEATING/AIR CONDITIONING						$0
725-23	DRESSING RM. INSTALL						$0
725-24	DRESSING ROOM RENTALS						$0

Fig. 9–1. (continued)

Acct#	Description	Amount	Units	X	Rate	Subtotal	Total
725-00	**SET OPERATIONS (CONT'D)**						
725-25	MISCELLANEOUS EXPENSE						$0
725-30	LOCATION LOAD AND UNL...						$0
						Total For 725-00	$0
730-00	**ELECTRICAL**						
730-01	GAFFER						$0
730-02	BEST BOY						$0
730-03	LAMP OPERATORS/ELECT...						$0
730-04	LOCATION RIGGING/STRIKE						$0
730-05	GLOBES/CARBONS/SUPP...						$0
730-06	POWER						$0
730-07	GENERATOR RENTAL						$0
730-08	ELEC. EQUIP. RENTAL						$0
730-09	ELEC. EQUIP. PURCHASE						$0
730-10	BOX RENTAL						$0
730-11	STUDIO GENERATOR OPE...						$0
730-12	LOCATION GENERATOR OP...						$0
730-13	MISC. EXPENSE						$0
730-15	LOC. ELEC. MAINTENANCE						$0
730-20	LOSS, DAMAGE, AND REP...						$0
						Total For 730-00	$0
735-00	**SPECIAL EFFECTS**						
735-01	CO. SPECIAL EFFECTS MAN						$0
735-02	ASST SPECIAL EFFECTS...						$0
735-03	MANUFACTURING - SHOP...						$0
735-04	STANDBY PROPMAKERS						$0
735-08	SPEC. EFFECTS EQUIP RE...						$0
735-09	SPEC. EFFECTS PURCHAS...						$0
735-10	SPECIAL EFFECTS BOX R...						$0
735-11	ADDED SPECIAL EFFECTS						$0
						Total For 735-00	$0
740-00	**SPECIAL SHOOTING UNITS**						
740-01	UNIT #1						$0
740-02	UNIT #2						$0
740-03	UNIT #3						$0
740-04	UNIT #4						$0
740-05	UNIT #5						$0
						Total For 740-00	$0
745-00	**SET DRESSING**						
745-01	SET DECORATOR						$0
745-02	LEADMAN						$0
745-02	SWING GANG						$0
745-03	SET DRESSING - ALTER/M...						$0

Fig. 9–1. (continued)

Acct#	Description	Amount	Units	X	Rate	Subtotal	Total
745-00	**SET DRESSING (CONT'D)**						
745-04	SET DRESSING PURCHASED						$0
745-05	SET DRESSING RENTALS						$0
745-07	SET DRESSING CLEAN & ...						$0
745-08	DRAPERY RENTALS						$0
745-09	DRAPERY PURCHASES						$0
745-11	DRAPERY INSTALL & STRI...						$0
745-12	DRAPERY MANUFACTURE						$0
745-13	DRAPERY CLEAN & DYE						$0
745-14	CARPET-INSTALL-STRIKE						$0
745-16	CARPET PURCHASES						$0
745-20	LOSS, DAMAGE & REPAIR						$0
745-25	MISCELLANEOUS EXPENSE						$0
						Total For 745-00	**$0**
750-00	**PROPERTIES**						
750-01	PROPERTY MASTER						$0
750-02	ASSISTANT PROPERTY M...						$0
750-03	EXTRA PROP MEN						$0
750-04	PICTURE VEHICLE - L&M						$0
750-05	PICTURE VEHICLE RENTALS						$0
750-06	ANIMALS & LIVESTOCK						$0
750-07	HANDLERS/WRANGLERS						$0
750-08	PROP RENTALS						$0
750-09	PROP PURCHASES						$0
750-10	PROP BOX RENTALS						$0
750-11	ANIMAL FEED & STABLING						$0
750-12	EXPENDABLES						$0
750-19	PICTURE VEHICLE PURCH...						$0
750-20	LOSS, DAMAGE & REPAIRS						$0
						Total For 750-00	**$0**
755-00	**WARDROBE**						
755-02	ASSISTANT WARDROBE						$0
755-03	ASSISTING WARDROBE						$0
755-04	COSTUME DESIGNER						$0
755-05	WARDROBE MANUF - L&M						$0
755-06	ALTERATIONS - L&M						$0
755-07	CLEANING & DYEING						$0
755-08	WARDROBE RENTALS						$0
755-09	WARDROBE PURCHASES						$0
755-10	HAND BOX RENTALS						$0
755-20	LOSS, DAMAGE & REPAIRS						$0
						Total For 755-00	**$0**

Fig. 9–1. (continued)

Acct#	Description	Amount	Units	X	Rate	Subtotal	Total
760-00	**MAKEUP & HAIRSTYLISTS**						
760-01	MAKE-UP ARTISTS						$0
760-02	EXTRA MAKE-UP ARTISTS						$0
760-03	BODY MAKE-UP ARTISTS						$0
760-04	KEY HAIR STYLIST						$0
760-05	EXTRA HAIR STYLISTS						$0
760-06	WIG & HAIR PURCHASE						$0
760-07	WIG & HAIR RENTAL						$0
760-09	MAKEUP SUPPLIES/APPLI...						$0
760-10	MAKE-UP/HAIR KIT RENTA...						$0
						Total For 760-00	$0
765-00	**PRODUCTION SOUND**						
765-01	SOUND MIXER						$0
765-02	BOOM MAN						$0
765-03	SOUND RECORDER						$0
765-04	CABLE MEN						$0
765-05	PLAYBACK OPERATOR (A...						$0
765-06	SOUND EQUIP RENTALS						$0
765-07	PLAYBACK EQUIP RENTAL						$0
765-11	MISCELLANEOUS EXPENSE						$0
						Total For 765-00	$0
770-00	**TRANSPORTATION**						
770-01	MESSENGER SERVICE						$0
770-02	TRANSPORTATION COORD.						$0
770-02	DRIVER CAPTAIN						$0
770-03	STANDBY DRIVERS						$0
770-04	STANDBY VEHICLES						$0
770-05	MILEAGE ALLOWANCE						$0
770-06	FUEL						$0
770-07	PICTURE CAR DRIVERS						$0
770-08	LOCATION DRIVERS						$0
770-09	LOCAL HIRE DRIVERS						$0
770-10	LOC. VEHICLES/TRUCKS						$0
770-11	CAMERA DEPARTMENT						$0
770-12	CONSTRUCTION DEPART...						$0
770-13	DRAPERY DEPARTMENT						$0
770-14	SOUND DEPARTMENT						$0
770-15	ELECTRICAL DEPARTMENT						$0
770-16	GRIP DEPARTMENT						$0
770-17	LABOR DEPARTMENT						$0
770-18	PAINT DEPARTMENT						$0
770-19	PRODUCERS OFFICE						$0
770-20	LOSS, DAMAGE, REPAIRS						$0
770-21	PRODUCTION DEPARTMENT						$0
770-22	PROPERTY DEPARTMENT						$0

Fig. 9–1. (continued)

Acct#	Description	Amount	Units	X	Rate	Subtotal	Total
770-00	**TRANSPORTATION (CONT'D)**						
770-23	PUBLICITY DEPARTMENT						$0
770-24	SOUND DEPARTMENT						$0
770-25	SPECIAL EFFECTS DEPT						$0
770-26	WARDROBE DEPARTMENT						$0
770-27	ALL OTHER DEPARTMENTS						$0
770-28	ALL OTHER TRANSPORTA...						$0
770-35	STUDIO RENTAL CHARGES						$0
						Total For 770-00	**$0**
775-00	**LOCATION EXPENSE**						
775-01	SURVEY EXPENSE						$0
775-02	LOCATION STAFF						$0
775-03	SITE RENTALS/PERMITS/L...						$0
775-04	HOTEL & LODGING						$0
775-05	CATERING SERVICES						$0
775-06	MEAL ALLOWANCES/EXT...						$0
775-07	PRODUCTION EXPENDABL...						$0
775-08	TRASH FEES/CARTAGE						$0
775-11	FIREMAN/POLICE						$0
775-14	AIRPORT PICK UP/DELIVE...						$0
775-15	LOCATION LOAD & UNLOAD						$0
775-16	MISCELLANEOUS TRANSP...						$0
775-17	GRATUITIES						$0
775-18	OFFICE-RENT/FURNITURE						$0
775-19	LOCATION MEDICAL EXPE...						$0
775-20	SHIPPING						$0
775-21	LOCATION SECURITY						$0
775-22	PARKING LOTS						$0
						Total For 775-00	**$0**
780-00	**PROCESS PHOTOGRAPHY**						
780-01	INSTALL/HOOKUP EQUIP						$0
780-02	PROCESS CAMERAMAN						$0
780-03	VIDEO DESIGN & PLAYBACK						$0
780-04	OTHER PROCESS LABOR						$0
780-05	PROCESS BACKGROUND...						$0
780-08	PROCESS EQUIPMENT RE...						$0
780-09	RENT/PURCHASE/MFG. PL...						$0
						Total For 780-00	**$0**
785-00	**PRODUCTION DAILIES**						
785-01	NEGATIVE RAW STOCK						$0
785-02	DEVELOPING						$0
785-03	PRINT DAILIES						$0
785-04	SOUND RECORDING TAPE						$0
785-05	TRANSFER SOUND DAILIES						$0

Fig. 9–1. (continued)

Acct#	Description	Amount	Units	X	Rate	Subtotal	Total
785-00	**PRODUCTION DAILIES (CONT'D)**						
785-07	CODING DAILIES						$0
785-08	SCREEN DAILIES						$0
785-09	VIDEO TAPE TRANSFERS						$0
785-10	TAPE STOCK						$0
						Total For 785-00	**$0**
790-00	**LIVING EXPENSES**						
790-01	LIVING EXPENSES-CONTR...						$0
790-02	OTHER LIVING EXPENSES						$0
790-03	FARES-OTHER THAN TO L...						$0
						Total For 790-00	**$0**
795-00	**FRINGES**						
						Total For 795-00	**$0**
797-00	**TESTS**						
797-01	TEST #1						$0
797-02	TEST #2						$0
797-03	TEST #3						$0
797-04	TEST #4						$0
						Total For 797-00	**$0**
798-00	**FACILITIES FEES**						
798-01	STAGE CONSTRUCTION						$0
798-02	STAGE SHOOTING						$0
798-03	STAGE HOLDING						$0
798-04	OFFICE SPACE						$0
798-05	TESTS/INSERTS/PROMOS						$0
						Total For 798-00	**$0**
	Total Production						**$0**
800-00	**EDITING**						
800-01	FILM EDITOR						$0
800-02	SOUND EFFECTS EDITING						$0
800-03	MUSIC EDITING						$0
800-04	NEGATIVE CUTTING						$0
800-06	PROJECTION						$0
800-07	CONTINUITY SCRIPTS						$0
800-11	EDITORIAL FACILITIES						$0
800-12	EDITORIAL SUPPLIES						$0
800-14	POSTPROD. SUPERVISION						$0
800-17	OTHER COSTS						$0
800-18	ASSISTANT EDITOR						$0

Fig. 9–1. (continued)

Acct#	Description	Amount	Units	X	Rate	Subtotal	Total
800-00	**EDITING (CONT'D)**						
800-19	APPRENTICE EDITOR						$0
						Total For 800-00	$0
810-00	**MUSIC**						
810-08	COMPOSER						$0
810-09	CONDUCTOR						$0
810-10	SONGWRITER						$0
810-11	LYRICIST						$0
810-21	RECORDING MUSICIANS						$0
810-22	SINGERS & VOCAL COAC...						$0
810-23	ORCHESTRATORS & ARRA...						$0
810-24	COPYISTS & PROOFREAD...						$0
810-25	MUSIC SUPERVISOR						$0
810-26	MUSIC CLEARANCE SALA...						$0
810-27	MUSIC CLERICAL						$0
810-28	MASTER USE LICENSES						$0
810-29	MUSIC PUBLISHING LICEN...						$0
810-30	PRESCORE						$0
810-31	REHEARSAL MUSICIANS						$0
810-32	DEMO COSTS						$0
810-33	SCORE (FACILITIES)						$0
810-34	STUDIO EQUIPMENT RENT...						$0
810-35	MUSIC INSTRUMENT RENT...						$0
810-36	MUSIC INSTRUMENT CART...						$0
810-37	MUSIC TRANSFERS						$0
810-38	NEW USE/REUSE (MUSICI...						$0
810-39	NEW USE/REUSE (SINGERS)						$0
810-40	TRAVEL & PER DIEM						$0
810-41	PAYROLL TAXES/FRINGES						$0
810-42	PHONO						$0
810-43	MUSIC RESEARCH REPOR...						$0
						Total For 810-00	$0
820-00	**POSTPRODUCTION SOUND**						
820-01	DIALOGUE RECORDING (A...						$0
820-02	NARRATION RECORDING						$0
820-03	SOUND EFFECTS (FOLEY)						$0
820-06	DUBBING SESSION						$0
820-07	SOUND TRANSFERS						$0
820-09	PURCHASED SOUND EFFE...						$0
820-11	SOUND TRANSFER 35 & 3...						$0
820-12	MAGNETIC TAPE FOR EDIT						$0
820-13	OPTICAL NEG 35 & 35/32						$0
820-14	PREVIEW EXPENSES						$0
						Total For 820-00	$0

Fig. 9–1. (continued)

Acct#	Description	Amount	Units	X	Rate	Subtotal	Total
830-00	**STOCK SHOTS**						
830-01	LIBRARY EXPENSE						$0
830-03	LABORATORY PROCESSING						$0
830-09	RENTAL & PURCHASE						$0
						Total For 830-00	$0
840-00	**TITLES**						
840-01	TITLES (MAIN & END)						$0
840-02	MAIN TITLES						$0
840-03	END TITLES						$0
840-04	MISCELLANEOUS TITLES						$0
840-05	LABORATORY PROCESSING						$0
						Total For 840-00	$0
850-00	**OPTICALS, MATTES, INSERTS**						
850-01	OPTICAL EFFECTS/DUPE...						$0
850-02	MASTER POSITIVES						$0
850-03	LABORATORY PROCESSING						$0
850-04	SPECIAL PHOTO EFFECTS						$0
850-05	INSERTS						$0
850-11	PURCHASES						$0
						Total For 850-00	$0
860-00	**LABORATORY PROCESSING**						
860-01	REPRINTING & DEVELOPING						$0
860-02	1ST TRIAL COMPOSITE P...						$0
860-03	MASTER POSITIVE PRINT						$0
860-04	DUPLICATE NEGATIVES						$0
860-06	DEVELOP SOUND NEGATI...						$0
860-07	ANSWER PRINT						$0
860-17	LEADER & MISCELLANEOUS						$0
						Total For 860-00	$0
870-00	**FRINGES**						
						Total For 870-00	$0
	Total Post Production						$0
910-00	**ADMINISTRATIVE EXPENSES**						
910-01	ACCOUNTING & TERMINAL...						$0
910-02	MPAA CERTIFICATE						$0
910-03	POSTAGE & STATIONERY						$0
910-04	PHOTOCOPYING (No Scripts)						$0
910-05	LEGAL EXPENSE & FEES						$0
910-06	TELEPHONE/FACSIMILE						$0
910-09	MATERIAL MGMT PURCHA...						$0
910-12	PREVIEW EXPENSE						$0

Fig. 9–1. (continued)

Acct#	Description	Amount	Units	X	Rate	Subtotal	Total
910-00	ADMINISTRATIVE EXPENSES (CONT'D)						
910-14	PARKING LOT EXPENSES						$0
910-15	CELLULAR PHONES						$0
910-17	OFFICE RENT & OTH EXPE...						$0
						Total For 910-00	$0
912-00	PPC INTERNAL						
912-02	RENT-STUDIO OFFICES						$0
912-03	PARKING FEES-STUDIO						$0
						Total For 912-00	$0
920-00	PUBLICITY						
920-01	UNIT PUBLICIST						$0
920-02	SPEC. STILL PHOTOGRAP...						$0
920-03	STILL FILM & PROCESSING						$0
920-05	PUBLICITY STAFF - T&E						$0
920-09	SPACE MEDIA						$0
920-11	OUTSIDE SERVICES						$0
						Total For 920-00	$0
	Total Other						$0
	TOTAL ABOVE-THE-LINE						$0
	TOTAL BELOW-THE-LINE						$0
	TOTAL ABOVE & BELOW-THE-LINE						$0
	GRAND TOTAL						$0

Fig. 9–1. (continued)

the amount of money needed at any given time during the production. To ensure a continuing stream of money, the producer must be able to advise the financiers or bank on a weekly or monthly payment schedule. Because payroll is due weekly, the common cycle is a week. The cash-flow chart also helps to determine whether the production is still operating within budget. This financial blueprint serves as a cost-controlling device as well. Budgeted and actual expenses are compared, and differences are quickly spotted.

To create the cash-flow chart, the PM lists each function and major expense item as in the production budget, but structures this information after the production's timetable: the amount needed during the first week of preproduction, the amount needed four weeks before the start of production (perhaps the art department needs much money for construction), the amount needed two weeks before production (for down payments on location sites, for example), and so on. The bulk of the money is usually spent during principal photography for salaries, equipment rentals, location costs, film stock, and lab expenses.

The exact date when the payments will be required for particular items depends on the specific circumstances of the production. For example, equipment rental fees sometimes are due at the end of the rental period after a sizable down payment has been made at the beginning; all location permit fees are sometimes due before actual shooting; and the deposit to the SAG sometimes extends its permissible minimum. Because all these items are negotiated and determined anew for each production (some by the PM, some by the producer), these fees will vary each time. As a rule of thumb, the producer tries to delay actual cash expenses for as long as possible because interest on the money must be paid to the bank. The PM must bear this in mind when negotiating contracts and other legal agreements.

10

Insurance

Production companies are not legally required to carry any insurance other than (1) workers' compensation and employer's liability, and (2) comprehensive general and automobile liability (CGAL). The first is required at all times and everywhere; the second is required only when commercial filming is conducted outside a studio on state, county, city, or private property, or on any other location requiring a permit. It is customary and sensible, however, to put together an insurance package that addresses the potential problems and risks of the production. It is a good idea to have a broker put together the best deals, usually he or she researches a variety of different insurance companies and is not bound to any specific one.

When purchasing insurance, production companies generally ask an insurance company or broker to examine the screenplay and a detailed budget and provide estimated quotes for all coverages they should consider. Naturally, the ideal insurance package varies with each production, depending on the nature of the film. Documentary and commercial production companies usually obtain an annual producer's insurance policy (PIP) that combines various types of insurance.

Generally, a fee of about 2–3 percent of the total budget—the premium— is calculated. The actual fee will depend on the following:

- Size of budget;
- Location of shooting;
- Duration of principal photography;
- Number, ages, and physical condition of cast members; number, ages and physical key crew members such as Director or DOP;
- Value of equipment, props, sets, wardrobe;
- Unusual exposures and risks.

The final item is especially important and should be discussed with the insurance agent prior to filming. The existence of the following factors can strongly influence the premium to be paid:

- Distant locations (insurance coverage is usually in effect 24 hours a day);

- Unusual or dangerous activities (scenes involving airborne aircraft, motorcycles, violent stunts, etc.);

- Boats, ships, and harbors (production personnel scheduled to film on boats or ships or around harbors could fall within compensation areas with generally much broader benefits, reserved to U.S. federal law);

- Use of animals, railroad cars or equipment, underwater filming or pyrotechnics.

The different types of coverage generally offer deductibles of varying amounts, depending on the limits of the required insurance.

Based on the above criteria, the production company makes a deposit premium during the preproduction period. After the production period is complete, the insurance adjuster conducts a final audit and evaluates any changes made during production to the original screenplay, schedule, and estimate, and he or she adjusts the premium accordingly.

The insurance company issues certificates of insurance, which name the insured production company, the coverages, and the certificate holder, who is an additional insured party. The certificate holders generally comprise all the individual companies from which the production company rents equipment or to which it applies for filming permits. Copies of the certificates of insurance are kept by the insurance company, the production company, and the certificate holders.

Types of Insurance

The remainder of this chapter presents brief, nontechnical descriptions of the various types of insurance coverage available. For detailed contractual information, the production company should contact an insurance agent or broker.

Preproduction Cast Insurance

This policy reimburses the producer for legal liabilities that take place prior to the sickness, injury, or death of one or two principal actors and/or the director. However, this coverage is only in effect if the sickness, injury, or death causes the producer to abandon the project completely because of the unavailability of the insured.

Workers' Compensation and Employer's Liability

State laws require production companies to carry this coverage, which applies to all permanent and temporary cast and crew members. It pays for hospital and medical bills and provides disability or death benefits for any cast or crew member who becomes injured or dies in the course of employment. Specifically, this coverage provides the following benefits:

- Medical care. The employee is entitled to all medical and surgical expenses that might be required to cure or relieve injury. In a serious case, the employee is entitled to the services of a consulting physician of the employee's choosing.

- Temporary disability. An employee who misses work due to an on-the-job injury is entitled to compensation for time lost. Benefits generally begin on the fourth day following an injury. When the disability lasts longer than 21 days or results in the employee being hospitalized, benefits begin from the first day of injury. Currently, the weekly benefit is based on 66.33 percent of the worker's actual wages, subject to a maximum of $266 weekly.

- Permanent disability. If an employee's injury results in a permanent disability, the extent of the disability is determined, and the benefits are based on (1) the degree of total or partial disability, (2) the employee's earnings, (3) his or her age, and (4) his or her occupation. The determination of benefits is usually made by the Industrial Accident Commission.

- Death. When an on-the-job injury results in death, the benefit for the surviving spouse is subject to a maximum of $95,000. Where there is a surviving spouse and one or more dependent minor children, the award is $115,000. A burial allowance of $5,000 is granted in each case.

Workers' compensation and employer's liability insurance is usually in effect 24 hours a day while employees are on location away from their homes. This coverage can be obtained in one of three ways, depending on the state in which the production takes place: (1) through a private insurance company, (2) through a state fund, and (3) through a self-insurance program. People who classify themselves as independent contractors are usually considered employees as far as workers' compensation is concerned.

The California Workers' Compensation Act states that employees shall be entitled to medical expense and compensation for time lost from work due to injury or illness arising during the course of their employment. An employer who does not carry this insurance for an injured employee (1) is liable for any payments required by law, just as if the policy were in effect, (2) might be required to pay attorney's fees, and (3) might be subject to a 10 percent penalty, based on the amount of the award, if the failure to provide insurance is judged to be "willful". Failure to secure this coverage is, in itself, sufficient proof of "willfulness". (The provisions of this insurance may not necessarily apply to employers in other states, but most workers' compensation laws are quite similar nationwide.)

Payroll Considerations—Workers' compensation rates are based on job classifications, and the actual rates charged are based on the type of work employees perform. The production company is expected to maintain accurate payroll records that reflect which classifications apply. Employees may be assigned to one of three different job classifications. Each classification carries a description of the job function and has a code number assigned it. The classifications are as follows:

1.   Motion picture production (code 9610). This classification applies to all employees involved in filming operations, including talent and production crew. For payroll audit purposes, the entire production crew is reported on the basis of the total gross payroll. The payroll for the director, production manager, assistant directors, and talent is reported separately, subject to a maximum reportable salary of $1,000 per week per person regardless of actual salary. The current premium rate for this classification is $3.93 per $100 of salary. It is even higher when special hazards exist. Full-time permanent production employees are reported under this classification only when they are actually involved in film production activities.

2.   Motion picture development of negatives, printing, and editing (code 4360). This classification applies to all production personnel whenever they are not involved in film production duties and to all preproduction and postproduction functions, including editing employees. This classification carries a lower rate (currently $2.20 per $100 of payroll) than code 9610 due to a lesser degree of accident exposure.

3.   Clerical office employees (code 8810). This classification includes all office employees not involved in filming or editing activities. Corporate executives and most producers are eligible for this classification unless they have direct responsibilities during filming operations.

The insurance company requires the producer to submit periodic payroll reports, called voluntary audit reports, with payroll figures assigned properly to the respective classifications. All temporary production crew personnel or talent hired for a particular production are considered employees, and their salaries must be reported in the same manner as those of permanent employees.

Comprehensive General and Automotive Liability

Comprehensive General and Automotive Liability (CGAL) coverage is required before filming on any city or state road or at any location that requires filming permits or certificates. It protects the production company against claims for bodily injury and/or property damage caused by an employee during the course and scope of company business. The coverage includes the use of all nonowned vehicles, both on and off camera, including physical damage to these vehicles. Owned automobile insurance covers vehicles registered to, produced by, or purchased by the production company. The following are the minimum insurance coverages applicable in Los Angeles:

General city requirements, $1 million;

Department of Water and Power property, $2 million;

Harbor Department property (water areas), $3 million;

Aircraft use, $5 million.

Automobile liability "owned", "hired" or "nonowned" coverage in the amount of $500,000 (for student film productions reduced coverage of $100,000–300,000) is required.

The acceptable evidence of required insurance coverage is a city form called the Additional Insured Endorsement. This form must be filled out and signed by a representative of the insurance company, which also keeps copies of these on hand.

Cast Insurance

This coverage reimburses the production company for any extra expense necessary to complete the principal photography of an insured production due to the death, injury, or sickness of an insured performer or director. The insured individuals must undergo a physical examination before coverage begins, and the examination cost is paid by the production company. The coverage is usually subject to certain named exclusions, such as hazardous activities, stunts, and non-commercial flying. The coverage usually begins two to four weeks before the start of principal photography and covers seven people, including the director. Additional people can be added for a nominal cost. The cast furthermore may be insured covering the postproduction phase if they are needed for dubbing or other activities.

Props, Sets, and Wardrobe

This type of insurance covers company-owned property and the property of others, including props, sets, scenery, costumes, wardrobe, and similar theatrical property, against all risks of direct physical loss, damage, or destruction occurring during production.

Extra Expense

Extra expense coverage reimburses the production company for any additional out-of-pocket expenses needed to complete principal photography for an insured production due to the damage or destruction of property (props, sets, or equipment) or facilities (such as a location site) intended for use in the production. The damage must have led to the interruption, postponement, or cancellation of the production. This coverage includes losses due to faulty generator operation but excludes damage or interruption caused by rain.

Third-Party Property Damage

This coverage pays for the damage, destruction, and loss of property of others while the property is in the care, custody, or control of the production company and is used or would have been used in an insured production. For example, this insurance covers damage to a house being used as a location site. It does not cover liability for destruction or damage of property caused by the operation of a motor vehicle, aircraft, or watercraft, including damage to these vehicles, or liability for damage to any property rented or leased that may be covered under props, sets, and wardrobe or miscellaneous equipment insurance.

This coverage is not included under the comprehensive liability policy. The property damage coverage included in that policy excludes damage to property in the production company's care, custody, or control.

Miscellaneous Equipment

Miscellaneous equipment insurance covers the production company against all risks of direct physical loss, damage, or destruction to cameras, camera equipment, sound, lighting (including breakage of globes), and grip equipment owned or rented by the production company. This coverage is subject to certain exclusions, such as mechanical breakdown. It can be extended to cover mobile equipment vans, studio location units, and similar vehicles for an additional premium.

Negative, Film, and Videotape

This coverage protects against all risks and covers all costs incurred in reshooting as a result of direct physical loss, damage, or destruction of raw film or tape stock, exposed film (developed or undeveloped), recorded videotape, soundtracks and tapes, and work prints up to the amount of the insured production cost.

Coverage is continuous until the answer print is made, but it does not include losses caused by fogging; faulty camera or sound equipment; faulty developing, editing, processing, or manipulation by the camera operator; exposure to light, dampness, or temperature changes; errors of judgment in exposure, lighting, or sound recording; or use of the incorrect type of raw film stock or tape. This coverage, due to common postproduction workflow techniques, nowadays extends to computer-stored data as well.

Faulty Stock, Camera, and Processing

This insurance reimburses the production company for any additional out-of-pocket expenses incurred in reshooting as a result of damage to negative film, videotape, soundtracks, work prints, and tapes from faulty raw stock; faulty camera, sound recording, or editing equipment; faulty processing; or accidental erasure of videotape recordings. The coverage does not include loss caused by errors of judgment in exposure, lighting, or sound recording; use of the incorrect type of raw stock; or faulty manipulation by the camera operator or sound recordist. This coverage can only be purchased with the negative, film, and videotape coverage.

Money and Securities

This insurance covers cash on hand at any one location and cash on hand at all locations and usually is limited to $50,000.

Office Contents or Business Personal Property

This insurance generally is obtained on an annual basis and is more for the production company than the individual production.

Errors and Omissions

Errors and omissions insurance covers the production company's legal liability and defense against lawsuits alleging unauthorized use of titles, formats, ideas, characters, or plots; plagiarism; unfair competition; or breach of contract. It also protects against alleged libel, slander, defamation of character, invasion of privacy, wrongful portrayal, copyright infringement, and so on.

It does not cover punitive damages. Distributors usually require this coverage before they will release a theatrical or television production.

Clearance Procedures—Before applying for errors and omissions liability insurance, the production company should follow these clearance procedures:

1. The script must be reviewed by the applicant's attorney before commencement of the production to eliminate material that might be defamatory, that invades someone's privacy, or that might otherwise be actionable. The coverage cannot be bound until the insurance carrier's clearance attorney has approved the complete application.

2. Unless the work is an unpublished original not based on any other work, a copyright report must be obtained and submitted with the application. Both domestic and foreign copyrights and renewal rights should be checked. If a completed film is being acquired, a similar review should be made of copyright and renewals on any copyrighted underlying property.

3. If the script or story is an unpublished original, the origins of the work should be determined, including basic idea, sequence of events, and characterizations. It should be ascertained whether the applicant has received submissions of any similar properties, and if so, why the submitting party may not claim theft or infringement should be described in detail.

4. Before the final title selection, a title clearance should be obtained from a title clearance firm. The title of the production is excluded from coverage until a satisfactory title report is obtained. The fee for obtaining a title clearance may range from $150 to $250, depending on research time involved.

5. Whether the production is fictional, with identifiable locations, or factual, no names, faces, or likenesses of any recognizable living persons should be used unless written releases have been obtained. Release is unnecessary if a person is part of a crowd scene or is shown in a fleeting background shot. The term "living persons" includes thinly disguised versions of living persons readily identifiable because of the identity of other characters or because of the factual, historical, or geographic setting.

6. Releases are not required for members of the Screen Actors Guild, the American Federation of Television and Radio Artists (AFTRA), or the Screen Extras Guild because they are compensated for their performances. Releases obtained from living persons, as described in the preceding paragraph, should conform to the language used in the sample personal release (see Chapter 8).

7. If music is used, the applicant must obtain all necessary synchronization and performance licenses.

8. Written agreements must exist between the applicant and all creators, authors, writers, performers, and anyone else who provides material (including quotations from copyrighted works) or on-screen services.

9. If distinctive locations, buildings, businesses, personal property, or products are filmed, written releases should be obtained. This is unnecessary if non-distinctive backgrounds are used.

10. If the production involves actual events, the applicant must ascertain whether the author's sources are independent and primary (contemporaneous newspaper reports, court transcripts, interviews with witnesses, and so on) and not secondary (another author's copyrighted work, autobiographies, copyrighted magazine articles, and so on).

11. A final shooting script must be submitted with the complete application. If the production is a documentary, a shooting outline or treatment should be submitted.

Excess Liability

Excess liability insurance provides additional coverage in case the regular $1 million combined single limit is insufficient. For example, permits for the use of Los Angeles Harbor and Airport facilities involve a $5 million combined single limit.

Guild/Union Accident Insurance

This coverage meets motion picture and television guild and union contract requirements, including those of the International Alliance of Theatrical Stage Employees, Moving Picture Technicians, Artists, and Allied Crafts . . . (known as IATSE), the National Association of Broadcast Employees & Technicians (NABET), the SAG, and the DGA, for aircraft accidental death insurance for production company cast or crew members. The coverage is blanket, and limits of liability meet all signatory requirements.

Nonowned Aircraft Liability

This coverage is required when an airplane or helicopter is rented, leased, or borrowed for use as a picture plane for scouting locations or for aerial photography.

Animal Mortality

Animal mortality insurance protects the production company against loss or destruction of animals used in connection with a production. The value of the animals must be established before their use, and current veterinarian certificates are required for full mortality coverage.

Guild- and Union-Required Insurance Benefits

Table 10.1 provides an overview of the insurance provisions of various guild and union agreements. Individual cases should be discussed with an insurance agent or broker.

Table 10–1. Guild and Union Insurance Requirements

Guild/ Union	Regular Travel	Plane Travel	Helicopter Travel	Hazardous Work
DGA	$200,000	$250,000	$350,000	$350,000
SAG		100,000	250,000	1–2 million
SEG		50,000		
WGA	200,000	250,000	350,000	
IATSE	100,000		100,000	100,000
NABET	50,000		100,000	
AFTRA	100,000			
Teamsters	100,000	100,000		

11

Completion Bonds

Simply stated, a completion bond is a contractual agreement that guarantees that a film is finished and delivered or, if abandoned, that investors are reimbursed for out-of-pocket losses in case the production exceeds the budget. Spelled out more clearly this means that the completion guarantee assures the bank, Fonds or financiers that (a) the producers will complete and deliver the picture in accordance with the screenplay, budget and production schedule that the bank, Fonds or financiers approved; or (b) the guarantor will complete and deliver the picture in accordance with such pre-approved screenplay and production schedule, and advance any sums in excess of the pre-approved budget necessary to do so; or (c) in the event that the production is abandoned, the guarantor will fully repay all sums invested in the picture by the bank, Fonds or financiers. Of course, completion bond companies can only insure that the film is physically completed; no guarantee is made of its artistic, creative or commercial value. In addition, the completion bond company does not guarantee that additional funds will be provided for the project. When dealing with bank financing and/or private investor's financing it has become absolutely necessary for the producer to obtain a completion bond—while the procedure of arranging for a bond may be of little concern for the production manager, in preproduction and even more so during production and postproduction he will have to deal with the requirements posted by the completion company on a daily basis. The completion bond company is entitled to and usually demands daily production reports as well as thorough accounting at any time. The production manager needs to be aware that meeting the bond company's requests and/or attending to the bond company's agents is time-consuming.

Completion bonds, also called completion guarantees, originated in Europe in the late 1950s. Contrary to film production in the U.S., which was dominated by major studios with little or no use for completion bonds, overseas producers were truly independent and usually dealt with several outside sources of financing. Thus, the need for completion bonds arose to protect investors' interests.

With the current increased involvement of European banks and Film Investment Fonds in American film financing, completion bonds have become almost standard in every production with a budget of more than $2 million. Although a producer might want to secure a completion bond for a lower-budget production, completion bond companies show little enthusiasm for small films because the ratio of their overhead costs to the customary 3–4 percent fee (based on the overall budget, excluding the 10 percent contingency) is not very attractive. For the completion bond company, the same amount of work and risk is involved regardless of the size of the production to be insured. The risk of a low-budget production may actually be greater; of course; actual risk depends on the screenplay and on other elements of the production, such as cast, crew, director, and producer. However, due to ever-increasing competition among completion bond companies, it is worthwhile to shop around.

In recent years, the advent of video, television, and foreign presales and publicly or privately sold limited partnerships as a means of film financing has also increased the need for completion bonds to insure investors, financiers, and lenders against the failure to complete a picture. These parties generally have almost no possibility of effectively controlling the day-to-day use of their funds during production, and the completion bond company basically functions as their watchdog during all phases of preproduction, production, and postproduction. In addition, domestic banks will not lend money without a completion bond guarantee.

Although the responsibility for arranging for a completion bond belongs to the executive producer or the producer, it might be the production manager's job to fulfill or oversee the specific requirements of a completion bond. Obtaining a bond generally requires the producer to provide the completion bond company with the following documentation and information:

1. Shooting script;
2. Detailed production budget;
3. Shooting schedule (production boards);
4. Preliminary application for completion guarantee;
5. Résumés of key personnel and principal cast members;
6. Rights and underlying rights agreements in regard to script;
7. Producer's agreement between company and producer;
8. Director's agreement between production company and director;
9. Key crew agreements;
10. Production agreement/financing agreement;

11. Evidence of insurance coverage that includes filmmaker as additional loss payee;

12. Signed agreement by producer and director to cast, to budget, and to limit expenses;

13. Signed agreement by director that budget, shooting schedule, and postproduction schedule are achievable and that allocation of film stock in budget is sufficient;

14. Principal artists' contracts;

15. Postproduction schedule (to be provided as soon as practical but no later than two weeks before end of principal photography);

16. Signed agreement that music and all relevant clearances are obtained within budget;

17. Music agreements;

18. Signed agreement that any delivery requirements pursuant to distribution agreement and any publicity costs in excess of approved budget are considered distribution costs and expenses, and will not be chargeable to production;

19. Film and sound laboratory agreements;

20. Signed agreement that legal fees charged to production budget are limited to amount budgeted;

21. Distribution agreements, if any.

The completion bond company (guarantor) analyzes certain elements of the package—from budget to screenplay to choice of key personnel—to evaluate the soundness of the production. The guarantor's main concern is whether the production can be completed and delivered on time and within budget without substantially tapping into the contingency amount. Thorough discussions between the guarantor and the production's key personnel take place to review and evaluate the production schedule and other preparations for the production. The producer, director, and PM are asked to sign off on the screenplay, budget, and production schedule, confirming that all parties agree to produce the film in accordance with these elements. On the other hand—despite its triggering higher costs and financing—it is comforting to get a green light from a bond company because it shows that the project is sound in its planning and overall evaluation.

The completion bond is the final step a producer takes after complete financing, casting, staffing, production arrangements, presales, and distribution agreements, if applicable, are all in place. If a picture is completely privately financed or if none of the investors or lending parties requires a completion bond, the producer need not acquire one. Generally, a picture can be safely produced with an appropriate and adequate film insurance package, general contracts, and a competent staff and crew.

The completion bond company has the right to ask the producer to hire additional production personnel if it deems it necessary to guarantee the completion and delivery of the film. This is true during all phases of production; the company can recommend or install PMs and can dismiss or hire anyone during the course of the production, including producer, director, or star. However, very rarely is it necessary or desirable for the completion bond company to exercise these rights. Frequently, just the threat of doing so brings difficult personnel, directors, or actors into line. The producer generally has the same goal as the completion bond company—to finish the picture in time and within budget—and in cases of unavoidable delays (such as those caused by weather), even a completion bond company cannot do any better.

Completion Bond Contract

The following excerpts from a standard completion bond contract spell out in great legal detail the understanding, rights, and obligations between producer and completion bond company. The contract consists of the Producer's Agreement and the Completion Guarantee.

Producer's Agreement

1. Production of the Film

    a.   . . . Producer shall produce the film in accordance with the Approved Screenplay, the Approved Production Schedule, and the Approved Budget and in compliance with all of the provisions hereof and of the Production Agreement. Producer shall not, without the prior written consent of Guarantor, make or agree to make any variation or modifications in such Approved Screenplay, Approved Production Schedule, or Approved Budget or in the personnel or other details of Production that have been approved by Guarantor. Notwithstanding the foregoing, however:

    (i) To the extent permitted by the Production Agreement, Producer may make minor changes in the Approved Screenplay, Approved Production Schedule, and Approved Budget that are required by the customary exigencies of production and that, in Guarantor's sole discretion, individually and in the aggregate do not result and are not likely to result in either an increase in the cost of Production of the film, or a delay in the delivery thereof; and

    (ii) Producer may, after written notice to Guarantor, make such changes that may result in an increase in the cost of Production if

Producer deposits or causes to be deposited to the Production Account for the film sums that, in Guarantor's sole discretion, are at least equal to such increased cost of Production that may result.

b. The individual Producer, Executive Producer, Director, Production Supervisor, Production Accountant, principal members of the cast, Director of Photography, and all other key personnel for the film shall be subject to the written approval of, and engaged using forms of agreement approved in writing by, Guarantor. No changes in such personnel or modifications or amendments to any such agreement shall be made without Guarantor's written consent. No agreements for such personnel will contain any provision that will or might allow such personnel to be unavailable to the Producer after a stipulated date or by reason of any event or contingency, unless the Guarantor otherwise consents in writing.

c. Producer undertakes that the cost of each of the following items will not exceed the budgeted allowance therefore in the Approved Budget:

(i)   Personnel costs, including, but not limited to, directors, technical personnel, and cast;

(ii)   Living and/or travel expense;

(iii) Legal fees, bank charges, and/or loans;

(iv) Music, sound recordings, and all associated worldwide clearances;

(v)   Trailers, promotional films, and other advertising material included in the Approved Budget;

(vi) Additional or protective material (so-called "cover shots") required for the release of the film on network television or other exhibition requiring a particular rating, censorship clearance, or similar standards;

(vii) Foreign language versions included in the Approved Budget.

To the extent that the items set forth in c, (i) and (ii) exceed the allowances in the Approved Budget as a result of a force majeure event (as customarily understood in the motion picture industry), or such excess is recovered pursuant to any contract of insurance, the requirement set forth in the immediately succeeding sentence shall not apply thereto. . . .

d. . . . Producer shall prepare daily status reports that will be delivered to Guarantor in _____ or such other location as Guarantor shall specify every day during Production, shall prepare weekly cost statements and promptly submit copies thereof to Guarantor at such location as Guarantor shall specify and shall at all times keep Guarantor informed of the progress of Production and the plans for continuing Production and completing the film. Producer shall submit to Guarantor copies of any estimates, reports, or statements of costs that

Guarantor requests or that Producer submits or is required to submit to Beneficiary or any third party.

e.   . . .

f.   . . . Producer shall maintain an account called the "Production Account" in the _____ branch of the _____ bank, separate from Producer's other funds, into which shall be paid all funds advanced pursuant to the Production Agreement or otherwise advanced or invested for the production of the film. . . .

g.   . . . Guarantor or its representatives shall at all times have the right to visit studios, locations or elsewhere to observe production of the film and to view "dailies" or rough cuts and may at all reasonable times inspect Producer's accounts, books and records relating to the film and make copies thereof or take extracts therefrom. . . .

h.   . . .

i.   . . . Producer shall promptly and faithfully comply with Guarantor's directions with regard to the production of the film, including the dismissal of any person engaged in the production of the film or the engagement of other persons in addition to or in substitution for such persons, to correct, avoid, and ameliorate any matter that Guarantor, in its sole discretion, deems to involve a risk of liability being incurred under the Guarantee; provided, however, that no such instructions may require breach of the provisions of the Production Agreement or any other contractual obligation of Producer with respect to the film that has been approved in writing by Guarantor, unless the consent of the party with whom Producer has such contractual obligation has been obtained. . . .

2.   Insurance

a.   . . . Producer shall immediately obtain, pay the premiums for, and thereafter maintain in force, such insurance coverage with respect to the film as set forth in exhibit _____ attached hereto. Guarantor will be named as an additional insured under all liability insurance policies and as to the loss payee under all other insurance policies. . . .

Typical insurance coverage:

- Film Package: Cast;
- Props, Sets, Wardrobe;
- Extra Expense;
- Third-Party Property Damage;
- Miscellaneous Equipment;
- Negative Film Risk;
- Faulty Stock, Camera, and Processing;

- Union/Guild;

- Producer's Liability (a.k.a. Errors and Omissions);

- Comprehensive General;

- Excess Umbrella;

- Third-Party Property Damage;

- Workers' Compensation;

- Comprehensive Auto Liability and Property Damage.

b.   . . .

c.   . . . Producer shall provide, pay for, and maintain such further insurance in such amounts as shall be reasonably specified in writing by Guarantor from time to time and shall modify or extend its insurance policies to the extent necessary in order to ensure that full insurance is in effect at all times until completion and delivery of the film. . . .

3.   Takeover

a.   . . . Guarantor shall have the right, but not the obligation, to take over the production of and complete the film in compliance with the requirements of the Guarantee at any time after the occurrence of any of the following events:

(i)   Guarantor believes, in its sole discretion, that the course of Production will or might result in the liability of Guarantor under the Guarantee for costs or expenses of Production;

(ii)   Producer does not carry out instructions given by Guarantor pursuant to paragraph _____;

(iii)   Producer defaults as provided in paragraph _____ hereof or otherwise breaches any other provision of the Agreement and fails to remedy such default or breach immediately upon written notice thereof.

b.   Prior to taking over Production as foresaid, Guarantor shall notify Beneficiary and Producer. Within forty-eight (48) hours of receipt of such notice, Beneficiary may, but need not, take over Production of the film and/or Beneficiary or Producer may advance additional funds (or furnish a guarantee for such funds to be paid as and when required, in form and substance satisfactory to Guarantor) in an amount deemed by Guarantor, in its sole discretion, to be sufficient to cover the anticipated overbudget costs. . . .

c.   . . . If Guarantor takes over Production, it shall be deemed to do so as an assignee of Producer. Producer shall, concurrently with the execution hereof, execute a Production Account Takeover Letter and

Laboratory Access Letters, and deliver the same to the banks and laboratories referred to therein placing the Production Account and all film material at the disposal and under the sole control of Guarantor. In addition, upon Takeover of Production by Guarantor, Producer shall place at Guarantor's disposal and under its control all persons and equipment employed or used by Producer in connection with the film. . . .

d.   . . .

e.   . . .

f.   . . . Producer may, at any time, with the written consent of Beneficiary and Guarantor, relieve Guarantor of all of its obligations under the Guarantee, in which event Guarantor shall, if it has not theretofore expended or advanced any sums pursuant to the Guarantee, waive any rights of "takeover" it may have hereunder. . . .

Exhibit A: Production Account Takeover Letter

To

_____ Bank

Name of Account _____

Gentlemen and/or Ladies: _____

By countersigning this letter, you hereby acknowledge and agree that:

1.   In consideration of [Completion Bond Guarantor] guaranteeing completion of the film presently entitled _____ for which the above account was established, the undersigned has executed a Takeover Agreement giving Guarantor authority, in lieu of the undersigned, to exercise control over the account at any time it may so desire. Please confirm to Guarantor that upon presentation of a copy of the Takeover Agreement executed on the _____ day of _____ [year], a copy of which is attached hereto as exhibit, you will permit such signatories as may be designated by Guarantor to have exclusive control of the account and to operate on the account in lieu of all signatories authorized by the undersigned and that thereafter you will only pay checks signed by such designees of Guarantor in lieu of the undersigned.

2.   The undersigned hereby releases you from any and all claims, demands, and liabilities, without limitation, arising from your compliance herewith or with the instructions of Guarantor pursuant to the aforesaid Takeover Agreement.

3.   You will not exercise any right of "set-off" or similar right with respect to the account based upon any claims that you may have against the undersigned or any third parties and you acknowledge that Guarantor, in reliance upon such agreement, is agreeing to guarantee completion of the film.

Kindly acknowledge the within instructions and authorization and your acceptance thereof in the acknowledgment and acceptance space provided below.

Sincerely,

By _____

Acknowledged and accepted

_____ Bank

By _____

Exhibit B: Laboratory Access Letter Sender's address
[film laboratory]

To _____

Completion Bond Guarantor

Gentlemen:

We have been informed that you are about to enter into or have entered into agreements with Producer and Beneficiary pursuant to which you will guarantee completion of the now presently entitled film _____ and that pursuant to said agreements you have, under certain conditions, the right to take over production of the film.

At the request of Producer and in order to induce you to enter into the foregoing agreements with the Producer and the Beneficiary, we are executing this Agreement relating to the film for the benefit of you and the Producer. We represent to you that we have entered into arrangements with the Producer whereby we will have, as the same are produced, in our possession and under our control, at our laboratory located at _____, all film and sound materials and properties relating to the film including, but not limited to, the original film negative.

If you shall advise us in writing that you have taken over Production of the film under the aforesaid agreements:

a.   We agree that you and your duly authorized licensees and designees shall at all times have complete, free, and exclusive access to all materials and properties of or relating to the film now or hereafter in our possession or under our control;

b.   We acknowledge that you have the right to remove any or all of such materials and properties of or relating to the film from our laboratory, and we agree that our records shall indicate that all such materials and properties are being held by us in your name and exclusively for your account;

c.   We agree to fill all your orders and those of your duly authorized licensees and designees for prints or any other film materials of any kind as well as for any other laboratory work pertaining to the film at prices not higher than our then-prevailing prices. Except upon your written request or pursuant to your written direction, we shall not allow any of such materials or properties to be removed from our laboratory.

We represent and agree that we do not have, and shall not assert against you or any of your licensees and designees, any claim or lien, statutory or otherwise, against the film or any of the materials or properties of or relating thereto, which now or hereafter may be held by us by reason of any work, labor, service, or material that we may perform or furnish to any party other than yourselves.

We agree that we shall not permit the removal at any time, whether or not you notify us that you have taken over the production of the film from our laboratory of any of the original film negative or other original material of or relating to the film, without your prior written consent.

We agree that the instructions, authorizations, directions, agreements, and representations herein contained in favor of you and your licensees and designees are coupled with an interest on your part and may not be revoked, rescinded, or modified without written consent. We represent that the technical quality of the materials in our possession is suitable for commercially acceptable color prints.

Sincerely,

_____ Laboratory

By _____

Exhibit C: Takeover Agreement

As an inducement to [Completion Bond Company/Guarantor] to guarantee completion, and in consideration of the Guarantor guaranteeing completion of the film _____ described as follows:

Presently titled _____

Based on literary material consisting of a screenplay written by _____

based upon _____ written by _____

to be produced by _____

and directed by _____

The Producer and Beneficiary hereby agree that if the Guarantor, in its sole judgment, shall deem it probable that the film will not be completed as scheduled in compliance with the Approved Screenplay and within the Approved Production Schedule and Approved Budget, as defined in the Agreement dated _____ between Producer and Guarantor (the Producer's Agreement), with reference to Guarantor guaranteeing completion of the film, or if Producer, or any person or entity under its direction or control, violates any of the terms and conditions of the Producer's Agreement, . . . Guarantor may take and assume sole and exclusive possession of all property, assets, materials, facilities, contracts, and rights relating to or in connection with the film and the Production thereof, including, but not limited to, such funds as then remain in the Production accounts and including, but not limited to, the right to demand and receive from any person or entity the remaining amounts, if any, of their respective loans or advances committed to be advanced in connection with the film and use them in such manner as the Guarantor, in its sole discretion, may determine for the completion of the film, as provided in the Producer's Agreement and in the Guarantee.

In the event the funds remaining in the Production Account upon takeover and the remainder of the Beneficiary's committed loans or advances, duly and timely advanced, are not sufficient to complete the film, the Guarantor is required to advance sums to complete the film, or if Guarantor shall advance funds to complete the film without exercising takeover, Producer and Beneficiary hereby assign to Guarantor as it becomes due all of the income payable to Guarantor in accordance with the terms of the Producer's Agreement for the purpose of Guarantor's recoupment until such time as the entire amount contributed by Guarantor including reasonable and customary expenses (to be documented by Guarantor), plus interest to be computed at the prime rate of Guarantor's bank, plus one percent (1%), has been repaid, at which time the Guarantor's participation in such income shall cease.

Any entity which may owe the Producer any sums as a result of the production, distribution, exhibition, or other exploitation of the film is hereby irrevocably directed to pay directly to Guarantor any amount owed to the Producer until Guarantor has been repaid in accordance with the terms of the paragraph next preceding. In order to exercise the rights given Guarantor by this Agreement, Producer hereby gives the following power of attorney, which may be reproduced as necessary.

Executed this _____ day of _____, _____ [year]

By [Producer] _____

By [Beneficiary] _____

Exhibit D: Individual Producer/Director* Agreement

I understand that _____ (Guarantor) is guaranteeing completion of the presently entitled film _____ with respect to which I am to be the individual Producer/Director*, and that as a condition of providing such Guarantee, Guarantor has been given the right to have one or more representatives on the film who will have certain rights and privileges as defined in said Guarantee, and may, under certain circumstances, take over and complete the film.

I agree to exercise my best efforts to produce/direct* the film in accordance with the Production Agreement and in accordance with the Approved Screenplay, Approved Budget, and Approved Production Schedule. I agree to fully cooperate with and assist Guarantor at all times, to reply in writing within 24 hours to any questions relating to the film submitted by Guarantor and to cooperate with and assist Guarantor or its designees in the event Guarantor shall take over the film or otherwise. I have reviewed the Approved Screenplay, Approved Budget, and Approved Production Schedule, and in my professional opinion, the film can be completed in accordance with the Approved Screenplay on schedule and within budget as set forth in the Approved Production Schedule and Approved Budget.

Producer/Director* _____

Date _____

*Strike out if not applicable.

4.   Additional Affirmative Covenants

   a.   . . .

   b.   . . . Producer shall keep proper books and records in which full, true, correct, and timely entries will be made of all of its dealings in connection with the film in accordance with generally accepted accounting principles. Guarantor shall have the right at all times to examine such books and records and make extracts therefrom. . . .

   [Items c through g omitted]

5.   Representations and Warranties

   a.   . . .

   b.   . . . Guarantor and Beneficiary have approved the Approved Screenplay, Approved Production Schedule, and Approved Budget for the film and Producer has acquired all motion picture rights, television rights, and all ancillary, subsidiary, and allied rights, now known or hereafter devised, in respect of the source material (if any) and Approved Screenplay necessary for the production and distribution of the film as contemplated hereby and by the Production Agreement. . . .

   c.   . . .

   d.   . . . Producer has delivered to Guarantor fully executed copies of all studio and location agreements for the production of the film. Producer has not entered into any studio or location agreements that are not in writing and delivered to the Guarantor and will not enter into any further studio or location agreements without the written approval of Guarantor.

   e.   Producer has obtained and delivered to Guarantor fully executed copies of all agreements with the individual Producer, Executive Producer, Director, director of photography, production supervisor, production accountant, principal members of the cast, and all other key personnel for the film, all of whom have been approved by the Beneficiary and the distributors of the film (to the extent that they are subject to such approval) and by Guarantor in writing and each of whose agreements is binding and enforceable and in a form approved by Guarantor in writing. . . .

   [Items f through l omitted]

6. Negative Covenants

    a. . . . Producer shall not sell, assign, transfer, lease, license, or otherwise encumber all or any portion of the film, the Approved Screenplay, the source material, or the ancillary, subsidiary, and allied rights with respect thereto, or Producer's interest in any of the foregoing without the prior written consent of Guarantor.

    b. . . .

7. Indemnification and Recoupment

    [Recoupment provisions are generally negotiated in relation to the particular circumstances and conditions of each film. Customarily, recoupment occurs only after the cost of production of the film has been recouped first and after the recoupment of the financiers' and investors' interest as well. The completion bond company usually recoups any monies they have advanced toward the completion and delivery of the film in second position after recoupment of the principal financiers.]

8. Security Interest and Lien

    [If a film is financed through several sources, especially with the aid of bank loans, and, as is common, uses SAG actors, different security interests often are potentially in conflict. Discussions are necessary to order the competing security interests; for this the various guarantors, banks, or Screen Actors Guild have established individual forms of subordination agreements.]

9. Default

    a. . . . Producer shall be deemed in default if:

        (i) Producer defaults in the observance or performance of any covenant or condition contained or implied by law in this Agreement or in the Production Agreement or of any mortgage or lien to, or agreement with, any person relating to the film or any property used in connection with Production of the film. . . .

        (ii) . . .

        (iii) . . . Payment of any sum due hereunder is not made by Producer within five (5) days of written demand therefore by Guarantor. . . .

        (iv) . . .

        (v) . . .

    b. . . . If Producer is in default hereunder, in addition to all other rights and remedies that Guarantor may otherwise have hereunder or under applicable law:

        (i) All monies or sums payable by Producer to Guarantor hereunder shall become immediately due and payable together with interest thereon at the rate equal to the prime rate charged by Guarantor's bank plus one percent (1%);

(ii) Guarantor may appoint a receiver of the collateral upon such terms as to compensation and otherwise as Guarantor shall see fit and may, from time to time, remove the receiver so appointed and appoint another in his place;

(iii) Guarantor (or receiver) shall be the agent of the Producer and shall have the power in connection with the Production of the film and subject always to the terms and provisions hereof and of the Production Agreements:

> A.   to take possession of and collect collateral;
>
> B.   to take over Producer's functions in relation to the film for this purpose to raise or borrow any money that may be required upon the security of the whole or any part of the collateral;
>
> C.   to appoint managers, agents, and employees at such salaries and for such periods as it (the insurance company) may determine;
>
> D.   to sell, transfer, assign, or lease the interest of Producer in the film and rights relating thereto and all other collateral or otherwise to deal therewith in any manner that, in its discretion, it thinks is in the interests of Guarantor, the Beneficiary and the production of the film. . . .
>
> [Items E through H omitted]

10. Fees
[While the standard completion bond fee has been 5–6 percent of the production budget (excluding the 10 percent contingency), fees recently have come down, due to increased competition, to about 3–4 percent.]

11. Waiver

> a.   . . .
>
> b.   . . .

12. Notices

> a.   . . .

13. Credit

> a.   . . . The Guarantor shall be entitled to screen credit on the negative and all positive copies of the film on a separate card, in size (all dimensions) as large as the largest credit accorded in the end titles, as follows: Completion Guarantee supplied by _____ [name];
>
> b.   . . .

14. Miscellaneous

[Items a through d omitted]

Completion Guarantee

This Agreement made this _____ day of _____, _____ [year] by and between _____ (Beneficiary) and _____ (Completion Bond Company) _____ [address] is entered into with reference to the following facts:

A. Beneficiary has entered into an Agreement ("Production Agreement") dated _____ with _____ ("Producer"), a copy of which is attached hereto as exhibit _____, pursuant to which Beneficiary will provide or cause to be provided to Producer the sum of US$ _____ towards the cost of Production of a tentatively titled film _____ ("film"). Such sum shall be deposited in a bank account ("Production Account") established by the Producer for such purpose on an "as needed" basis in accordance with a cash-flow schedule to be approved in writing by Guarantor and Beneficiary, with Producer (or Guarantor in the event of "takeover") having the right to accelerate such payments if required by the exigencies of Production;

B. The sum to be provided by Beneficiary as set forth in paragraph A above equals the amount of the final budget dated _____ for the film including the contingency, both of which have been approved by Beneficiary and Guarantor (in the aggregate, the "Approved Budget");

C. Producer has entered into an agreement ("Producer's Agreement") dated concurrently herewith with Guarantor with reference to the Production of the film, and Beneficiary acknowledges that it has been furnished with a copy of the Producer's Agreement and has approved all the terms and conditions thereof.

For valuable consideration as set forth herein, Guarantor hereby guarantees the completion of the film and delivery thereof upon and subject only to the following terms and conditions:

1. The term "completion of the film" means production of the film in all material aspects in accordance with the Production Agreement, as amended from time to time with the prior written approval of Guarantor or in accordance with any other agreements substituted therefore with the prior written approval of Guarantor. "Delivery of the film" means delivery to Beneficiary or the laboratory designated by Beneficiary in the Production Agreement, of the items set forth in Schedule A attached hereto.

2. Guarantor hereby agrees and undertakes as follows:

   a. To advance to the Producer any sums in excess of the Approved Budget required to meet the cost of the delivery items of the film in accordance with the Production Agreement and the Approved Budget;

   b. To ensure that the Producer completes and delivers the film in the manner aforesaid;

c. If the Producer fails to complete and deliver the film in the manner aforesaid, the Guarantor will, at its sole election, and in lieu of its obligations under paragraphs 2(a) and 2(b) hereof, either:

(i) Complete and deliver the film or cause the same to be completed and delivered in the aforesaid manner and will provide such sums in excess of the Approved Budget as may be necessary to do so; or

(ii) Elect not to complete and deliver the film, declare an abandonment of the film, and pay the Beneficiary, from the monies remaining in the Production Agreement and from Guarantor's own funds, an amount equal to Beneficiary's actual out-of-pocket expenditures and guaranteed financial obligations to third parties with respect to the production of the film, which have previously been approved in writing by Guarantor and with respect to which Beneficiary has made or is required to make payment, upon receipt by Guarantor of evidence of the payment thereof by Beneficiary.

If Guarantor is required pursuant to this paragraph 2, Guarantor's obligation hereunder shall not in any event exceed _____.

3. The obligation of Guarantor under this Guarantee is subject to fulfillment of the following conditions precedent:

a. Guarantor shall have received its fee for this Guarantee in the amount of _____;

b. . . .

c. Guarantor shall have approved in writing all key personnel and other elements of the film, received, reviewed, and approved in writing the Approved Budget, Approved Screenplay, Approved Production Schedule (as those terms are defined in the Production Agreement), all insurance policies required in the Producer's Agreement, and final versions of all agreements with respect to the production of the film, including, but not limited to, the Production Agreement, music agreements, Director's agreements, facilities agreements, rights agreements, and key crew agreements. All of such agreements shall be delivered to the Guarantor immediately and Guarantor shall endeavor to review such documents as soon as practicable after receipt.

4. The Guarantor shall not in any way be responsible for any costs, damages, liabilities, expenses, or other sums caused directly or indirectly by:

a. Producer not having obtained title to, or license to use story, script, music, or other rights in connection with the film, including copyrights and titles, or the contents of the film infringing upon or violating, or claims being made that the contents of the film infringe upon or violate, the rights of others, including delay in the production or delivery of the film as a result thereof;

b. Failure of the film to conform with the requirements and standards of any group having censorship, seal, rating, or similar authority over films, wherever located;

c. (i) Hostile or warlike action in time of peace or war;

(ii) Any weapon employing atomic fission or radioactive force, whether in time of peace or war;

(iii) Insurrection, rebellion, revolution, civil war, usurped power, or action taken by governmental authority in hindering, combating, or defending against such an occurrence, seizure or destruction under quarantine or customs regulations, confiscation, nationalization, or destruction of or damage to property by order of any governmental or public authority, or risks of contraband or illegal transportation or trade;

d. The artistic quality of the film as a condition of delivery of the film or otherwise;

e. The requirement, or perceived requirement, of additional monies in excess of those expressly allocated in the Approved Budget for any of the following:

(i) Personnel costs, including, but not limited to, directors, technical personnel, and cast;

(ii) Living and/or travel expense;

(iii) Legal fees, bank charges, and/or loan costs;

(iv) Music, sound recordings, and all associated worldwide clearances;

(v) Trailers, promotional films, and other advertising material;

(vi) Additional or protective material (so-called cover shots) required for the release of the film on network television or other exhibition requiring a particular rating, censorship, clearance, or similar standard;

(vii) Foreign-language versions.

To the extent that the items set forth in subparagraph 4 e. (i) or (ii) exceed the allowance therefore in the Approved Budget as a result of a force majeure event (as customarily defined in the motion picture industry), or such excess is recovered pursuant to any contract of insurance, the exclusions set forth in subparagraphs 4 e. (i) and/or (ii), as the case may be, shall not apply.

f. Expenses for cutting, editing, reediting, rerecording, scoring, rescoring, dubbing, subtitling, or making any other changes in, or additions to, the film after delivery unless previously approved in writing by Guarantor;

g. Expenses incurred in providing, supplying, or delivering delivery items not set forth in the delivery items and not provided for in the Approved Budget;

h. Consequential damages (including, but not limited to, lost or deferred tax benefits) resulting from delay in the delivery of the delivery items beyond the delivery date specified in the Production Agreement;

i. Nuclear reaction or nuclear radiation or radioactive contamination, and whether such loss be direct or indirect, or be in whole or in part caused by, contributed to, or aggravated by the peril(s) covered by this Guarantee;

j. Claims or losses that are or would be covered by insurance that Producer has agreed to provide in the Producer's Agreement, which claims are not paid by the insurer because of some action or inaction of Producer or some act, event, or situation that Producer has permitted to occur or continue;

k. The bankruptcy or insolvency of Producer or beneficiary, any dishonest, fraudulent, or criminal act or omission of Producer or Beneficiary, or any material breach by Producer or Beneficiary hereof or of the Producer's Agreement;

l. Any category of cost not expressly provided for in the Approved Budget;

m. Changes in the Approved Budget, Approved Screenplay, or Approved Production Schedule that increase the cost of production of the film;

n. Abandonment by Producer or Beneficiary as the result of loss of any element or aspect of the film if such loss and cost of abandonment could have been insured.

5. . . .

6. . . .

7. Beneficiary acknowledges and agrees that any sums advanced or expended by Guarantor pursuant hereto, together with interest thereon at a rate equal to the prime rate charged by Guarantor's bank plus one percent (1%), shall be recouped by Guarantor out of the "gross receipts of the film" (as said term is defined in the Production Agreement) after the deduction of the following items only:

a. Distribution fees;

b. Distribution expenses;

c. Recoupment by Beneficiary of its actual out-of-pocket investment in the film up to the amount set forth in _____.

Such recoupment by Guarantor shall be made prior to the payment of any share of gross receipts to Producer or any other party or the payment to any party of any deferment or participation in the net profits or gross receipts of the film. No termination of this Agreement pursuant to any of the terms hereof shall affect in any way Guarantor's right to recoup any sums advanced or expended by Guarantor prior to such termination in the manner provided herein.

8.   Beneficiary shall promptly notify Guarantor regarding any knowledge that Beneficiary might have any material change(s) in the Producer's financial situation that might affect the film or the production thereof or that Producer has changed any key employee or other element of the film, has materially deviated from the Approved Screenplay, Approved Budget, or Approved Production Schedule, or has otherwise breached any term or condition of the Producer's Agreement.

9.   . . .

10. Notwithstanding anything to the contrary contained herein, if Guarantor either (a) believes Beneficiary is in breach of this Guarantee; or (b) anticipates exercise of its "takeover" rights under paragraph 2 c. (i), Guarantor shall deliver to Producer and Beneficiary written notice of either (a) the facts upon which Guarantor considers Beneficiary to be in breach; or (b) the facts upon which Guarantor anticipates exercising its "takeover" rights.

   Beneficiary shall have forty-eight (48) hours from the receipt of such notice to cure any alleged breach and/or to remedy the facts upon which Guarantor anticipates a takeover. . . .

   If beneficiary exercises its "takeover" rights, Guarantor shall (a) be relieved of its obligations hereunder; (b)shall retain the fee paid to it hereunder; and (c) shall retain the right to recoup any sums advanced by it hereunder as provided in paragraph 7 hereinabove.

11. If Guarantor shall take over production of the film pursuant to paragraph 2 c. (i) hereof, Beneficiary and Producer shall provide Guarantor with all reasonable assistance required by Guarantor and shall cooperate with Guarantor in the completion and delivery of the film, including the replacement of any element involved in the film. If Guarantor intends to replace any element involved in the film that has been approved by Beneficiary, Guarantor shall consult with Beneficiary with respect thereto, but Guarantor's decision with respect to such replacement shall be final. In addition, Beneficiary and Producer shall cooperate with Guarantor in pursuing any valid claims against third parties responsible for delaying the delivery, or otherwise increasing the costs, of the film. In the event Beneficiary shall fail to provide, or shall fail to exercise its best efforts to have Producer provide, such cooperation and assistance as required by Guarantor, Guarantor shall so advise Beneficiary in writing and Beneficiary shall have forty-eight (48) hours from receipt of such

notice to cure such failure. This Guarantee and Guarantor's obligations hereunder shall terminate upon written notice from Guarantor, provided that such termination shall not be effective unless Beneficiary has not cured any such failure to cooperate or to use best efforts as aforesaid within such time period and provided that such failure materially affects the production and/or delivery of the film. Guarantor shall not be responsible for any costs incurred as a proximate result of Guarantor's waiting, under the provisions of this paragraph, for Beneficiary to cure any such failure.

[Items 12 through 17 omitted]

As completion bond companies and American studio and independent producers are looking toward the future, and as they anticipate ever-increasing international coproductions and international cofinancing, the global need for completion bonds will further increase. So will the need of completion bond companies to have seasoned production managers on their staffs to evaluate such productions to be bonded beforehand as well as monitoring them while they are in production and postproduction.

12

Film Festivals and Markets

Once the motion picture is complete—and if theatrical distribution or a television airdate is not set—you must show your picture to obtain exhibition, or if only to obtain some audience reaction. While this is really not part of a production manager's job, it might be of interest to you, the producer, anyway.

One of the few and relatively inexpensive ways to get your picture seen is during film festivals and (more expensive) film markets. It may happen that you and your film get invited; usually, however, you must attend to deadlines, send prints or tapes, and pay processing fees.

While film festivals are usually attended by a film-enthusiastic crowd (generally local or national, but sometimes international), television markets are for professionals only. Attendance fees are fairly high, and if you want to exhibit your product and rent a booth, very quickly expenses will exceed several thousand dollars. Markets are clearly delineated as motion picture, television product, music and multimedia, or interactive.

Literally hundreds of film festivals run throughout the world, and each tries to carve its special niche, to become known for its particular profile. Competition may get fierce. Despite, and because of this, many major and traditional film festivals insist they will show only local, regional, national, or world premieres. That of course means you must be very careful where you show your motion picture and how you plan to have the film and print "travel." A film older than two years very rarely has a chance of getting shown at a festival. Some festivals are known for cultural and publicity values, others are good places to make deals, and some offer both. By reading the trade papers or various trade magazines on a regular basis, you very quickly will get a feel for each festival's specializations; hence you can decide which festival or market serves your needs best. Information on festivals (deadlines, time of competition, fees, categories, awards, addresses, and so on) can easily be obtained via specialized books or the Internet. The search term "film festival" will give you links to hundreds of festivals throughout the world, many of which have their own websites.

In general, some criteria a producer should look for in a festival are as follows:

1.   Are the technical standards flawless? Will the festival guarantee that the projection of the film or the video presentation is state-of-the-art?

2.   Is it easy and convenient to communicate with prospective buyers of your product? Are rooms or facilities set aside where you can show materials, and meet with national and international clients and possible future partners? More and more festivals are involving themselves in arranging for possible coproducers to get to know each other: they schedule meetings well in advance, invite producers and their projects to pitch and be publicized in special "co-production-markets" booklets to be sent to every participating producer and production company. Independent producers may take advantage of the fact that producers from other parts of the country or world are there to meet for international coproductions. Especially in Europe, where film subsidies are part of almost every film-financing structure, these co-production markets are popular; however, everyone is looking for international partners from overseas too. Usually these markets are also attended by decision-makers from television stations, film subsidy agencies, world-sales agents, and film commissioners.

3.   Is the festival well attended by prospective buyers and future partners concerning coproductions and deal-making? What is the basic audience and participant structure at the festival? Are the audiences local, regional, national, or international? Is the press local, regional, national or international? Are the deal-makers local, regional, national or international?

4.   Does the festival have the infrastructure to effectively accomplish national and international public relations and press-work?

5.   Does the festival give out awards and prizes? If so, how good is their standing and are they attached to cash awards?

6.   Of what professional or cultural caliber is the committee that selects the program?

To obtain the maximum benefit from a festival, some or most of the following criteria should be fulfilled:

1.   Are personal boxes for professional visitors set up so you effectively can get in touch with anybody you want?

2.   Do press boxes allow you to share yourself and your motion picture effectively with the press?

3.   Can festival staff get you in touch with persons you want to meet?

4.   Are special events like dinners, invitations, and excursions planned, which you may attend?

5.   Does the festival provide press conferences regarding your film?

6.   Do guest lists exist that give you an overview of the attendees and how to get in touch with persons you want to meet?

7.   Does a festival catalog provide space and advertising possibilities for your film?

8.   Does the festival have office communication like phone, fax, and e-mail available for you?

These criteria have contributed to developing a certain ranking that shows how the U.S. entertainment business judges festivals and markets:

Top Ten for Executives	Top Ten for Film/TV Buyers	Top Ten for Film/TV Sellers
1. Cannes	1. Cannes	1. Cannes
2. AFM (American Film Market)	2. AFM	2. Mifed
3. Mifed	3. Mifed	3. AFM
4. Berlin	4. Berlin	4. Mip-TV
5. Venice	5. Mipcom	5. Mipcom
6. Toronto	6. Mip-TV	6. Berlin
7. Mip-TV	7. Toronto	7. Venice
8. Sundance	8. Venice	8. Toronto
9. Montreal	9. Sundance	9. NATPE
10. Tokyo	10. Tokyo	10. Tokyo

(*Source:* compiled from various articles in *Variety*)

CILECT lists the following festivals as especially interesting for student films and filmmakers:

Angers	European First Film Festival
Bologna	European Festival of Film Schools
Cannes	Cinéfondation
Clermont-Ferrand	International Short Film Festival
Lodz	Cameraimage

Munich	International Festival of Film Schools
Poitiers	Festival International des Ecoles de Cinéma
Potsdam	Worldwide Student Film Festival
Tampere	International Short Film Festival
Tel Aviv	International Student Film Festival

(*Source:* Centre International de Liaison des Ecoles de Cinema et de Télévision/International Association of Film and Television Schools, 2002)

Festivals are an excellent opportunity to get to know the players in the business. Networking is vital and essential to get future productions off the ground.

13

Film Schools

One way to gain experience and to break into the entertainment business is to study filmmaking at one of the many colleges, universities, or film schools. To find the most effective or appropriate school, be very specific about what personal goals you hope to achieve. Many schools offer a wide variety of courses, so be as clear as possible about your professional goals—whether you wish to become a screenwriter, director, director of photography, animator, producer, or scholar (a Master of Fine Arts degree will qualify you to teach at universities); these are but a few of the more prominent and clearly defined professions in the industry. Many of the qualifications you may obtain studying to become a producer however may be of value if you decide to move to a different professional field, for example into distribution or marketing. The better and the more thorough professional studies are, the better you will be qualified to change from your original career goal into fields related within the entertainment business. You may well find out that your interests are changing and you feel more comfortable in a profession you did not know much about when you started your studies.

Most colleges and universities offer courses in media studies, communication, or filmmaking, on both undergraduate and graduate levels, but very few actually teach standards and practices as they are in the film industry and as they are described in this book. Nevertheless, most school programs will give you enough training in screenwriting; video or film production; critical studies; film, video, or computer animation; and filmmaking to allow you at least to finish a feature-length screenplay or a short film that can serve as a calling card into the industry. The opportunity to make at least one short film is the biggest motivation that draws students to universities. Mostly, winning awards at film festivals presents opportunities for student films to gain some attention, possibly leading to more exposure at additional festivals or local television channels.

Everything that distinguishes you from other filmmakers is helpful in gaining attention and possible entry into Hollywood mainstream filmmaking. Some film schools or universities traditionally have ties to film festivals, as most major cities have their own festivals with national or international recognition.

Because networking is an essential part of becoming successful in the business, carefully evaluate any ties the school may have to the industry. These ties may be part of the curriculum, as when guest speakers or teachers are themselves active parts of the film industry, or they may be established by field trips or through film festivals.

Attending a film school, university, or college, however, is quite expensive, and usually you must pay for your film (material, lab costs, expenses, and so forth) in addition to tuition and other expenses. The school normally will supply equipment and postproduction facilities; also, you will meet other ambitious filmmakers who can help you with your own film. In evaluating a film school, check the level of technical equipment, cameras used, and postproduction equipment available. To what extent are the latest digital features part of the equipment? How up-to-date is the equipment you will use? To what extent is this equipment used in mainstream filmmaking?

Whether the required money and time to attend school is well spent, or whether it may be better trying to break into the business by becoming an intern at a film company, is a dilemma everyone must decide for themselves. It will be answered mainly by whether you possess a strong desire to make your "own" film right away, or if you prefer the slow, steady climb up the corporate ladder.

According to personal tastes and wishes, film schools and courses can be distinguished into mainly three different types:

1. *So-called "industry" schools that train students to become part of Hollywood filmmaking standards and enable them to fit requirements made by professional industry-like productions smoothly.* Students at these schools are trained to become either writers, directors, producers, or members of other clearly defined professions. Such schools are usually located at production centers such as Los Angeles, have strong ties to the industry, and are interested in gaining new talent from such a pool. These schools offer full-time graduate studies and fund student productions to a large degree.

2. *So-called "independent" schools that train students to become filmmakers familiar with all phases of filmmaking.* Students at these schools write, direct, and produce to the best of their capabilities and finish films in the best way possible—generally under low-budget restrictions and not necessarily in accordance with industry standards.

3. *So-called "experimental" schools that view filmmaking as an art form and the filmmaker as an artist who largely follows his or her*

own vision and who may not adhere to Hollywood-type filmmaking.
These departments are often situated at liberal arts colleges.

There is no safe way to a career in the Hollywood-type motion-picture film-making industry. While film schools in category 1 can provide connections into the business this does not automatically guarantee a job as desired by the student—competition is fierce and the industry usually already has all the talent it needs. The industry—they say—is always on the lookout for the fresh new vision, the bold idea, the concept that will gather large audiences—but in reality such wishes frequently are on paper only. If you want to pursue fresh new visions and bold ideas you may consider going to a type 2 or type 3 school where the restrictions of commercial filmmaking may be much less ingrained with teachers, personnel and fellow students.

The Internet offers ample information on film schools; almost every school or university can be accessed via their websites, which give a detailed picture of the studies and courses offered. For the industry-standard-oriented purpose of this book, only the first category of above-described schools is relevant. These are as follows: University of Southern California (USC), American Film Institute (AFI), University of California, Los Angeles (UCLA), Florida State University, Columbia University, and New York University (NYU) Interactive Telecommunications Program.

Indeed, many other schools offer the qualification and opportunity to obtain training and to make films that will attract attention. These are as follows: Bard College; California Institute of the Arts; Chapman University; City University of New York, City College; Columbia College, Chicago; Columbia University; Howard University; New York University; Northwestern University; Ohio University; San Francisco Art Institute; San Francisco State University; Savannah College of Art and Design; School of the Art Institute, Chicago; Southern Illinois University at Carbondale; Syracuse University; Temple University; University of Miami; University of New Orleans; University of Texas at Austin; University of Utah; University of Wisconsin, Milwaukee.

While the first set of schools mentioned has very close ties to the respective production communities and is regarded by those communities as the professional breeding ground where the first and foremost look for new talent, new scripts, new directors, or new producers, you still should be very aware that the need for new talent is far less than the amount of students trained at these and other schools.

If you cannot attend college or university, for example because you are already working and cannot find the time, you may find training opportunities at special courses, private schools or extension programs from established film schools designed just for professionals like you. Usually they are scheduled at weekends or at evenings; they may well suit your needs and will advance your career goals.

Appendix 1:
Selected Addresses

This appendix provides addresses for the national guilds, producers' organizations, relevant government offices, location scouting and permit services, and state film commissions.

National Guilds

American Federation of Musicians
7080 Hollywood Blvd, Suite 1020
Hollywood, CA 90028
(323) 461-3441

American Federation of Musicians
1501 Broadway, Suite 600
New York, NY 10036
(212) 869-1330

American Federation of Television &
  Radio Artists
5757 Wilshire Blvd, 9th Floor
Los Angeles, CA 90036
(323) 634-8100

American Federation of Television &
  Radio Artists
260 Madison Ave., 7th Floor
New York, NY 10016
(212) 532-0800

American Federation of Television &
  Radio Artists
One East Erie, Suite 650
Chicago, IL 60611
(312) 573-8081

Directors Guild of America, Inc.
7920 Sunset Blvd.
Los Angeles, CA 90046
(310) 289-2000

Directors Guild of America, Inc.
110 W. 57th St
New York, NY 10019
(212) 581-0370

Directors Guild of America, Inc.
400 N. Michigan Ave., Suite 307
Chicago, IL 60611
(312) 644-5050

Producers Guild of America
400 S. Beverly Dr., Suite 211
Beverly Hills, CA 90212
(310) 557-0807

Screen Actors Guild
5757 Wilshire Blvd
Los Angeles, CA 90036-3600
(323) 954-1600

Screen Actors Guild
1515 Broadway, 44th Floor
New York, NY 10036
(212) 944-1030

Screen Actors Guild
One East Erie, Suite 650
Chicago, IL 60611
(312) 573-8081

Screen Extras Guild, Inc.
5757 Wilshire Blvd
Los Angeles, CA 90036-3600
(323) 954-1600

Songwriters Guild of America
6430 Sunset Blvd, Suite 705
Hollywood, CA 90028
(323) 462-1108

Writers Guild of America, Inc.
7000 West 3rd St
Los Angeles, CA 90048
(323) 782-4520

Producers' Organizations

Alliance of Motion Picture and
    Television Producers
15503 Ventura Blvd
Encino, CA 91436
(818) 995-3600

Association of Independent
    Commercial Producers
11 East 22nd Street, 4th Floor
New York, NY 10010
(212) 475-2600

Contract Services Administration
    Trust Fund
15503 Ventura Blvd
Encino, CA 91436
(818) 995-3600

Government Offices

California State Information
601 Sequoia Pacific Blvd
Sacramento, CA 95814-0282
(213) 620-3030

Institute of Museum Services
1100 Pennsylvania Ave., NW, Room 510
Washington, DC 20506
(202) 786-0536

Los Angeles City Motion Picture/
    Television Affairs Office
6922 Hollywood Blvd, Suite 612
Los Angeles, CA 90028
(213) 461-8614

Los Angeles County Information
    Switchboard
(213) 974-4321

United States Information Agency
Television and Film Service
Patrick Henry Bldg, Room 5118
601 D St, NW
Washington, DC 20547
(202) 501-7764

Location Scouting and Permit Services

Association of Film Commissioners
    International
c/o Wyoming Film Office
I-25 & College Dr.
Cheyenne, WY 82002
(307) 777-3400

County of Los Angeles
Filming Permit Coordination Office
6922 Hollywood Blvd., Suite 606
Hollywood, CA 90028
(213) 957-1000

Los Angeles City
Film Permit Office 6922
Hollywood Blvd., Suite 602
Los Angeles, CA 90028
(213) 485-5324

United States Forest Service
National Media Office
444 E. Bonita Ave.
San Dimas, CA 91773
(818) 332-6231

State Film Commissions

Alabama Film Office
401 Adams Ave.
Montgomery, AL 36130
(800) 633-5898

Alaska Film Office
3601 C St, Suite 700
Anchorage, AK 99503
(907) 562-4163

Arizona Film Commission
3800 N. Central Ave.
Building D
Phoenix, AZ 85012
(800) 523-6695

Arkansas Motion Picture
   Development Office
I State Capitol Mall, Room 2C-200
Little Rock, AR 72201
(501) 682-7676

California Film Commission
6922 Hollywood Blvd, Suite 600
Hollywood, CA 90028
(213) 736-2465

Los Angeles Motion Picture and
   Television Division
(213) 461-8614

Colorado Motion Picture &
   TV Commission
1625 Broadway, Suite 1975
Denver, CO 80202
(303) 572-5444

Connecticut Film Commission
865 Brook St
Rocky Hill, CT 06067
(203) 258-4301

Delaware Development Office
99 Kings Hwy
P.O. Box 1404
Dover, DE 19903
(800) 441-8846

District of Columbia Mayor's Office
   of TV & Film
717 14th St, NW, 10th Floor
Washington, DC 20005
(202) 727-6600

Florida Film Bureau
107 W. Gaines St
Tallahassee, FL 32399
(904) 487-1100

Georgia Film & Videotape Office
P.O. Box 1776
Atlanta, GA 30301
(404) 656-7830

Hawaii Film Industry Branch
P.O. Box 2359
Honolulu, HI 96804
(808) 586-2570

Idaho Film Bureau
700 W. State St, 2nd Floor
Boise, ID 83720
(800) 942-8338

Illinois Film Office
100 W. Randolph, Suite 3-400
Chicago, IL 60601
(312) 814-3600

Indiana Tourism and Film
  Development Division
1 N. Capitol, Suite 700
Indianapolis, IN 46204-2288
(317) 232-8829

Iowa Film Office
200 E. Grand Ave.
Des Moines, IA 50309
(800) 779-3456

Kansas Film Commission
700 S.W. Harrison St
Topeka, KS 66603
(913) 296-4927

Kentucky Film Office
2200 Capital Plaza Tower
Frankfort, KY 40601
(800) 345-6591

Louisiana Film Commission
P.O. Box 44320
Baton Rouge, LA 70804-4320
(504) 342-8150

Maine Film Office
State House Station 59
Augusta, ME 04333
(207) 289-5707

Maryland Film Commission
601 N. Howard St
Baltimore, MD 21201
(410) 333-6633

Massachusetts Film Office
Transportation Building
10 Park Plaza, Suite 2310
Boston, MA 02116

Michigan Film Office
525 W. Ottawa
P.O. Box 30004
Lansing, MI 48909
(800) 477-3456

Minnesota Film Board
401 N. 3rd St, Suite 401
Minneapolis, MN 55401
(612) 332-6493

Mississippi Film Office
1200 Walter Sillers Bldg
P.O. Box 849
Jackson, MS 39205
(601) 359-3297

Missouri Film Office
P.O. Box 1055
Jefferson City, MO 65102
(314) 751-9050

Montana Film Office
1424 9th Ave.
Helena, MT 59620
(800) 548-3390

Nebraska Film Office
301 Centennial Mall, S.
P.O. Box 94666
Lincoln, NE 68509
(800) 228-4307

Nevada Motion Picture &
  TV Development
3770 Howard Hughes Pkwy,
Suite 925
Las Vegas, NV 89158
(702) 486-7150

New Hampshire Film and
  TV Bureau
172 Pembroke Rd
P.O. Box 856
Concord, NH 03302
(603) 271-2598

New Mexico Film Commission
1050 Old Pecos Trail
Santa Fe, NM 87501
(800) 545-9871

New York State Governor's Office for
    Motion Picture & TV Development
Pier 62
W. 23rd St & Hudson R.
New York, NY 10011
(212) 929-0240

North Carolina Film Office
430 N. Salisbury St
Raleigh, NC 27611
(919) 733-9900

North Dakota Film Commission
604 E. Blvd
Bismarck, ND 58505
(800) 437-2077

Ohio Film Office
77 S. High St., 29th Floor
P.O. Box 1001
Columbus, OH 43266
(800) 848-1300

Oklahoma Film Office
440 S. Houston, Room 505
North Tulsa, OK 74127
(800) 766-3456

Oregon Film Office
775 Summer N.E.
Salem, OR 97310
(503) 373-1232

Pennsylvania Film Bureau
Forum Bldg, Room 449
Harrisburg, PA 17120
(717) 783-3456

Puerto Rico Film Institute
P.O. Box 362350
San Juan, PR 00936
(809) 758-4747

Rhode Island Film Commission
7 Jackson Walkway
Providence, RI 02903
(401) 277-3456

South Carolina Film Office
P.O. Box 927
Columbia, SC 29202
(803) 737-0490

South Dakota Film Commission
711 E. Wells Ave.
Pierre, SD 57501
(800) 952-3625

Tennessee Film, Entertainment &
    Music Commission
320 6th Ave., N., 7th Floor
Nashville, TN 37243
(800) 251-8594

Texas Film Commission
P.O. Box 13246
Austin, TX 78711
(512) 469-9111

United States Virgin Islands Film
    Promotion Office
P.O. Box 6400
Saint Thomas, VI 00804
(809) 775-1444

Utah Film Commission
324 S. State St, Suite 500
Salt Lake City, UT 84111
(800) 453-8824

Vermont Film Bureau
134 State St
Montpelier, VT 05602
(802) 828-3236

Virginia Film Office
P.O. Box 7981021
E. Cary St
Richmond, VA 23206
(804) 372-8204

Washington State Film &
  Video Office
2001 6th Ave., Suite 2700
Seattle, WA 98121
(206) 464-7148

West Virginia Film Industry
  Development Office
2101 Washington St, E.
Charleston, WV 25305
(800) 225-5982

Wisconsin Film Office
123 W. Washington, 6th Floor
Box 7970
Madison, WI 53707
(608) 267-3456

Wyoming Film Commission
I-25 & College Dr.
Cheyenne, WY 82002
(800) 458-6657

Appendix 2:

Example Agreement Forms

Directors Guild of America
7920 Sunset Blvd.
Los Angeles, CA 90046
310-289-2000 / FAX 310-289-2029

Unit Production Manager and Assistant Director Deal Memorandum—FILM

This confirms our agreement to employ you on the project described as follows:

AD/UPM INFORMATION

Name _____   SS Number ____-__-_____

Loanout (corp. name)_____   Federal ID Number_____

Address _____   Telephone Number_(___)___-_____

Category:
- ☐ Unit Production Manager
- ☐ First Assistant Director
- ☐ Key Second Assistant Director
- ☐ 2nd Second Assistant Director
- ☐ Additional Second Assistant Director
- ☐ Technical Coordinator
- ☐ Assistant Unit Production Manager

Photography ☐ Principal ☐ Second Unit ☐ Both

Salary (dollar amount) $ _____ (Studio) $ _____ (Location)   ☐ per week ☐ per day

Production Fee (dollar amount) _____ (Studio) $ _____ $ _____ (Location)

Start Date _____   Guaranteed Period_____

PROJECT INFORMATION

Film or Series Title_____

Episode/Segment Title_____

Length of Program
- ☐ 30 min.
- ☐ 60 min.
- ☐ 90 min.
- ☐ 120 min.
- ☐ Other _____

Produced Primarily for
- ☐ Theatrical
- ☐ Network
- ☐ Basic Cable
- ☐ Syndication
- ☐ Disc/Cassettes
- ☐ Pay-TV (service) _____

Other conditions _____
(e.g., credit, suspension, per diem, etc.)

☐ Studio ☐ Distant Location ☐ Both   ☐ Check if New York Amendment Applies

This employment is subject to the provisions of the Directors Guild of America Basic Agreement of 1999.

Accepted and Agreed   Signatory Co (print) _____

Employee _____   By _____

Date _____   Date _____

LOCATION AGREEMENT

Film _____   Scripted Location _____
Production Company _____   Scene Number(s) _____
Address _____   _____
_____

Phone Number (___) ___ - _____   Date _____

Dear Ladies and Gentlemen:

1. I, the undersigned owner or agent, whichever is applicable, hereby irrevocably grants to _____
("Producer"), and its agents, employees, contractors and suppliers, the right to enter and remain upon and use the property, both
real and personal, located at:_____
_____
(the "Property"), including without limitation, all interior and exterior areas, buildings and other structures of the Property, and
owner's name, logo, trademark, service mark and/or slogan, and any other identifying features associated therewith or which
appear in, on or about the Property, for the purpose of photographing (including without limitation by means of motion picture, still
or videotape photography) said premises, sets and structures and/or recording sound in connection with the production, exhibition,
advertising and exploitation of the _____ tentatively entitled _____
(the "Picture").

2. Producer may take possession of said premises commencing on or about _____ subject to
change because of weather conditions or changes in production schedule, and continuing until the completion of all scenes and
work required.

3. Charges: As complete and full payment for all of the rights granted to Producer hereunder, Producer shall pay to Owner
the total amount of $_____ , broken down as follows:

	Number of Days			
Prep	_____	X $_____	= $	_____
Shoot	_____	X $_____	= $	_____
Strike	_____	X $_____	= $	_____
Hold	_____	X $_____	= $	_____
Other	_____		$	_____
	_____		$	_____

All charges are payable on completion of all work completed, unless specifically agreed to the contrary. Producer is not obligated
to actually use the property or produce a _____ or include material photographed or recorded hereunder in
the Picture. Producer may at any time elect not to use the Property by giving Owner or agent 24 hours written notice of such
election, in which case neither party shall have any obligation hereunder.

4. Producer may place all necessary facilities and equipment, including temporary sets, on the Property, and agrees to remove
same after completion of work and leave the Property in as good condition as when received, reasonable wear and tear from uses
permitted herein excepted. Signs on the Property may, but need not, be removed or changed, but, if removed or changed, must
be replaced. In connection with the Picture, Producer may refer to the Property or any part thereof by any fictitious name and may
attribute any fictitious events as occurring on the Property. Owner irrevocably grants to Producer and Producer's successors and
assigns the right, in perpetuity, throughout the universe, to duplicate and recreate all or a portion of the Property and to use such
duplicates and recreations in any media and/or manner now known or hereafter devised in connection with the Picture, including
without limitation sequels and remakes, merchandising, theme parks and studio tours, and in connection with publicity, promotion
and/or advertising for any or all of the foregoing.

(continued)

5. Producer agrees to use reasonable care to prevent damage to the Property, and will indemnify and hold Owner harmless from and against any claims or demands arising out of or based upon personal injuries, death or property damage (ordinary wear and tear excepted), suffered by such person(s) resulting directly from any act of negligence on Producer's part in connection with the work hereunder.

6. All rights of every nature whatsoever in and to all still pictures, motion pictures, videotapes, photographs and sound recordings made hereunder, shall be owned by Producer and its successors, assigns and licensees, and neither Owner nor any tenant, or other party now or hereafter having an interest in said property, shall have any right of action against Producer or any other party arising out of any use of said still pictures, motion pictures, videotapes, photographs and or sound recordings, whether or not such use is or may claimed to be, defamatory, untrue or censurable in nature. In addition, neither Owner nor any tenant, nor any other party now or hereafter having an interest in the Property, shall have any right of action, including, but not limited to, those based upon invasion of privacy, publicity, defamation, or other civil rights, in connection with the exercise of the permission and/or rights granted by Owner to Producer. If there is a breach by Producer hereunder, Owner shall be limited to an action at law for monetary damages. In no event shall Owner have the right to enjoin the development, production, distribution or exploitation of the Picture.

7. Force Majeure: If because of illness of actors, director or other essential artists and crew, weather conditions, defective film or equipment or any other occurrence beyond Producer's control, Producer is unable to start work on the date designated above and/or work in progress is interrupted during use of the Property by Producer, then Producer shall have the right to use the Property at a later date to be mutually agreed upon and/or to extend the period set forth in Paragraph 2, and any such use shall be included in the compensation paid pursuant to Paragraph 3 above.

8. At any time within six (6) months from the date Producer completes its use of the Property hereunder, Producer may, upon not less than five (5) days prior written notice to Owner, reenter and use the Property for such period as may be reasonable necessary to photograph retakes, added scenes, etc. desired by Producer upon the same terms and conditions as contained in this agreement.

9. Owner warrants neither he or anyone acting for him, gave or agreed to give anything of value, except for use of the Property, to Producer or anyone associated with the production for using said Property as a shooting location.

10. Owner represents and warrants that he/she is the owner and/or authorized representative of the Property, and that Owner has the authority to grant Producer the permission and rights granted in this agreement, and that no one else's permission is required. If any question arises regarding Owner's authority to grant the permission and rights granted in this agreement, Owner agrees to indemnify Producer and assume responsibility for any loss and liability incurred as a result of its breach of the representation of authority contained in this paragraph, including reasonable attorneys' fees.

AGREED AND ACCEPTED TO

_____

Production Company ("Producer")

By _____

Its Authorized Signatory

By _____

("Owner")   Its _____

_____

Social Security or Federal ID No.

Address

(   )   -   (   )   -

Phone No.   Fax No.

LOCATION INFORMATION SHEET

SHOW _____   PRODUCTION NUMBER _____
LOCATION MANAGER _____   (SCRIPTED) LOCATION _____
PERMIT SERVICE _____
       CONTACT _____   DATE(S) _____
       PHONE # ( ) - _____   ☐ INTERIOR ☐ EXTERIOR ☐ DAY ☐ NIGHT

ACTUAL LOCATION
(Address & Phone #)

( ) - _____

DATE & DAYS

	Number of days	dates
Prep:		
Shoot:		
Strike:		

LOCATION OF NEAREST EMERGENCY MEDICAL FACILITY

CONTACTS

Owner(s)   Name(s) _____
                 Address _____
Phone/FAX Number ( ) - _____
Beeper Number ( ) - _____

Representative(s) _____

Company: _____
Contact: _____
Address: _____
        _____
Phone/FAX Number ( ) - _____
Beeper Number ( ) - _____

LOCATION SITE RENTAL FEE

Full Amount	$ _____	O.T. after _____ hours per day @ _____ per hour
Amount for PREP days	$ _____	_____ Additional days @ $ _____ per day
Amount for SHOOT days	$ _____	Additional charges: Phone $ _____
Amount for STRIKE days	$ _____	Utilities $ _____
Deposit $ _____ Due on _____		Parking $ _____
☐ Refundable ☐ Apply to total fee		(Other) _____ $ _____
Balance $ _____ Due on _____		

CHECKLIST

☐ Location Agreement
☐ Certificate of Insurance
☐ Permit
☐ Fire Safety Officer(s)
☐ Police
☐ Location Fee
☐ Security
☐ Intermittent Traffic Control
☐ Post for Parking
☐ Signed Release from Neighbors
☐ Prepared Map to Location

☐ Heaters/Fans/Air Conditioners
☐ Lay-out Board/Drop Cloths
☐ Utilities/Power Supply
Allocated Areas For
☐ Extras
☐ Dressing Rms.
☐ Eating
☐ Hair/Makeup
☐ School
☐ Equipment
☐ Special Equipment
☐ Animals

Allocated Parking For
☐ Equipment
☐ Honey wagons
☐ Motor Homes
☐ Catering Truck
☐ Cast Vehicles
☐ Crew Vehicles
☐ Buses
☐ Picture Vehicles
☐ Extra Tables & Chairs
☐ Locate Parking Lot if Shuttle is Necessary

© ELH

SCREEN ACTORS GUILD

TAFT/HARTLEY REPORT

#15

ATTENTION: _____ ATTACHED?: ☐ RESUME*   ☐ PHOTO

EMPLOYEE INFORMATION

NAME _____ SOCIAL SECURITY NUMBER ___ - ___ - _____

ADDRESS _____ AGE (IF MINOR) _____

CITY/STATE _____ ZIP _____ PHONE (___) ___ - _____

EMPLOYER INFORMATION

NAME _____ Check one: ☐ AD AGENCY
                                                   ☐ STUDIO
ADDRESS _____   ☐ PRODUCTION COMPANY

CITY/STATE _____ ZIP _____ PHONE (___) ___ - _____

EMPLOYMENT INFORMATION

Check one: CONTRACT: ☐ DAILY   CATEGORY: ☐ ACTOR
                         ☐ 3-DAY   ☐ SINGER   ☐ OTHER
                         ☐ WEEKLY   ☐ STUNT

WORK DATE(S) _____ SALARY _____

PRODUCTION TITLE _____ PROD'N/COM'L NUMBER _____

SHOOTING LOCATION (City & State) _____

REASON FOR HIRE (be specific) _____

_____

_____

_____

_____

Employer is aware of General Provision, Section 14 of the Basic Agreement that applies to Theatrical and Television production, and Schedule B of the Commercials Contract, wherein Preference of Employment shall be given to qualified professional actors (except as otherwise stated). Employer will pay to the Guild as liquidated damages, the sums indicated for each breach by the Employer of any provision of those sections.

SIGNATURE _____ DATE _____
           Producer or Casting Director—Indicate which

PRINT NAME _____ PHONE (___) ___ - _____

*PLEASE BE CERTAIN RESUME LISTS ALL TRAINING AND/OR EXPERIENCE IN THE ENTERTAINMENT INDUSTRY.

THE PERFORMER MAY NOT WAIVE ANY PROVISION OF THIS CONTRACT WITHOUT THE WRITTEN CONSENT OF SCREEN ACTORS GUILD, INC.

SCREEN ACTORS GUILD

**DAILY CONTRACT
(DAY PERFORMER)
FOR THEATRICAL MOTION PICTURES**

Company _____   Date _____

Date Employment Starts _____   Performer Name _____

Production Title _____   Address _____

Production Number _____   Telephone No.: (_____)_____

Role _____   Social Security No. _____

Daily Rate $_____   Legal Resident of (State) _____

Weekly Conversion Rate $ _____   Citizen of U.S. ☐ Yes ☐ No

COMPLETE FOR "DROP-AND-PICK-UP" DEALS ONLY:

Firm recall date on _____

or on or after *_____

("On or after" recall only applies to pick-up as Weekly Performer)

As   ☐ Day Performer   ☐ Weekly Performer

*Means date specified or within 24 hours thereafter.

Wardrobe supplied by Performer   Yes ☐   No ☐

If so, number of outfits _____ @ $_____

(formal) _____ @ $_____

Date of Stunt Performer's next engagement: _____

The employment is subject to all of the provisions and conditions applicable to the employment of DAY PERFORMER contained or provided for in the Producer-Screen Actors Guild Codified Basic Agreement as the same may be supplemented and/or amended.

The performer does hereby authorize the Producer to deduct from the compensation hereinabove specified an amount equal to   per cent of each installment of compensation due the Performer hereunder, and to pay the amount so deducted to the Motion Picture and Television Relief Fund of America, Inc.

Special Provisions:

PRODUCER _____   PERFORMER _____

BY _____

Production time reports are available on the set at the end of each day. Such reports shall be signed or initialed by the Performer.

Attached hereto for your use is Declaration Regarding Income Tax Withholding.

NOTICE TO PERFORMER: IT IS IMPORTANT THAT YOU RETAIN A COPY OF THIS CONTRACT FOR YOUR PERMANENT RECORDS.

CAST DEAL MEMO

PRODUCTION COMPANY _____ DATE _____

ADDRESS _____ PHONE # _____

_____ FAX # _____

SHOW _____ EPISODE _____

CASTING DIRECTOR _____ PROD # _____

CASTING OFFICE PHONE # _____ FAX # _____

ARTIST _____ SOC. SEC. # _____

ADDRESS _____ PHONE # _____

_____ MOBILE # _____

ROLE _____ START DATE _____

☐ ACTOR   ☐ THEATRICAL   ☐ DAY PLAYER
☐ STUNT   ☐ TELEVISION   ☐ 3-DAY PLAYER
☐ SINGER   ☐ CABLE   ☐ WEEKLY
☐ PILOT   ☐ MULTIMEDIA   ☐ D/PU—DAILY TO WEEKLY
☐ DANCER   ☐ INTERNET   ☐ D/PU—DAILY TO DAILY

COMPENSATION $ _____ Per ☐ DAY ☐ WEEK ☐ SHOW

	NO. OF DAYS—WEEKS	DATES
TRAVEL	_____	_____
FITTINGS	_____	_____
REHEARSAL	_____	_____
PRINCIPAL PHOTOGRAPHY	_____	_____
ADDITIONAL SHOOT DAYS	_____	_____
POST PRODUCTION DAYS	_____	_____

DRESSING ROOM _____

PER DIEM—EXPENSES _____

TRANSPORTATION—TRAVEL _____

HOTEL ACCOMMODATIONS _____

OTHER _____

BILLING _____

© ELH

☐ PAID ADVERTISING

AGENT _____ OFFICE # _____

AGENCY _____ FAX # _____

ADDRESS _____ MOBILE # _____

_____ PAGER # _____

MANAGER _____ OFFICE # _____

MANAGEMENT CO. _____ FAX # _____

ADDRESS _____ MOBILE # _____

_____ PAGER # _____

PUBLICIST _____ OFFICE # _____

P.R. FIRM _____ FAX # _____

ADDRESS _____ MOBILE # _____

_____ PAGER # _____

☐ LOANOUT

CORP. NAME _____ FED. ID # _____

ADDRESS (If different from above) _____

_____

EMPLOYER OF RECORD _____

ADDRESS _____ PHONE # _____

_____ FAX # _____

APPROVED BY _____

TITLE _____ DATE _____

© ELH

CREW DEAL MEMO

PRODUCTION COMPANY _____ DATE _____

SHOW _____ PROD # _____

EMPLOYEE'S NAME _____ SOC. SEC. # _____

ADDRESS _____ PHONE # _____

_____ MOBILE # _____

START DATE _____ FAX # _____

JOB TITLE _____ PAGER # _____

UNION/GUILD _____ ACCOUNT # _____

RATE (In town) _____ Per ☐ Hour ☐ Day ☐ Week for a ☐ 5- ☐ 6-day week

(Distant location) _____ Per ☐ Hour ☐ Day ☐ Week for a ☐ 5- ☐ 6-day week

ADDITIONAL DAY(S) @ _____

OVERTIME _____ After _____ hours & _____ After _____

hours _____   _____   _____

☐ BOX/EQUIPMENT RENTAL _____ Per ☐ Day ☐ Week

☐ CAR ALLOWANCE _____ Per ☐ Day ☐ Week

☐ MILEAGE REIMBURSEMENT _____ Per Mile

| Note: Any equipment rented by the Production Company from the employee must be inventoried before rental can be paid |

TRAVEL & HOTEL ACCOMMODATIONS _____

_____

_____

_____

EXPENSES—PER DIEM _____

☐ LOANOUT

CORP. NAME _____ FED. ID # _____

ADDRESS (If different from above) _____

_____

AGENT _____ AGENCY _____

ADDRESS _____ PHONE # _____

_____ FAX # _____

EMPLOYER OF RECORD _____

ADDRESS _____ PHONE # _____

_____ FAX # _____

IF AWARDED SCREEN CREDIT, HOW WOULD YOU LIKE YOUR NAME TO READ?

_____

_____

APPROVED BY _____ TITLE _____

ACCEPTED BY _____ DATE _____

© ELH

Index

Entries in *italics* denote films.